The Bourgeois Charm of Karl Marx and the Ideological Irony of American Jurisprudence

Studies in Critical Social Sciences Book Series

Haymarket Books is proud to be working with Brill Academic Publishers (www.brill.nl) to republish the *Studies in Critical Social Sciences* book series in paperback editions. This peer-reviewed book series offers insights into our current reality by exploring the content and consequences of power relationships under capitalism, and by considering the spaces of opposition and resistance to these changes that have been defining our new age. Our full catalog of *SCSS* volumes can be viewed at https://www.haymarketbooks.org/series_collections/4-studies-in-critical-social-sciences.

Series Editor
David Fasenfest (Wayne State University)

Editorial Board
Eduardo Bonilla-Silva (Duke University)
Chris Chase-Dunn (University of California–Riverside)
William Carroll (University of Victoria)
Raewyn Connell (University of Sydney)
Kimberlé W. Crenshaw (University of California–LA and Columbia University)
Heidi Gottfried (Wayne State University)
Karin Gottschall (University of Bremen)
Alfredo Saad Filho (King's College London)
Chizuko Ueno (University of Tokyo)
Sylvia Walby (Lancaster University)
Raju Das (York University)

The Bourgeois Charm of Karl Marx and the Ideological Irony of American Jurisprudence

Dana Neacşu

Haymarket Books
Chicago, IL

First published in 2019 by Brill Academic Publishers, The Netherlands
© 2019 Koninklijke Brill NV, Leiden, The Netherlands

Published in paperback in 2020 by
Haymarket Books
P.O. Box 180165
Chicago, IL 60618
773-583-7884
www.haymarketbooks.org

ISBN: 978-1-64259-367-9

Distributed to the trade in the US through Consortium Book Sales and Distribution (www.cbsd.com) and internationally through Ingram Publisher Services International (www.ingramcontent.com).

This book was published with the generous support of Lannan Foundation and Wallace Action Fund.

Special discounts are available for bulk purchases by organizations and institutions. Please call 773-583-7884 or email info@haymarketbooks.org for more information.

Cover design by Jamie Kerry and Ragina Johnson.

Printed in the United States.

10 9 8 7 6 5 4 3 2 1

Library of Congress Cataloging-in-Publication data is available.

Cu dragoste, *I dedicate this book to my daughters
Absy, ZouZou, and Izzie*

Ironically, the relationship between status quo and ideology is the same as that between revolutions and ideology. Whether willingly or not, academia is called upon to decipher it.

∴

Contents

Acknowledgments XI
List of Illustrations XII

Introduction 1
  1 Marx, Irony and Ideology – Negotiating Meaning 5
  2 Meaning as a Result of Textual Instigation and Interpellation 9

1 **Contextualizing Marx: Differentiating to Embrace or to Reject?** 17
  1 Marx and Dewey 23
  2 Linguistic and Cultural Barriers to Marx's Works 29
  3 The Cultural Lifespan of Scholarship 31
  4 Marxian Ideology as Soviet, *ergo*, Undesired, Subjectivity 36
  5 Marx's Un-American Attitude toward Religion 37
  6 Marx's Unshaken Belief in Human Progress 40

2 **Marxian or Marxism: Labels Differentiating Content or Fabricating Difference?** 43

3 **Textual Differences and Marx's Interdisciplinary Dialectics** 50
  1 Dialectics and Ideology: Thinking, Researching and Incorporating Observations 51
  2 Marxian Interdisciplinary Dialectics 53
  3 Dialectics and Post-Marxian Scholarship 66

4 **Private Subjectivity – Alienation and Theory Production** 72
  1 Alienation as Creative Reification 74
  2 Alienation and Ideological Resistance to Power Structures 78
  3 Alienation and Scholastic Needs 81

5 **Ideology as Public (Political) Subjectivity** 85
  1 Ideology through the Ages 86
  2 The Case against (Academic) Ideological Purges 94
  3 Mass Media – Technology Actuating Ideology 106
  4 Ideological Meaning-Making 113

6   The Irony of Scholarship Production   118
    1   Encoded Irony in T_1 119
    2   Dormant Irony as T_1's Textual Omissions   125
    3   Textual Irony and Rorty's Intellectual Ironist   127

7   Ideological Irony – S_2's Ideology Actuating T_1's Irony   131
    1   Irony and Direct Scholastic Criticism   135
    2   Scholarship as (Ironic) Polite Criticism   137

8   The Bearable Lightness of Jurisprudential Irony   141
    1   Jurisprudential Irony as an Inescapable Trade-Off between Scholastic Ambition and Reality   143
    2   Jurisprudential Irony and the Socratic Method of Teaching Law   145
    3   Jurisprudential Irony – Byproduct of Legal Hegemony   147
    4   Encoded Jurisprudential Irony   153
    5   Jurisprudential Irony and the Supreme Court: The Case of Justice Antonin Scalia and Justice Neil Gorsuch   159

9   Philosophical Camaraderie, Ideological Difference, and Irony   167
    1   Plato's Concepts of Just and Justice   170
    2   Aristotle's Dialectical Universals   173
    3   Thomas Hobbes and John Locke's Ideological Differences Lead to Diverse Epistemological Conclusions   176
    4   The Intersection between the Abstract and Concrete Facets of the Law according to Montesquieu, Kant and Rousseau   180
    5   Jeremy Bentham's Common Sense and Grotius' Technocratic Approach to Law   184
    6   American Jurisprudence and Marx: Strange Bedfellows … Not   188

10 Irony, Jurisprudential Meaning-Making and Ideological Camaraderie   192
    1   Classical Liberalism and Marx   194
    2   Law as Science or the Rejection of Ideology   200
    3   Formalism and Realism: Two Sides of the Same Coin   204
    4   The Limits of Rawls and Dworkin: Justice and Historical Contingency   206
    5   Critical Legal Studies and Marx   213
    6   Feminism, Queer Theory and Marx   217
    7   Intersectionality – Pragmatic Bridge between Theory and Reality   220

Summary and Conclusion: Ideological Irony and Liberal Scholarship 229

References 237
Index 262

Acknowledgments

This book would not have been possible without the help of so many. I am profoundly indebted to David Tse-Chien Pan for accepting my paper on ideology for the 2018 Telos-Paul Piccone Institute Conference, as well as, to the organizers of the 2018 Caribbean Studies Association (CSA), held in La Habana, Cuba. I have rarely encountered a group of scholars more dedicated to engaging each other in the meaning-making process than the CSA family. Bernard Harcourt provided inspiration when I had only three chapters to show. Timothy Luke encouraged me to re-write parts that seemed amiss. Peter Goodrich pointed me to more sources on Marx and irony. Michael Schudson wondered if Stuart Hall's name was properly spelled (it was not). John Pavlik recommended inter-personal communication research and braved reading the finished draft. Peter Strauss valiantly engaged my views about Justice Scalia. Joe Gerken thought my proposed attribution of Scalia's point of view to his "pre-Vatican II Roman Catholicism" was insightful. Călin Liviu Georgescu, a friend and former classmate at the National University of Theatre and Film "I.L.Caragiale" (though Călin did not drop out), helped me conceive the cover art. I am indebted to David Pozen, both for his scholarship and his generosity shown during his replies to my many painfully cryptic emails. Encouragingly, Katharina Pistor showed interest in my project. Moshe Adler found it interesting. George Fletcher, bemused by my Marxian views given my Eastern-European roots, never ceased to show optimism that I would eventually find a publisher. I did, and David Fasenfest could not have been a more supportive editor. Without Kaia N. Shivers and Cal Brisbin's attention for detail, this book might have looked differently. The support received from the Barnard College – Environmental Science Department, as well as the commitment from my former Barnard College student, and current T.A., Alissa Lampert have been nothing less of remarkable. Thank you.

Illustrations

Figures

1. The relation between Individual Scholarship (T_1) and the Paradigm of Knowledge (K) 3
2. The relation between Individual Scholarship (T_1) (flour waiting to be sifted), the existing Regime of Truth (sifter), and the Paradigm of Knowledge (K) (sifted flour) 4
3. S_1's alienation and its role in Theory Production, T_1 73
4. Theory Production T_1, S_1's research, alienation and ideology 73
5. Hobbes' *Leviathan*. Engraved title page (London, 1651) 124
6. T_1's meaning 133
7. T_1's meaning = $f[T_1 + \text{Irony} \, (f S_1\text{'s} + S_2\text{'s Ideology})]$ 133

Table

1. Most-cited legal periodicals: U.S. and selected non-U.S. 83

Introduction

Marxian theory seems best situated to explain scholarly meaning-making in terms of ideological irony. Ironically, such an integrated interpretation minimizes the impact of the very accusations of dogmatism imposed on Karl Marx, making their ideological bias transparent.

Generally speaking, the concept of meaning, though far from clear, enjoys a prominent place in popular culture and everyday life (Campbell and Nyholm 2015: 694). Meaning-making occupies a similar position in the academe. Through theory production, scholars make sense of the world and participate in building the Knowledge Paradigm and Regime of Truth of their age (Lorenzini 2013):

> The most interesting text, before 1980, with regard to Foucault's use of the concept of regime of truth – leaving aside a short passage in The Birth of Biopolitcs [...], is without a doubt the 1976 interview The political function of the intellectual, where Foucault argues, in contrast to a certain philosophical myth, that "truth isn't outside power, or deprived of power": on the contrary, truth "is produced by virtue of multiple constraints [a]nd it induces regulated effects of power." This is to say that "each society has its regime of truth," and by this expression Foucault means:
> (1) "the types of discourse [society] harbors and causes to function as true";
> (2) "the mechanisms and instances which enable one to distinguish true from false statements" and
> (3) "the way in which each is sanctioned";
> (4) "the techniques and procedures which are valorized for obtaining truth";
> (5) "the status of those who are charged with saying what counts as true" [...].
>
> Therefore, "truth" is "a system of ordered procedures for the production, regulation, distribution, circulation and functioning of statements"; it is linked "by a circular relation to systems of power which produce it and sustain it, and to effects of power which it induces and which redirect it." And right at the end of the interview, Foucault adds that the essential political problem for us, today, is trying to change our "political, economic, institutional regime of the production of truth" (where truth is modeled on the form of scientific discourse), in order to constitute a new "politics of truth." (Id.)

Ferdinand de Saussure argued that "meaning comes from the relationship that exists between concepts" (Berger 2006: 142), thus defining meaning-making as relational. Mikhail Balkin suggested that meaning stems from "the give and take" dialogue "between different speakers" (id.). Like Stuart Hall (1997), Algirdas Greimas noticed that meaning emerges from "difference" (Keršytė 2017). Going a step further, Hall suggested meaning-making comes from opposites (id.). In this way, the color black has meaning because "we can contrast black with white, and it is the difference between the two that generates meaning" (Berger 2006: 142).

Applied to scholarship, including jurisprudence, the root of Hall's difference of meaning, I contend, is ironic and ideological. That difference springs from the interaction between the theory (T_1) and its meaning-making negotiators: the text-instigator (author, S_1), and the text-interpellator (scholarly audience, S_2). The more outside the hegemonic cluster of meaning that negotiation outcome lies, the more obvious its ideological irony becomes.

Within the public sphere, T_1 interpellates the scholarly community, S_2 et al. and the process of meaning-making, with its natural emphasis on the difference between T_1 and the existing scholarship, ensues. At the end of this process, the result is often ironic because it differs from what S_1 expressly proposed as the meaning of T_1, or, it might even oppose it. This unexpected aspect of meaning, especially jurisprudential meaning, captivates my interest because in addition to exposing the ambiguity of jurisprudence, it deflates any expectations of inherent objectivity. While ideas are necessary to explain reality and promote change, explaining meaning-making as a negotiation between two equally flawed (because subjective) negotiators, S_1 and S_2, emphasizes the dynamic nature of any existing Knowledge Paradigm (K) and adds transparency to how all regimes of truth are built (Foucault 1972).

The S_1's private subjectivity, which I call intellectual and emotional alienation, comprises private feelings, desires, frustrations and interests. S_1's public subjectivity, which I call ideology, is a personal interpretation of S_1's cultural positioning within the public sphere. This private and political subjectivity is actuated within the process of meaning-making once S_1 publishes or otherwise communicates the text, T_1, and makes it public.

Half-a-century ago, Foucault acknowledged,

> truth isn't outside power, or deprived of power (contrary to a myth whose history and functions would repay further study, it isn't the reward of free spirits, the child of prolonged solitudes, or the privilege of those who have been able to liberate themselves). (Id.)

Foucault's words are visually explained in Figure 1. T_1, in our example, will be incorporated in the Knowledge Paradigm (K), and used as reference for future knowledge production only if it fits the historical (hegemonic) normativity of the accepted Regime of Truth within which political power is exercised.

Similarly, Leila Brännström recently noted the nefarious impact of hegemonic normativity, where knowledge is calibrated to fit within the political goals of the particular power structure of the moment:

> Neoliberal governmentality brings about a fundamental transformation of the objective of the exercise of political power (not the proper balance between the numerous interests of individuals, groups and the collective, but economic growth by way of encouraging competition and projecting market principles onto social life in general) as well as of the regime of truth within which political power is exercised (not primarily the "truth of nature," but normative market behavior in relation to every dimension of human life).
> BRÄNNSTRÖM 2014: 186

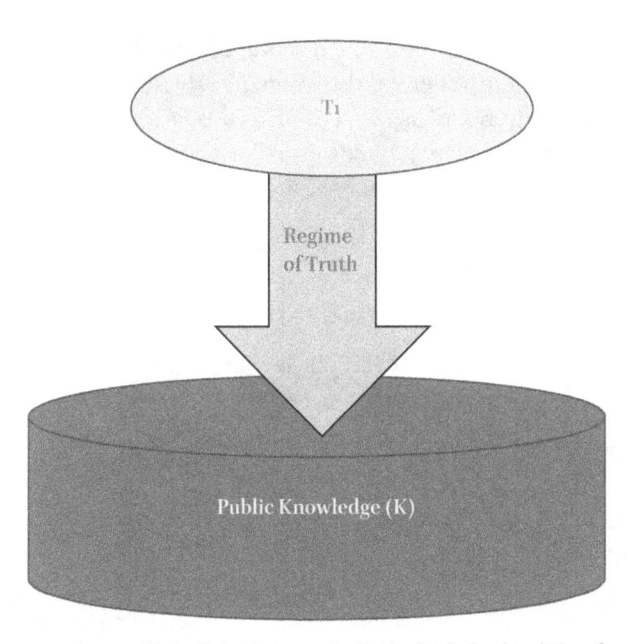

FIGURE 1   The relation between Individual Scholarship (T_1) and the Paradigm of Knowledge (K)
SOURCE: CREATED BY AUTHOR

S_1 is thus dependent on S_2 et al to give meaning to T_1 within the specific Regime of Truth. While perhaps counter-intuitive, it makes sense because T_1 will be incorporated into the Pantheon of Knowledge (K), if subsequent scholars (S_2 et al.) will accept its meaning-making gambit, and then engage it in their own scholarship. Marx's works (T_1) made it into and remain in the Pantheon of Knowledge to the extent that scholars (S_2 et al.) can refer to them today, because they fit the liberal Regime of Truth at the time that they were written, and today. Ironically, without their bourgeois charm, Marx's works would have been lost. Visualizing this, the Regime of Truth acts as a sifter for all theory (e.g., Figure 2). The Regime of Truth brings theory to the attention of the scholarly community. Thus sifted, scholars can interperllate and incorporate it in their subsequent theory production, the way flour is incorporated in breadmaking, for instance.

Scholarship production is a complex political process, which plays a crucial role in meaning-making. The scholarly community, S_2 et al., will focus on the well-reasoned narrative of the facts, called here, "philosophy," when it interpellates the text. This narrative segment of T_1 can be scientific, ontological, epistemological, a theory about theories, or even a descriptive or normative interpretation of reality. When S_2 et al interpellate T_1, its philosophy is immediately compared with the existing Regime of Truth, which acts as the standard of T_1's "objectivity." Absent any threatening difference between the established hegemonic normativity and the "philosophy" of T_1, T_1 is hailed as "objective." When S_2 et al interpellate T_1 and its outcome is an oppositional meaning-making negotiation then, T_1's "literal meaning" becomes exposed against the suddenly

FIGURE 2   The relation between Individual Scholarship (T_1) (flour waiting to be sifted), the existing Regime of Truth (sifter), and the Paradigm of Knowledge (K) (sifted flour)
SOURCE: THE AUTHOR'S PERSONAL PHOTO COLLECTION

visible Regime of Truth. S_1's subjectivity becomes a point of discontent and T_1 is often described as "lacking objectivity."

However, S_1's subjectivity enrobes all theory production, while S_2's its textual interpellation. T_1's reasoned narrative (philosophy) is soaked in S_1's private state of mind, described here as alienation, as well as in S_1's view about hierarchy and their position within it, described as ideology. Ironically, S_1's subjectivity becomes a visible element in meaning-making when S_2's subjectivity engages it, because they are different. The more S_1's and S_2's subjectivities clash, the more consequential they are to the T_1's meaning-making process. However, if there is incompatibility, the Regime of Truth rejects T_1 from joining the Knowledge Paradigm. That is not the case for Karl Marx's work, and I credit ideological irony for that.

Jurisprudential meaning-making has the same private and public subjectivity as any type of social scholarship. Some schools of jurisprudential thought emphasize subjectivity. For instance, *Critical Legal Studies* and their members, *the Crits*, highlight the political, thus subjective, nature of the law. *Law and Literature* focuses on the ambiguous nature of law as text. These are the schools that talk about the Regime of Truth, or the hegemonic role of jurisprudence. To a lesser degree, they also touch upon the monolithic, liberal, nature of all-American schools of jurisprudence. Certainly, neoliberalism has added some diversity to American jurisprudence, but within the same realm of individualism and its resolute values.

That scholarship production and communication are embedded within the foundation of knowledge and thus the Regime of Truth and that jurisprudence supports the political status-quo of its time are not new topics. What is new is the presentation of theory production T_1 and its meaning-making as ironic actuation of the subjectivity of S_1 and S_2. Their private subjectivity is identified here as creative alienation, and public subjectivity is their ideology.

This book is a structural argument focused on meaning-making as a multilayered process, whose core is ideological irony. To that extent, it is a new meaning-making proposal.

1 Marx, Irony and Ideology – Negotiating Meaning

The Bourgeois Charm of Karl Marx is a direct ironic reference to Luis Buñuel's surreal fantasy, *The Discreet Charm of the Bourgeoisie* (1972). Scholarship (T_1) and art exist through the meaning built by their instigators (S_1, authors) and intepellators (S_2, audience). Their meaning is fluid, and varies according to many factors, including the authors' subjectivity, itself a variable of contingency.

If Buñuel's movie questions the face value of the bourgeoisie, this book is a commentary on the face value of (legal) scholarship.

Marx used linguistic irony, because, as Robert Paul Wolff (1988) noted, that was the only tool that would permit him to do three things at once: (1) express the mysteriousness of our daily experience of commodity production and exchange; (2) lead us to confront its mystery; and (3) help us dispel it and move beyond appearances (43). That required language that expressed more meaning than at first brush. Sometimes, Marx relied on specific ironic language to work on particular arguments. For instance, his masterpiece, the first volume of *Das Kapital*, referred to here as *Capital* (1887), overflows with such language when explaining commodity production and exchange. Additionally, as shown here, his theory is an ironic response to his predecessors' work, including Hegel's and Ricardo's.

Moreover, I find Marxian work ironic because, despite the fear it still incites, it is a bourgeois product of a thoroughly bourgeois author, and one may add, the prototype of a misogynist white male. To that extent, the irony in the Marxian text comes from my own subjectivity, when it negotiates and actuates Marxian meaning.

Buñuel's movie contains ironic language and lends itself to ironic meaning-making. It is built as a twisted ode of the bourgeois lifestyle which reads as a scathing pamphlet. Engaging the movie reveals that its irony is explicit and it elicits the viewer to decipher its meaning opposite to the apparently eulogizing one.

Despite the fact that at first brush, Marx's and Buñuel's work appear unrelated, they both share common features. First, they vied for the attention of sophisticated audiences who were able to understand "high culture" references – whether it was German philosophy, for Marx, or restaurants with refined wine lists on their menu, for Buñuel. Second, topically, both focused on alienation: Marx on the worker's alienation, while Buñuel on the boredom of the *haute bourgeoisie* and their ilk. Buñuel's movie relates the numbing effects of routine on the privileged – e.g., dining with friends – and credits alienation as influencing their behavior. Marx's travails of harnessing new technologies within the free-market environment unveil their alienating effects on the oppressed, and he credits that alienation as the root of social revolutions. Finally, their works underline the fact that left to their own devices, capitalist free markets produce alienation for both the privileged and the oppressed: for Marx, its root was the ever-increasing inequalities between the two.

In this inquiry, alienation and ideology are the two sides of creative subjectivity, while irony actuates them in the process of meaning-making. For the text-instigator, subjectivity is mediated by their research methods. For instance,

Marx transformed dialectics, a mode of analysis traced to Socrates, and used it ideologically to create a theory about the course of human history. Marx used "concepts that we think we understand and take for granted inside out" (Menand 2016). Consequently, a scholar's subjectivity, which is essential to meaning-making, becomes apparent upon engaging their scholarship, T_1. This statement, like so many in this book, bypasses lengthy explanations and becomes obvious in the case of Marx and his body of work.

Irony here is more than mere ironic language. As a structural part of meaning-making it actuates subjective difference between text-instigators and text-interpellators, which contingency often amplifies. Buñuel's literal irony makes this point valiant because relying on ironic language whose rules are easier to grasp, it remains untouched irrespective of the variations in contingency. With characters built to be easily derided, he invites his viewer to read the opposite in their actions, and we easily accomplish the task. To the contrary, Marx's irony is multilayered, and its meaning is vastly dependent on the interpellators' subjectivity and their contingency – whether it is actuated by followers, including Friedrich (Frederick) Engels and Vladimir Ilyich Ulyanov (Lenin); epigones, such as Karl Kautsky and Georgi Plekhanov, or progressive thinkers like Antonio Gramsci and György Lukács. This also includes the likes of Isaiah Berlin, Michel Faucault, Leszek Kolakowski or Jon Elster, who form a class apart of Marxian readers. Some believe that if Lenin had not arrived in Petrograd in 1917 and taken charge of the Russian Revolution, Marx would probably be known today as "a not very important nineteenth-century philosopher, sociologist, economist, and political theorist" (Ryan 2014). Ironically, the Russian Revolution made the world take Marx's criticism of capitalism seriously, Louis Menand (2016) suggests. The work of Marx's true followers, pretenders, as well as that of his opponents exposes the irony of Marxian writings. Vice-versa, Marx exposes the irony in the work of his epigones, the creators of Marxism. His work also reveals his opponents' irony, what I would call a liberal irony of good intentions.

Last century, Wolfgang Friedmann (1967) wrote that jurisprudence was reasoned narrative, which he labeled as "philosophy," and ideology. I incorporate most of Friedmann's textualism and generalize it to all social scholarship, and add a third ingredient, irony. Irony, textual and subjective, cannot be totally controlled by S_1. S_1 might even ignore it. But, subsequent text-interpellators (S_2) use it (often unknowingly) as fertile area for meaning-making.

Marx's body of work is ideal to promote this perspective because its complexity and its singularity make all elements easier to identify. In the process, I also argue for a renewed interest in primary theories, and especially for using the Marxian frame of thinking when contemplating the Rule of Law as the symbol of the legitimate legal order of the moment. Its century-long theoretical resilience seems as best suited to forge a complex understanding of our reality as one could imagine.

An additional bonus for my undertaking is that many have some knowledge about Karl Marx and his work on socio-economic interaction in the capitalist market place. His ideological perspective of the economically disadvantaged marked the meaning of his writings two centuries ago, and even now. Ironically, despite having penned his work for a hyper-educated, economically prosperous readership, it did not increase his popularity with the North American academy either then or now.

Marx's political subjectivity, his ideology, reflects his views on societal power. If Marx becomes our S_1, and his work T_1, then his ideology steers the meaning of T_1. S_2 starts negotiating T_1 through Marx's ideology, which positions T_1 within a particular set of ideas, as well as through S_2's subjectivity, including their ideology. The irony is that the subjectivity of those interpellating Marxian tests – S_2 at al. – is unpredictable but also dynamic. Theory production is actuated with every act of textual engagement, an act whose subjectivity changes the meaning of the text. That Marxian texts (T_1) became the basis of a wild array of Marxist texts, such as Gramsci's or Lukács' Marxism, as well as Lenin's and even Stalin's Marxism is the product of S_2's unpredictable private and political subjectivity, and of its ironic impact on meaning-making.

More generally speaking, a process and a result, irony gives voice to S_1's and S_2's subjectivity, actuating them. Irony thus creates meaning S_1 never expected. Irony gives voice to what has been ignored or omitted in the context of the existing body of scholarship at a specific moment. S_1's ideology and the irony surrounding their work form what could be called the aura of ideological irony of meaning. I posit that it affects meaning production irrespective of S_1's awareness of its impact. The meaning that ideological irony adds to social scholarship, especially jurisprudence, goes beyond Wittgenstein's penumbra of ambiguity (Davis and Neacşu 2014). Wittgenstein referred to the language of expressed reasoning, philosophy for instance, which despite its various degrees of obviousness, somehow, sometimes "may become the hardest of all to understand" (id.: 489).

Ideology, S_1's ideatic baggage of social and political hierarchy, influences meaning in its pre-creation manifestation. It actuates thinking into the act of scholarship by guiding S_1's choice of concepts. Subsequently, the ambiguity that surrounds those concepts might affect their meaning, but it is S_1's ideology, among other factors, which dictates their choice.

Irony anchors the process of thinking post-creation, connecting it to the surrounding circumstances, to its contingency. For instance, S_1 may engage that aura of ideological irony, or perhaps ignore it, but nothing would make it disappear. Through various research methods, such as the use of data, statistical or other empirical support, scholars have been known to attempt to distance themselves from the ideological irony of scholarship production. Some scholars, such as Jon Elster (2017), in a discussion with this author, asserted that their ideology cannot be ascertained from their writings, and thus could not have any meaningful influence. Aside from the fact that objectivity in scholarship is only a flight of Icarus, ironically, attaining it would only empty the hallways of the academia: so much has already been written on everything.

Marx's ideology affected the meaning of his work at the outset by embedding his view of the world. Marx consciously embraced it, and in his more mature work he used it and subjected his philosophy to his ideology. Irony wanted it that Marx did not contemplate the limitations his ideology had on meaning-making.

> "Irony" simultaneously describes a form of consciousness, a rhetorical trope, a mode of aesthetic representation, a characteristic of historical events, and a disposition toward various modes of signification...
> STRATTON 2013

Contingency affixes all scholarship, whose meaning is further contextualized by the existing scholarship. Irony is actuated post-creation, as if residing in the eye of the beholder, the text-interpellator, S_2. Paradoxically, while the aura of ideological irony attaches itself to scholarship irrespective of the scholars' self-awareness, the scholars who embrace their scholarly limitations – eventual irrelevance and transience – are those who would exercise the most control over their work. At a minimum, they avoid the ridicule of ignorance when they deny the perennial role of subjectivity in meaning-making.

2 Meaning as a Result of Textual Instigation and Interpellation

Marxian work is an example of the structure I propose for all scholarship. As it will become obvious, the structure of his scholarship I promote here has no connection to the structure Lenin and other scholars have suggested for the Marxian narrative. They viewed it as a compound of three elements: (a) German philosophy; (b) English political economy; and (c) French socialism, which do stand proof to Marx's interdisciplinarity (Lenin 1913). Here, Marx's work is an example of scholarship with a different tripartite structure: reasoned text, ideology and irony.

The choice seems obvious in light of its ideological transparency and embedded dormant irony. I shall explain. When Marx believed the engine of human progress through history rested with the exploited classes, whose actions could be channeled in the direction of progress once they acquired class consciousness, he made a huge leap of ideological faith. He dismissed the off chance that one day the working class might become extraneous to historical progress. Not only might their class consciousness never mature, but they might stop being the engine of social progress.

Ideology, in addition to his historical contingency, might have impeded Marx from envisioning a future where factory-type exploitation would cease demarcating a social class in certain geographical areas, such as those where exploitation would cease looking like torture and would escape the confinement of the public space. It was too far-fetched for him to see that exploitation would not happen traditionally, or in a unidirectional fashion. He could not envision profits being channeled to capitalists and corporations, systemically, in a diffused manner from a variety of centers. Civilized exploitation has nurtured more or less permanently temporary and freelancing classes, as well as the unemployed welfare class (underclass), at the expense of the organized (but tortured) market-place proletariat.

Marx imagined one type of violence that capitalism required to exist, like Michel Foucault would do when he exposed the system of discipline imposed on the work force in his own scholarship on punishment (Laval et al. 2015). While impressive, Marx's imagination could not surpass certain limitations, including the cognitive confines built into the existing Knowledge Paradigm (K) by its Regime of Truth. Understandably, Marx did not conceive of exploitation as naturally fluid, much like age, gender, or sexual orientation, which could be experienced emotionally, as vulnerability or violence. Similarly, Foucault could not conceive discipline as a result of disruption and the fear of temporary employment. Today, that could be the narrative of progressive post-identity politics. Ironically, while breaking the public versus private binary, with few exceptions, identity-based theories have ignored the very lessons they noticed Marx missed – the reality outside of his comfort zone, which regarded the gendered exploitation taking place in the private sphere.

Unfortunately, no scholarship goes beyond what is (ideologically) comfortable to confront its own "unfamiliar narrative." From this perspective, Marx's critical limits are obvious, despite his interdisciplinary dialectics; his inability to envision the complex diversity of the exploited. Perhaps that was due to his ideology – his public subjectivity – his most limiting boundary. It confined Marx's studies to the market place (public space); a mistake seemingly avoided by his contemporary, John Stuart Mill (1869), when he addressed women's bondage in *On the Subjection of Women*.

Applying an Althuserian term, Marx used theory to interpellate reality. More than reflect reality in his work, Marx interpellated it to make it manageable, or even to tame it:

> This is a proposition which entails that we distinguish ... between concrete individuals on the one hand and concrete subjects on the other, although ... concrete subjects only exist insofar as they are supported by a concrete individual.... [I]deology "acts" or "functions" in such a way that it "recruits" subjects among the individuals (it recruits them all), or "transforms" the individuals into subjects (it transforms them all) by that very precise operation ... called interpellation or hailing, and which can be imagined along the lines of the most commonplace every day police (or other) hailing: "Hey, you there!" ... [T]he hailed individual will turn around [and] by this mere one-hundred-and-eighty-degree physical conversion, he becomes a subject. Why? Because he has recognized that the hail was "really" addressed to him, and that "it was really him who was hailed" (and not someone else).
>
> ALTHUSSER 1971: 174

This term very aptly visualizes the role of theory regarding the social reality it analyzes. Theory subordinates reality in its service, transforming it into a narrative.

Unquestionably, Marx sublimated reality into his scholarship, and fetishized his work for the cause of the proletariat. By writing the *Communist Manifesto* (1848), a guide for the proletariat's *praxis*, Marx openly incorporated what he identified as the ideology of the proletariat in his analysis of the objective contingency. Ironically, in that moment the correlation between the surrounding material circumstances, history, and scholarship reversed roles in the theoretical interpellation of reality. Contingency became, using Hegelian vocabulary "sublet," or replaced by ideas. Marx overturned one of his tenets so crucial to his misguided followers: the supremacy of structure over superstructure, which includes ideology without any explanation, as if unaware of it.

Marx observed that the material conditions of life are justified, legitimized, and stabilized by whatever overarching theory dominates the Knowledge Paradigm. By offering a solution in the *Manifesto*, he was elevating his theory over reality, the superstructure over the structure, thus reversing their roles. And, this might the supreme irony his writing entails. Marx's work became an example of "distorted" applied dialectics. Instead of letting social dynamism dictate theoretical changes, Marx let ideology control his narrative. Ironically, his position is not unlike Hegel's before him.

This ironic discrepancy between what a scholar (S_1) sets herself up to achieve (T_1) and what she actually achieves is not unique to Marx and his work, but to all theory relevant enough so others scholars (S_2) engage it. What is unique to Marx is the extremely vast terrain of meaning-making his work occupies because of the vastly different subjectivity of the generations of scholars interpellating it. Furthermore, in today's bastion of liberalism, which is most of the world's academe, there is so little allegiance to it that Marx's work is best suited to provide the clearest example of the transiency of scholarship – from both a descriptive and prescriptive view. In the process, it also provides support to my claim that scholarship, including jurisprudence, is composed of philosophy (methodologically reasoned narrative), ideology (public subjectivity outgrowing from its private counterpart), and irony (actuating the difference between the text-instigator and interpellator's subjectivity).

Additionally, from a pragmatic perspective, Marx's work offers an ideological mirror to measure how far to the right American jurisprudence has turned lately. We might even start wondering whether the Rule of Law, paraphrasing Thomas Paine, the jewel of the crown of our American King, isn't somehow deeply ideological and fraught with problems (Paine 1922: 35–36). Moreover, by holding Marx's theoretical mirror to our legal liberalism, we might see its ideology and stop attempting to export our particular point of view to circumstances where it cannot fit. Or, as Paine said, for only in

> absolute governments the king is law [...] and there ought to be no other. (Id.)

Marx's theory can be understood as the ironic response to muscular, individual, manly liberal narratives, which promoted individual freedom to the level of religion and were built on the concept of a free market, whose participants have private resources and can freely agree about its disposition (as in contracts) or restoration (as in torts). In his ponderings, Marx seemed to have noted the irony that all free-market theories contained, including their nascent irrelevance which can be ascribed to their authors' ideology, research methods, or inability to grasp reality. At times, Marx pointed out to all three as missing, like in his criticism of Proudhon's work, or like in his criticism of the Young Hegelians in *The Holly Family* (1844), co-written when he was only twenty-six (Wolf 1988).

Liberalism, in its classic laissez-faire mode, ignored the government's role in establishing and enforcing the rules defining the very existence of the market. Furthermore, it disregarded that the government, and not the market, sets the parameters of what is free to possess, control, and dispose of in a well-determined manner (Boucke 1932).

During that time, the Jacksonian era in the United States was based on the universal belief that the economy would thrive if the government adopted a "hands-off" attitude. In Europe, liberal economic theorists, particularly David Ricardo (2000), building on the work of Adam Smith (1993), sought to demonstrate that free markets, unfettered by state regulation, would result in the greatest prosperity for all (Davis and Neacşu 2001). While the official narrative, what is left unsaid seems far more intriguing: "Why have a government at all?" Or, "Why not shuffle the cards, come up with a new set of players, and then take your hands off, again and again?"

Marx noted the irony of that liberal storyline. Markets exist as a legitimizing function of the Rule of Law. Norms sanctioned by the state in charge make profits legal. Theories imbued with liberal ideology then further present this legitimation as unquestionable. Regrettably, Marx stopped short from owning the limiting impact his own ideology would have on future negotiations of Marxian meaning by bringing up its inherent irony.

What this book adds to meaning theory, and especially to jurisprudential meaning, is its contention about ideological irony. The text-instigator has substantial control over the meaning of the text (T_1). That control transpires through S_1's expressed reasoned narrative as determined by the existing Knowledge Paradigm (K), and, when S_1 is aware of it, as limited by their subjectivity. What is undisclosed – often inadvertently or ideologically unaddressed – as well as what T_1's subsequent interpellators bring to the textual negotiation table, is deeply ideological. That meaning unveils irony, which explains how Marxian text could be used, now infamously, by Lenin to promote his Soviet, state-planned economy response to the free-market theory, and by me, here, as an illustrious example of bourgeois charm. Ironically, even Soviet theory is, alas, bourgeois, although its depravity is so undesirable that instead of labeling it state capitalist theory, we called it Soviet, and thus foreign. It mirrored its economy, which installed its own set of players – proletariat and bureaucracy – who first appeared to be extrinsically opposed to the laborer-capitalist binary of the classical version of world capitalism. However, Soviet proletariat soon became the exploited counterpart to Generalissimo Stalin's *nomenclatura* (Berlin 1952). The language was different – proletariat for labor and nomenclatura for capitalist – while the game had the same rules.

Antonio Gramsci's theory could be seen as the ironic response to the early twentieth century Soviet theory, and the liberal theory of that time. Jurisprudentially, though, there is a generalized want of non-liberalism. For instance, free-market theory is behind all American jurisprudence. A more recent incarnation is Judge Richard Posner's brand of law and economic jurisprudence. Like all theories, it is reasoned narrative, ideology and irony. Its irony is not linguistically built in the text, but it is post-creation. It comes from what Judge Posner ignored, but yet, S_2, the scholar T_1 interpellates, imagined. For instance, Judge Posner explained the 2008 depression as a failure of capitalism to self-regulate.

> In sum, rational maximization by businessmen and consumers, all pursuing their self-interest more or less intelligently within a framework of property and contractual rights, can set the stage of an economic catastrophe.
> POSNER 2009

Posner supplemented that statement by saying,

> [I]t is inexcusable that there was [a] failure of the Federal Reserve and other economic agencies within the federal government to have prepared contingency plans for the possibility, remote as it seemed, that a crumbling of the banking industry would set the stage for a depression. (Id.)

Judge Posner's statements convey meaning beyond what is explicit and despite his ideological choices. If intelligent businessmen and consumers pursuing their self-interest set the stage for economic catastrophes, is not Posner's reliance on government agencies to wait to clean up their mess, ironically, paternalistic and the very opposite of what he proposes? And when Posner attempted to protect himself from the ironic irrelevance of his partial explanation by acknowledging the complexity of the problem, although not as a systemic, insurmountable one, is not that equally illiberally paternalistic, and contradicting his narrative?

> [T]he trillions of dollars that the government has spent to speed recovery, and the restructuring of banks and its reforms that will bring in their train untold problems and uncertainties, will overhang the economy for years to come, as when an expensive treatment cures a deadly illness but leaves the patient debilitated. (Id.)

Judge Posner could not retreat from his absolutism of free-market laissez-faire. He needed the government as the incompetent scapegoat to save his own ideological explanation. But at the same time, Posner realized that like a (Maytag) washing machine someone has to play the role of the competent repairman. Ironically, Judge Posner's (Maytag) repairman is the state.

Poignantly, Posner-*fils*, Professor Eric Posner, co-wrote a piece with Professor Adrian Vermeule, that comes up with an equally ironic explanation for what I identify to be his father's failure of understanding. In a similar assessment, which I attribute to the same lack of imagination among younger scholars, legal problems remain well-delineated squares on a linear continuum of social problems. Eric Posner (Posner and Vermeule 2013) talks about the inside/outside fallacy, brought about the inherent contradiction between adopting an analysis (outsider's) for a situation where that analysis is not suited (the insider's behavior) *ab initio*.

Posner and Vermeule (2013) use Madisonian writings with as much awe and frustration as Marxists use and blame Marx for his nineteenth-century shortcomings. James Madison pointed out to the institutional ambition as a problem to be overcome by our federal constitution (inside/outside fallacy), while their objection to Madison's scholarship in the name of bipartisanship is equally a fallacy. Furthermore, their writing happens in a different contingency than Madison's, but they seem to ignore that. Certainly, there are principles of law for the ages, redistributive justice for instance, but even they are ideologically questionable. Moreover, there are no legal problems outside of the political realm, unless life is treated as cookie dough and law is its cookie cutter. Ironically, Posner and Vermeule criticize others for using a cookie cutter they do not like, thinking that no one would notice that what they offer is just a different cookie cutter: as fraught as any. Instead, they might have opted for an integrated explanation, but then their inside/outside premise would have been incorporated in their systemic approach.

In the same way there is plenty of non-Marxian space, there is plenty of non-Posnerian space for the next scholarly narrative to explain the crisis caused by intelligent business people acting in their own interest. Moreover, there is plenty of space to explain social relations in a more comprehensive, dialectical way, or just from another ideological perspective to promote another set of norms. Oftentimes, liberal legal theories criticize each other on methodological shortcomings, as if the method of research is an objective standard. But much like the work of the late Justice Antonin Scalia, whose originalism was what he deemed to be the original meaning of the Constitution, the inside/outside fallacy is deeply personal, almost a pictorial perspective.

The fallacy is an illusion, which could be tempered if the authors used dialectics as a method of research – much better suited for a comprehensive theory about public law.

In sum, it is likely that scholarship production is possible only because scholars are unaware of their work's transiency (or if aware, because they ignore it for a while), or because its moment of transcendence from revelatory into reactionary is not obvious to the text-instigator. Marx engaged the social reality in an interdisciplinary and dialectical manner seeking its contradictions and explaining them while he acknowledged his ideology. Although, ironically, he was unable (or more likely, intentionally unwilling) to see ideology as a limiting bias of his own scholarly enterprise (applying Marx to Marx, a wonderfully intriguing and inviting enterprise), its presence hopefully makes us aware of our own ideological preferences.

To the extent that all scholarly breadth of investigation is a consequence of S_1's skill and confidence but also ideology, the scope and value of that work, as well as its descriptive and normative significance can be assessed from these perspectives. Such scholarly awareness makes its nascent irrelevance ironically obvious. Rather than ignored, irrelevance becomes a possibility open to subsequent interpretation and meaning-making negotiation.

As with free-market liberalism and its once-innovative but soon much-reviled and globally-destructive laissez-faire theory, all liberal jurisprudential schools comprise, at times, hard-to-notice, irony. The implications of what is written (the meaning of T_1) is not limited to what is said on the text of T_1, but it is often changed by what is not, at least explicitly, considered – which S_2 nevertheless finds meaningful. By accepting this subjectivity, S_1 puts themselves on equal footing with S_2 in the meaning-making process. The next chapter will point out how irony actuates meaning in context and tips the balance in favor of the scholar most aware of their subjectivity. Dewey and Marx have created a body of work both similar in its pragmatism and dissimilar in practical implications. Both thought they could be objective and ignore their subjectivity. Ironically, because neither one saw the limiting implications of their subjectivity on meaning-making, each opened the door to rich subsequent interpretations of their work.

CHAPTER 1

Contextualizing Marx: Differentiating to Embrace or to Reject?

Hall's meaning-making theory supports my argument in favor of introducing Marx to legal academia: teach Marx to better teach *Law and Economics,* for instance. Hall's difference promotes making space for non-liberal scholarship in today's liberally monolithic academia to better emphasize liberal theories.

From this perspective, *The Bourgeois Charm of Karl Marx*, which mimics Buñuel's literal irony, feeds two perceived needs with one book. It applies Marxian critique to Marx, and in the process, it develops Hall's theory of meaning. All while it engages the legal scholarship market place from a non-liberal, feminine angle.

Aside from its content, Karl Marx's work is hence attractive to my project because it is so objectionable to the American bourgeois (legal) academia. However, the mere juxtaposition of identifiers in *The Bourgeois Charm of Karl Marx*, rather than underline the opposite, will make following the point salient: Marx is a thoroughly bourgeois author, despite the fact that the members of the current legal academe consider Marx's work to be the epitome of bourgeois antagonism. For starters, using a Buñuel image – his film canvases many dinners – Marxian theory needs little introduction because, in fact, it is part of the world's patrimony of knowledge (Knowledge Paradigm, K) – patrimony sanctified by liberalism, a bourgeois ideology.

Nevertheless, within the last two decades, capitalism seems to have swallowed the Marxian revolutionary class, the factory-contained proletariat, the way Cronus ate all his children. Would this render Marxian thought quaint rather than programmatic? While we have witnessed mass leadership within the last decades, the very idea of leading masses to victorious revolts seems moot. Again, appearances need to be demystified, and the more complex the reality the more complex the theory explaining it needs to be. Thus, while no one can deny the success of identity politics and their openness for infinitesimal individuality, while no other woman can speak on my behalf as a woman, so many could speak on my behalf as an uprooted, working immigrant, parent of two minors and an abused spouse, and many could do it so much better and more effectively. From this perspective, Marxian thought, with its engrained emphasis on integrated contingency, brings dialectics, and interdisciplinary studies of reality to the forefront. Starting from the premise that the politics of exploitation, while often opaque, exist and need to be demystified, Marxian thought remains relevant because it is socially unconfined.

For a multi-layered meaning-making approach, Marx's work is ideal because it represents his answer to an interpretation of Hegelian philosophy, French socialism, and Ricardian political economy. Written through the lens of German nationalism irked by British imperialism, his theory is filled with ideological irony. Mix that with Marx's awareness of the plight of the masses of liberated laborers caught in the servitude of farm and factory work, and its attraction to this book's project of unveiling the irony embedded into meaning-making becomes obvious. This is enough difference to explain meaning-making at so many levels. In light of this, Marxian theory becomes a sounding board for engaging all social scholarship, including legal theory. Its textual complexity (Wolff 1988), (1) history of the development of capitalism, (2) philosophy, (3) literary criticism, and (4) economic theory, also provides the best tool I could imagine to support my triptych view of all scholarship as philosophy, ideology, and irony.

Moving on, Karl Marx is also suited for my project because his life and work are filled with irony.

> Paradox, irony and contradiction, the animating spirits of Marx's work were also the impish trinity that shaped his own life. He would, one guesses, have applauded Ralph Waldo Emerson's defiant creed: "A foolish consistency is the hobgoblin of little minds […]."
> WHEEN 2000: 349

Ironically, without bourgeois patronage from his friend Frederick Engels, much of his theory would have never been produced (id.). Some, Robert Paul Wolff (2018) included, pointed out that Marx, the man, was no stranger to exploiting family members and friends for his personal gain. Furthermore, Marx's literary style had always been filled with humor due to his use of unexpected metaphors. For example, sarcasm and irony are pervasive in his unfinished comedic novel, *Scorpion and Felix* (1837), which he wrote when he was only nineteen years old:

> Poor Boniface! You are constipated with your holy thoughts and reflections, since you can no longer relieve yourself in speech and writing! O admirable victim of profundity! O pious constipation! (Id.)

Moreover, despite their diversity, the scholarly interpellation of Marxian writings has been somewhat even. Although his theory does not form a uniform body of ideas, with few exceptions in the economics departments, the

American academia uniformly dismissed it. His earlier writings might be different (in assumptions and goals) from his later works, but they are filled with the same Marxian analytical insight acknowledging historical contingency and ideological bias, which for me represent the template for engaged scholarship, the only way to produce honest knowledge. Placed next to our liberal scholarly production which often ignores its ideological bias and historical contingency, it brings Hall's difference of meaning to the forefront.

Thus, rather than engage in some Marxian revisionism, and answer the question "Which Marx?" I choose everything. The earlier works, as well as his later work, stand for the same radical scholarship of challenging the status quo while preserving their "bourgeois charm." Living a life of exile, Marx was expelled from Belgium and France while Prussia refused to welcome him, and eventually, he settled in London. However, his work found readers in all those countries and more. In fact, with the very few geographical exceptions of those who ask, "Marx, who? Groucho?" his work has received worldwide publication.

Ironically, the difference of meaning proposed here highlights the remarkable similarities between Marxian thought and North America pragmatism. Marx's work is steeped in pragmatism, including his earlier writings, which were only accessible to their initial German audience, or remained unpublished: *On the Jewish Question* (1844), *The Critique of Hegel's Philosophy of Right* (1844), *Critique of Hegel's Doctrine of State*, as well as the *Economic and Philosophic Manuscripts of 1844*. They all provide proof of Marx's liberating attitude towards theory. Like the rest of his work, his earlier writings testify to his revolt against the stultifying effect of theory. Marx opposed generic speculation and favored the moment's contingency to understand what is possible, and especially what is needed for the good of humanity, which he saw as an all-inclusive community.

> Hitherto men have constantly made up for themselves false conceptions about themselves, about what they are and what they ought to be. They have arranged their relationships according to their ideas of God, of normal man, etc. The phantoms of their brains have got out of their hands. They, the creators, have bowed down before their creations. Let us liberate them from the chimeras, the ideas, dogmas, imaginary beings under the yoke of which they are pining away. Let us revolt against the rule of thoughts. Let us teach men, says one, to exchange these imaginations for thoughts which correspond to the essence of man; says the second, to take up a critical attitude to them; says the third, to knock them out of their heads; and – existing reality will collapse.
> MARX 1845

Despite its muscular pragmatism and refreshing historical contingency, Marx's work was labeled as dogmatic, suffering of Big Theory Dogmatism, unlike any of the theories that influenced him and unlike Dewey's pragmatism, for instance. I argue that when Marx wrote his explanation of mid-nineteenth-century capitalism, he stumbled over his own greatness. While criticizing liberal theories, and noticing their ideological irony, his work did not incorporate his own ideological biases. Ironically, his detractors, as well as his imitators duplicated his misgivings, which points out that while all theoretical constructs are ideological, and thus, ironically transient, scholars are rarely aware of that. Scholarship is called upon to promote knowledge and, sometimes, that knowledge can be used to guide action. However, whether aware of it or not, scholarship is circumscribed by the contingency which made it possible. To aspire to something transcendental is often miserably doomed. But being doomed constitutes the modest aspirations as well as the magnificent ones: reality changes for both. Certainly, there are ways to make a theory more relevant than others. One way is the research methods employed, a process deeply affected by the textual instigator's ideology and sense of irony.

As this book also shows, Marx is witnessing a comeback. "And irony made Marxism," one could say, paraphrasing the French movie ... *And God Created Woman* (*Et Dieu créa la femme*). At times, it seems that scholars have created this bin-like conceptual label, Marxism, so we can say with impunity that Marx stands for anything we need to reject without the trouble of explaining the reasons. Within that label, Marx can stand for everything deemed Marxist.

We know that a text does not consist of a line of words, releasing a single "theological" meaning (the "message" of the Author-God), but is a space of many dimensions, in which we wed and contest various kinds of writing, no one of which is original. We know that the text is a tissue of citations, resulting from the thousand sources of culture (Barthes 1968).

Interestingly, when it comes to Marx, his authorship has never seemed to be in doubt. His position has always been treated as the singularly in charge of its theoretical meaning-making – with one exception. In in early 1976, for one of his most indebted readers, none other than the French philosopher Michel Foucault, Marx ceased to exist:

> Marx, pour moi, ça n'existe pas. Je veux dire cette espèce d'entité qu'on a construite autour d'un nom propre, et qui se réfère tantôt à un certain individu, tantôt à la totalité de ce qu'il a écrit, tantôt à un immense processus historique qui dérive de lui. Je crois que ses analyses économiques, la manière dont il analyse la formation du capital sont pour une part

commandées par les concepts qu'il dérive de la trame même de l'économie ricardienne.

FOUCAULT 1976–1979: 38–39

> *Marx, for me, does not exist. I mean this type of entity that has been built around a proper name, and which sometimes refers to a certain individual, sometimes to the totality of what he has written, sometimes to an immense historical process that is derived from him. I believe that his economic analyses, the way in which he analyzes the formation of capital, are to a large extent controlled by the concepts of what is derived from the very fabric of the Ricardian economy.*

Hall's meaning-making theory relies on difference. In my take on it, that difference stems from the meaning-making negotiation conducted by those interpellating or engaging the text. That Marx is witnessing a comeback has more to do with us, perhaps, than with his work. Roland Barthes wrote last century that "the true locus of writing is reading," (Barthes 1968) much like the *New Critics* when they disavowed the intent of the author as a fallacy of meaning: "the poem belongs to the public" (Wimsatt and Beardsley 1946: 470).

This is not to deny that the scholar's input is crucial to meaning-making by the very production of the textual reasoned narrative (its philosophy). Wittgenstein's penumbra of meaning undoubtedly enlarges the scope of the reasoned narrative, as does the scholar's subjectivity. Interestingly though, Foucault negated this role for Marx. Foucault temporarily annihilated the Marxian space of meaning. When Foucault mentioned some of the intellectual influences of Marx, and many of them, such as Ricardo, who have influenced North American scholarship, Foucault used that observation as support for his position when he stated, *"Marx, for me, does not exist."*

But, like many other instances, this one should not be taken at face value. Foucault's reading of Marx contradicts Foucault's position on Marx, rejecting to "academise" Marx, to reduce his work to a rigid subject of academic investigation. He declined to ignore Marx's impact, or in Foucault' words, he refused to academise Marx, because that way, his brilliance would have been misunderstood.

This academic rejection should be read within the larger context of Foucauldian work, wherein he presented the scholar as "initiator of discursive practices" (Foucault 1969) because, through theory production, the theorist enables "the endless possibility of discourse" (id.). Nonetheless, Foucault remains critical of Marx. He would view the Marxian erudition as a lack of originality. Ironically, Foucault himself would forget to trace his own intellectual roots in Marxian work. As, for instance, is the case of the Foucauldian "regime of truth" and "discourse" all indebted to Marx's work on ideology (Asiai 2002; Copin 2003).

Whether through the difference built in his text or through the difference of subsequent scholars – such as Cornel West (1991), who noted in Marx's work – Marx influenced the progressive North American thought tradition (1991). As West explains, Marxian thought fits within the historical "conditionedness of human existence" (1991: xvii), and its major contribution is the request for theory to produce action. Pragmatic, West's call resonates with Dewey's as well as with Marx's *Eleventh Thesis on Feuerbach*:

> The philosophers have only interpreted the world in various ways; the point, however, is to change it.
> MARX 1845: 170

Written in 1845, Marx's words called for the practical role of theory and meaning beyond that of legitimizing the power status quo. Centuries later, when engaging it, West (1987) decried the "political impotence" (942) of theory. Roberto Mangabeira Unger (1987), also denounced the "experience of acquiescence without commitment" (41). This Marxian belief in the role of theory has not necessarily been embraced by all American progressive thought, and clearly not by legal theorists. Another progressive colleague of West's, Duncan Kennedy, believed that passivity (political impotence) was sometimes appropriate:

> Sometimes it makes sense to strategize, not the best result within the discourse that will leave the discourse and its implicit metanorm of moderation intact, but the politicization of the setting. Sometimes it doesn't make sense, in which case passivity by all means.
> KENNEDY 1997: 374

Academic acquiescence and subsequent passivity, or mere *intellectual ennui*, as Cornell West persuasively demonstrated, do not ensure social inaction. But contrary to expectations, academic acquiescence produces irresponsible action, which has only intensified since West described it:

> sporadic terrorism for impatient, angry, and nihilistic radicals; professional reformism for comfortable, cultivated, and concerned liberals; and evangelical nationalism for frightened, paranoid, and accusatory conservatives.
> WEST 1987: 942

By studying the work of Karl Marx, one of the most influential and misunderstood of Western scholars, from a legal perspective, the student of his work might be better able to ponder the role of any school of jurisprudence. Using the symbolism of Thomas Paine's *Law* as *King* (1776), explained some chapters later, the anatomy of Marx's work might make it easier to spot the flaws in our legal system: our only King.

Paradoxically, though, much like pragmatism, Marxian thought has been rejected by most American thinkers of all stripes (Wolff 2018). After all, this is the land of "Marx, who? Groucho?" Much like pragmatism, a thoroughly American school of thought, Marxian work has a propensity for connecting theory to action. This incongruity is noteworthy in light of the fact that the work of John Dewey, arguably the prototypically American social thinker, shares immeasurable similarities with that of Marx. Analyzing their work, what differentiates them rests within their historical contingency and political subjectivity. Chapters later, the same will be noted between Marxian thought and American jurisprudence.

1 Marx and Dewey

It is well known that the leading pragmatists are John Dewey, William James, and Charles S. Peirce. Their views are similar because they regarded practical knowledge – available through social experiments or practical educational work, for instance – as the source of true knowledge. This was to be achieved through the pragmatic method of investigation, which according to James meant "looking away from first things, principles, 'categories,' supposed necessities; and of looking towards last things, fruits, consequences, facts." Pragmatism was to do for the business community what maids did for their homes: "sweeps away the cobwebs." Only these were "windy sophistries of the politician and the doctrinaire" (James 1912: 1009).

Michael Dorf refers to philosophical pragmatism as a "form of contextualism" (Dorf 1999: 596), while I prefer Rorty's term of contingency because of the attention given to both spatial and temporary transiency. Through both terms, the idea of normative consequences becomes clear, and through it, the inescapable end of all theoretical pursuits: social action. Written with an eye towards social action and social consequences, Marxian and Deweyan theories reinforce each other.

Marx's work is his response to social reality and provides both a descriptive and normative account, aiming to guide the action necessary to fix the problems it describes. Marx set the stage for his "pragmatic" view as early as 1845 with his "Thesis One" of *Theses on Feuerbach*. There, he pointed out that both Hegelian idealism and Feuerbachian materialism shared the same shortcomings: treating human beings as if they were simply thinking creatures, and forgetting that thinking was just one of the many ways humans engage reality.

> The chief defect of all hitherto existing materialism (that of Feuerbach included) is that the thing, reality, sensuousness, is conceived only in the form of the *object or of contemplation*, but not as *sensuous human activity*, *practice*, not subjectively.
> MARX 1998: 167

Marx clarified that reality could be both contemplated through thought and experienced through senses. He appended philosophical thought, bringing it from the realm of the imaginary (even materialist thought was circumscribed to the imaginary) to the seeds of experienced reality that fertilized the scholarly mind, and through it, to human activity.

Not unlike Marx, American pragmatism is also a call to apply theory to practice, and then incorporate it, as experienced, to build theory. For instance, in 1917, John Dewey famously situated theory within practice, and practice within every changing present, in *The Need for a Recovery of Philosophy*:

> (...) experiencing means living; and that living goes on in and because of an environing medium, not in a vacuum. Since we live forward; since we live in a world where changes are going on whose issues means our weal or woe; since every act of ours modifies these changes and hence is fraught with promise, or charged with hostile energies – what should experience be but a future implicated in the present!
> DEWEY 1917: 8

Marx attempted to explain human history and map out its future, eschewing any false humility, while offering it as a guide to social action, to praxis. American pragmatism is in fact not so different from Marx's theory of praxis once the ideological disparities are set aside. Scholars such as Douglas McDermid believe that Columbia University's own John Dewey thought "epistemology the opium of modern philosophers, numbing fine minds and filling them with world-denying dream" (McDermid 2016: 234), and offered his own brand of naturalism as the answer.

> Old ideas give way slowly; for they are more than abstract logical forms and categories. They are habits, predispositions, deeply engrained

> attitudes of aversion and preference. Moreover, the conviction persists – though history shows it to be a hallucination – that all the questions that the human mind has asked are questions that can be answered in terms of the alternatives that the questions themselves present.
> DEWEY 1951: 19

Would it be reasonable to see this Deweyan belief influenced by Marx's theory? If I were to guess, I believe so, although Dewey often betrayed his lack of first-hand knowledge of Marx's writings (Cork 1949: 438). But Dewey was able to accept "alternative answers" to the same question, and his position on truth could not be closer to Marx's. Furthermore, "Marx was in the air," and Dewey's stance is clearly made in the vein of Marx's own conviction as stated in his *Second Thesis on Feuerbach* (1845). There, Marx wrote that the "question whether objective truth can be attributed to human thinking" was not a theoretical question, but a practical one.

> Man must prove the truth – i.e. the reality and power, the this-sidedness of his thinking in practice. The dispute over the reality or non-reality of thinking that is isolated from practice is a purely scholastic question.
> MARX 1998: 168

In his conflation of Marx with Marxism, and his confusion of the latter with Stalin's perception of truth, Dewey showed hostility to both. Ironically, though, the more one reads Dewey, the more one notices that the American philosopher developed an uncanny affinity for Marx. Sidney Hook, a John Dewey disciple (Eastman 1934: 42), upon studying the original sources, cogently asserted that, doctrinally, Karl Marx and John Dewey were basically similar (Cork 1949: 438).

As pragmatism is undoubtedly the most American school of philosophy, John Dewey's work incongruously stands out as a remarkable form of American Marxism. Both Dewey's skeptical pragmatism and Marx's dialectical inquiry welcome social action.

Theories, as products of rationally organized inquiry, interpellate reality from the scholar's subjectivity, which necessarily includes the observer's education, political views, and cultural foundation. Legal theories, for instance, reflect the mind of the observer. They are highly analytic, and pick a problem apart (as well as initially choosing the problem itself) so they can select what is considered relevant.

Well before Marx, Immanuel Kant introduced the idea of the surrounding reality. Kant's object, or Dorf's contextualism, was mediated by the properties of the subject. In his preface to *The Critique of Pure Reason,* Kant noted how our theories are contingent to our surroundings and to our *experience*. For Kant, the choice was simple: either we make our ideas conform to "the nature of the objects" (our material contingency) or we make ideas conform to our older ideas (our Knowledge Paradigm) (Kant 1890: xxix). Kant chose the latter:

> Either, first, I may assume that the conceptions, by which I effect this determination, conform to the object – and in this case I am reduced to the same perplexity as before; or secondly, I may assume that the objects, or, which is the same thing, that experience, in which alone as given objects, they are cognized, conform to my conceptions – and then I am at no loss how to proceed… (Id.)

Marx similarly noted that we conceive of reality "in the form of objects of observation." But for him, experience was not a mere "mode of cognition" as it was for Kant. For Marx, the subjective impact, – the thinking – was made through the lens of a deeply contextualized and historicized existence, which Kant lacked. Through the Hegelian lens of the man viewed as a process, as the result of his own labor, Marx developed the concept of praxis, which Dewey also embraced in his work.

Marx's view of praxis, while embracing empiricism, was far more complex than those embraced at that time. His was similar to what we might call today "applied thinking," and it first appeared in his *Fifth Thesis on Feuerbach*.

> Feuerbach, not satisfied with abstract thought, wants empirical observation, but he does not conceive the sensible world as a practical, human sense activity.
> MARX 1998: 168

Unlike Kant, Marx did not conceive of subjectivity only in terms of consciousness and abstract knowledge. Unlike Feuerbach, empirical observation subsumes a theoretical position. Theory production for Marx comes also in terms of action, and is deeply immersed in the historical moment. In *German Ideology*, Marx clarified his position and added that humanity was an "historical product." Humanity for Marx was open to our observations and open to be changed through our interactions.

Dewey, too, connected the author's individual subjectivity to the surrounding historical, or collective, subjectivity, and pointed out that all inquiry proceeds within the cultural matrix ultimately determined by the nature of the topic studied. For him, that was social relations. Dewey noted that certain problems could not have arisen in the context of institutions, customs, and interests that existed at a specific moment in time. As he correctly explained, there is a historically set framework of conceptions – called here, the Paradigm of Knowledge or Knowledge Paradigm – which is, so to speak, practically ready-made by society at each point in time because it is not threatening to the existing status quo. Within this transient paradigm, all theories have an obvious and a less obvious epistemological utility. They can offer a means to examine a subject matter as rigorously as possible and make that reality knowable to the student.

Within that framework, all theories face the difficulty of representing reality in such an organized manner that it can be understood and duplicated if the methodology is repeated. Sometimes, their subject matter is so complex and so intricately interwoven with the organizing method that their frame of reference has to adapt to the ever-changing reality. In such cases, the existing, widely accepted theoretical paradigm becomes constraining, and the observing scholar has to find an alternative paradigm or invent a new one.

Though, as nothing comes out of nothing, even new paradigms would have to be imagined or imaginable from within the scholars' subjectivity. Therefore, all theory is both a product of an individual's subjectivity and a result of an existing paradigm. That paradigm shifts with time. To create a theory that is more than transiently useful, scholars have to imagine future paradigms to make it fit them. Marx successfully built a theory which fit multiple paradigms, including a liberal, Euro-centric paradigm and a Soviet-style paradigm. It is up to all scholars to remember theory production as a process affecting theoretical paradigm shifting and opening the door to subsequent theory production.

Both Marx and Dewey viewed all theories as profoundly impacted by the scholars' desire to explain a specific phenomenon, and their utility was determined by individual and social subjectivity: e.g., the scholar's education, political sympathies, and cultural background, as well as the existing theoretical paradigm. Marx implicitly viewed theoretical structure containing both creativity and praxis – its practical aspect. He located its usefulness in its potential to help the subject express herself through a "real mode of affirmation," or action. In *German Ideology*, Marx makes clear his view about theory (philosophy) as moving from contemplation to human activity:

> In direct contrast to German philosophy which descends from heaven to earth, here it is a matter of ascending from earth to heaven. [...] We set out from real, active men, and on the basis of real life-process we

demonstrate the development of the ideological reflexes and echoes of this life-process.
>   MARX and ENGELS 1998: 68–69

Marx's criticism of scholars with whom he had been previously affiliated up to 1844 is reminiscent of Dewey's own view of intellectual progress. That Marx's viewed the role of scholars as ending their contemplation of reality by engaging it for a purpose, through praxis, is further reminiscent of pragmatism.

More on point, David Rubinstein recently explained Marx's entire epistemological view in terms of praxis (1981). Rubinstein viewed it as the result of a dialectical interaction between human and nature at a specific historical moment.

Dewey's paradigm can be viewed as a practical approach to theoretical utility, a concept confined to the historical moment in which a theory appears. Dewey's theoretical paradigm begs for flexibility, so a greater array of theories can appear and serve as useful reflections of the reality they study. Through "observations and experiments … utilizing the existing body of ideas available for calculations and interpretations," Dewey's pragmatism enables scholars to find out "something about some limited aspect of nature."

> [I]n fact intellectual progress usually occurs through sheer abandonment of questions together with both of the alternatives they assume – an abandonment that results from their decreasing vitality and a change of urgent interest. We do not solve them; we get over them. Old questions are solved by disappearing, evaporating, while new questions corresponding to the changed attitude of endeavor and preference take their place.
>   DEWEY 1951: 19

Thirty years ago, the jurisprudential narrative outside the works of Marx and his followers re-imagined the influence of Dewey and Gramsci over our way of thinking. Today, I complement their work with West's call for demystifying patriarchal North Atlantic radicalism. West's observation about super-theories, which from their pedestal "had ignored the specificity of racial and gender subordination," needs to stay with us. West understood that lofty, well-articulated goals are as scholarly interesting as is incessant talk about the internal contradictions of the Rule of Law, but devoid of more. For all its abstractions, Unger's is the anchor that the American progressive narrative has to deal with, and for all its specific contingency, West's relevance remains actual and programmatic. Any struggle to ensure that our American King is not a mere jester in the evolution of natural order has to reckon with Unger's intellectual position that all society is both "made and imagined," and what is imagined encompasses both what is explicitly expressed and, ironically, what is identified by exclusion.

Paradoxically, American jurisprudence has explicitly rejected Marx, hoping that its liberal criticism would deflect any claims of "acquiescence." West never asked for such a mistaken approach. The goal is not the problem – its realization is. Critical Legal Studies, once *the* left-leaning liberal legal theory, disparaged talks about the ability of any rule to determine the scope of its application. It went further, exemplifying that saying "close the door at five" made it apparent that any quest for the logic of this rule could not be found in itself, because it would "require judgments about whether particulars in the order of events correspond or don't correspond to the concepts 'close,' 'door,' and 'five'" (Kennedy 1997: 31). The irony is that it missed the logic offered by "why not close the door at five?," or even clearer, "why not at any other time?" Rejecting the pragmatic outlook at rules in favor of incessant talks about the lack of determinacy is an implicit distraction and a call to passivity.

This book is a call to the opposite of distraction, thus belonging to what Dardot and Laval call the "oppositional" trend (2016). It uses Marx because lofty goals are the way to go. It is not a Marxist book, because lofty goals cannot be used as an excuse to ignore the specificity of the vulnerable individual. While written with a clear understanding that all scholarly constructs are transient, it is proof that nothing needs to be nascently irrelevant.

To the extent that Marx's work is incorporated in support of my theory of meaning-making, my efforts would be too minuscule if I had not tried to explain the many reasons for his original rejection. Some were stated. Others I guessed from how his detractors attempted to discredit his work.

2 Linguistic and Cultural Barriers to Marx's Works

In 1932, Max Eastman wrote that the Russian Revolution of 1917 had increased the popularity of Marxist thought in the United States. This may be so, but only if we were to judge by its popularity at the time Marx died, which was highly limited, most certainly because of linguistic barriers.

Marx's influence stayed insignificant here during the twentieth century for both linguistic and historical reasons. During the first third of the century, Marxism was discarded because of its association with the much-hated Bolshevik Revolution. Then, as soon as the Soviet State was recognized, World War II started. The necessary distance between Marxism and the Stalinist horrors was never established, for obvious political reasons: F.D.R. and Stalin became partners in the war against Hitler and Nazi Germany. As for the latter part of the twentieth century, so much baggage had accumulated behind the label of "Marxism," that, with few exceptions, no one seemed motivated to do any justice to the revolutionary, unique theory that the work of Karl Marx proposes.

A century ago, metaphysics was blamed for Marx's lack of popularity. "Marx was educated in the atmosphere of German metaphysics, as a follower of Hegel, and that way of German thinking is totally alien to the American mind," Max Eastman (1955) wrote. Today, more than ever, we can understand how that might have been a problem given the reality that metaphysics requires both patience and education from the reader: it cannot be conveyed via a tweet. But such an explanation does not seem sufficient for my argument, which is directed to a sophisticated audience. Legal theory is indisputably part philosophy, and some of the metaphysical philosophies discussed here have clearly influenced American jurisprudence.

Karl Marx epitomized nineteenth-century radical brilliance, but like Buñuel's iconoclastic surrealism, his influence remained largely confined to Europe. Marx's *Economic and Philosophic Manuscripts* (1844) and the *Communist Manifesto* (1848) overlapped with John Stuart Mill's *Principles of Political Economy* (1848). Both writers were highly aware of the San Andreas fault-like gap developing between the Victorian status quo of the British Empire and the upcoming crash enabled by the technology-driven capitalist system. While John Stuart Mill became the liberal mind Americans chose to emulate, probably because he settled for exporting the status quo of British domination globally, Marx remained marginalized. I believe that his use of German kept his pre-1848 work in the "foreign" scholarship section, while his later work remained foreign for conceptual reasons. Marx promoted the well-being of the toiling masses at a time when America was lurching towards laissez-faire capitalism, so clearly epitomized by the United States Supreme Court decision in *Lochner v. New York*, 198 U.S. 45 (1905), that later it became described as the *Lochner* era.

Every time scholars engage Marx and his writings, they engage the issue of scholastic rejection, while plantings the seeds of re-evaluation. Marx's work, once almost unanimously ignored by American legal academe, because of its linguistic barriers, is currently re-evaluated. For so many years, it remained marginalized and expediently vilified by association with Soviet-style dictatorships, while no one had ever discredited liberalism because of the innumerable dictatorships it has and continue to inspire, perhaps due to our regime of private property.

This initial minimal exposure of his work may explain its subsequent misappropriation under the label of so-called "Marxism." For many, they tell the story of the most profound Marxian contribution to scholarship – Marx at work engaging the existing body of knowledge and its descriptive and normative role within the particular German circumstances of his youth. His ideology was not an issue. He was building his interdisciplinary approach to reality. Not until later would Marx subsume his findings into his overarching ideology: both in terms of promoting a theoretical point of view (ideological) but also thinking that all points of view (ideologies) are truth-distorting, rather than scope-limiting.

In his later works, Marx's ideology is more on display, as if it seems to have subordinated his historical dialectics to his ideological allegiances. In the *Communist Manifesto* (1848), for instance, Marx both offered a salient explanation of capitalist exploitation and a less supported – though definitely – striking solution for ending that exploitation: the abolition of private property. Marx explained exploitation as the forced taking of an economic surplus from those producing it, by the capitalist. This taking is in exchange for a wage which is determined in connection to the goods needed to be ready for work the following day. In *The Critique of the Gotha Program*, based on a letter by Karl Marx written in early May 1875, he further explained his solution to the societal problem of exploitation: communism and its two stages.

Marx might have been driven by his own experience and ideology to choose exploitation as the societal problem of his time and communism as the appropriate solution. But his work, whether the one produced before 1864, before the creation of the International Working Men's Association, or afterward, remains relevant because its aim to decipher and then engage social reality in its integrated, complex, contingency. Marx's work employed the most ambitious research method to discover what differentiates social relations, historically and during his lifetime, and then to explain his findings in a persuasive, interdisciplinary narrative. It is no secret that the solutions he picked were clearly determined by his specific political interests. And that is what I call the legal charm of Marx, which, like Buñuel's movie, is ironic. Usually, text-instigators, first-tier creators of meaning, have only partial control of the knowledge their theoretical constructs would produce. Knowledge production is the outcome of the meaning-making negotiation between text-instigators and text-interpellators, the second-tier creators of meaning. In retrospect, Marx's work, like Buñuel's surreal fantasy, *The Discreet Charm of the Bourgeoisie* (1972), made the scope of all intellectual gambits clearer.

3 The Cultural Lifespan of Scholarship

If we can imagine and understand intergenerational conflict, with children needing to outdo or outshine their parents, we should be able to understand how theories, as human products, can work along similar lines. Certainly, trends are not alien to theory production, and what is fashionable one day may easily become revolting the next.

For instance, Max Eastman went from Marx devotee to denigrator within his lifetime. Decades later, and on a different continent, Michel Henry followed Eastman's trajectory. In the 1980s, Henry wrote (1983) that no thinker had been more influential than Marx, and no one had been more misunderstood, only to recant this position just before his earthly demise (2014).

Another trend in scholarship production is to omit intellectual debts. Some debts, such as those to Marx, are often overlooked in order to sanitize one's work and better fit within the perceived Paradigm of Knowledge. The work of Michel Foucault, one of the most influential postmodern theorists within the critical studies club membership, is imbued with Marxist sensibility even though he intentionally omitted references to it:

> Given the period in which I write those books, it was good form … to cite Marx in the footnotes. So, I was careful to steer clear of that.
> FOUCAULT 1988

Explicitly, Foucault denied any relevance to Marx on the grounds that Marx belonged culturally to nineteenth-century epistemology. Playing the role of an art critique snapping at admirers of Dali's or Buñuel's, Foucault's position was that their devotees wasted their time with works of art that were "so last century."

> Marxism exists in nineteenth-century thought like a fish in water: that is, it is unable to breathe anywhere else.
> SHERIDAN and FOUCAULT 1980: 70

Had it not been Foucault uttering that statement, it would have been discarded as mere envy. But, culturally, Foucault's attitude proved everything American critical studies circles (*Crits*) needed. It provided them with the reason for their knee-jerk rejection of Marx, often visible in the writings of that circle. Not very innovative, often acting as the "[b]lindfolded Justice [who] never cracks a smile" (Frankenberg 2011) in search of their relevance, the *Crits* borrowed Foucault's vocabulary, forgetting to attribute it to the source, Marx. Ironically, Foucault's compelling and poetic methodological manifesto, describing the nature of "critique" and the proper role of the critic, is full of Marxist-inspired concepts of "power," "truth," and "discourse." This is what became the *Crits*' vocabulary.

This selective attitude towards acknowledging one's intellectual roots is certainly not new and not necessarily limited to the American left, but I did not look for parity across the border. One of its origins may be, as Noam Chomsky explained (2017), the surrounding meta-narrative of liberalism and neoliberalism. The latter, Chomsky expounded, with its thorough flattery of individualism, has succeeded in making everybody happily retreat into the intellectual solitary confinement of their choice. No one has to bow or reckon with the influence of any other's theory when everybody can come up with their own.

That Marx is irrelevant to the legal academia may also be explained by a lack of rigor in identifying intellectual debts, which can be a byproduct of the apathy white tolerance has encouraged in scholarship production. In this atmosphere of everything goes, even radical story-telling becomes emasculated: a voice among the many narratives which ultimately promote, rather than denounce, the current status quo. Ironically, in this atmosphere of factory-like scholarship production, the singular radical voice is ultimately punished because its effects are canceled by so much individual expression.

Think only about Patricia Williams' fantastic book, *Alchemy of Race and Rights: Diary of a Law Professor* (1991). When published, it made racism visible in such a way that it could not be denied. The book was written from her unique perspective of the great-great-granddaughter of a slave and a white southern lawyer. For almost three decades it has become the threshold for eloquent autobiographical essays on the intersection of race, gender, and class. Her work uses the tools of critical literary and legal theory to set out her views of contemporary popular culture and current events, from Howard Beach to homelessness, from Tawana Brawley to the law-school classroom, from Civil Rights to Oprah Winfrey. Merely Googling it brings up elegiac appreciation, but what is its ultimate impact?

> Taking up the metaphor of alchemy, Williams casts the law as a mythological text in which the powers of commerce and the Constitution, wealth and poverty, sanity and insanity, wage war across complex and overlapping boundaries of discourse. In deliberately transgressing such boundaries, she pursues a path toward racial justice that is, ultimately, transformative. (Third Review Google Books)

Did Marx need to be crucified to make space for academic storytelling? Who in the academy believed that the only way to address racial subordination was to appeal to the White Man's emotional intelligence? My fears are that without a larger framework, such as a rigorous Big Theory, any attempt to promote radically different scholarship is seriously crippled. Can we be sure that the current storytelling paradigm does not promote the existing status quo of "whiteness" and "subordination"?

> The paradox for many Black people is that we have defined who we are and who our communities are within the system of subjugation. To the extent that building community based on racial identity has been the only thing separating us from extinction, Black people have done everything possible with what we had. Many Black people creatively have done wonders with the concept of race – the non-genetically, non-biologically, non-geographically, non-spiritually based, a-historical identity that was given to us by our oppressors. Race was a means of oppression, a pacifier when our mothers' breasts were literally torn from our mouths so that they could be raped or killed and tossed into the ocean or sold to the highest bidder to toil in someone's field or scrub someone's floor.
> cunnigham 2007: 804–805

Worse, what if the embedded restraint of not articulating more than our personal story has minimized any attempt to forge theoretical alliances based on ideas, rather than interpretation of experience? e. christi cunnigham (2007) seems to sense the same powerlessness in the present identity dialogue. More complexly she adds the racial aspect to it.

> We have the power to create our own prosperity. Prosperity, including equality, will not be conceded by whiteness. And a racial strategy that stays in relation to whiteness – attempting to reason, litigate, march, guilt, plead, legislate, sit-in, fast, demand, boycott, or otherwise negotiate prosperity, including equality, from whiteness – will most likely fail. Despite the delusion propagated by the race paradigm, whiteness is not the center of all things, and it does not control prosperity. Whiteness only controls the racial relationship, and only as long as people choose to remain in that relationship rather than focusing on our own power and prosperity. (Id.)

> Growth and healing from an abusive relationship often begins with the choice to leave. My grandfather left the sharecropping field. In *The Matrix*, Morpheus offers Neo a choice between the blue pill (staying in the matrix) and the red pill (leaving the matrix). He tells Neo that the matrix "is the world that has been pulled over your eyes to blind you from the

truth.... That you are a slave." The first step to prosperity is making the choice to leave. (Id.)

Theories have relevance if they engage their contingency while exposing their biases. That is their author's ideology. Storytelling is often a ticket to bypass ideological awareness because it is a personal story about exceptional people who engage and conquer their personal reality. They do not necessarily engage reality theoretically as a Kantian object, to study, and then in a Marxian or even Dewean manner to envision change for all.

From this perspective, cunnigham's power to create prosperity is limited to "follow my lead." When storytelling succeeds it is because the stories they tell are inspirational. That is extraordinary and rare.

So, is Marx over for the left? Storytelling does not seem to need his Big Theory, and if we believe that Marxian theory brings in everything without explaining anything then it is not useful in terms of meaning-making, which is the role of any theory. Dewey once denounced, there is "no theory of Reality in general" (Dewey 1917: 2). He forgot to add that because all theories are specific, their specificity can be due to many reasons. The one that is common to all is their ideology. All theories espouse a point of view. Dewey denounced any need for a complete account of reality "*überhaupt*" (id.), perhaps a wink at Marx, thinking, "what would be the need for a replica of reality?" For Dewey, "reality" was a denotative term, a

> word used to designate indifferently everything that happens. Lies, dreams, insanities, deceptions, myths, theories are all of them just the events which they specifically are. (Id.)

In making sense of reality, theories use observation, and various empirical, inductive methods, upon which they develop a deductive approach. This approach is not set in stone for present and future scholarship production. But, what is set is meaning-making, and as Stuart Hall eloquently explained, meaning resides in the difference between T_1 and T_2. The meaning of Marxian theory comes from its interdisciplinary dialectics and its ideological explanation of reality. Marx might have equated his ideology with an absolute standard of ethics, which in itself is Kantian and anti-Marxian, but that is a difference of meaning with which scholars can reckon. Furthermore, Marx built a grand theory while assuming a public point of view, thus challenging those whom his text interpellated to show their own views rather just passively display them, and that again is a difference of meaning which we, the academy, would be misguided to overlook.

4 Marxian Ideology as Soviet, *ergo*, Undesired, Subjectivity

Marx openly engaged reality through the lens of his ideology. That political subjectivity became synonym with the outspokenly non-liberal political system of its time, the Soviet system and Soviet politics. Due to the crimes against humanity perpetrated by the Soviets, few had the inclination to disentangle Marx from its successors, whether legitimate or not.

It comes as no surprise that postmodern philosophers of Michel Foucault's caliber, while having recognized the value of Marx's work, including his non-liberal ideology, have distanced themselves from his work. Their rejection was not of Marx's work in itself, but of what their public persona might have become, had they continued to be associated with Marx.

Subsequent commentators, such as Michèle Barrett, explained Foucault's actions. Rejecting Marx conceptually as "passé," Foucault was rejecting a political posture and a political association with an ossified political party (Barrett 1991: 135). This public rejection proved fruitful: Foucault was emphatically embraced by the Marxphobe Left-leaning American Academe. Interestingly, Foucault never really discarded his Marxian roots to accommodate his more famous, alas liberal, public persona, because, as Etienne Balibar sensed, without Marx there would have been no Foucault.

> Étienne Balibar a écrit que l'œuvre de Foucault se caractérise par une sorte de "véritable combat" avec Marx, cette lutte apparaissant comme une des sources principales de sa productivité.
> LEMKE 2004; FOUCAULT 1988

> Étienne Balibar wrote that Foucault's work is characterized by a sort of "real fight" with Marx, this struggle appearing as one of the main sources of his productivity.

At first blush, the trepidation caused by the ideological association with Marx may be another reason for a lack of academic enthusiasm for his work, especially in the legal academe. One could easily imagine teaching many basic liberal institutions (i.e., private property) would have felt incongruous if Marxian theory would have also been taught in the vicinity. That is unfortunate, because, as argued here, all theories incorporate, in one form or another, the political ideology of their time. So, if the legal academe feels that liberalism is a twenty-first-century ideology, Marxian ideology could easily be described in Foucauldian terms as a nineteenth- and twentieth-century ideology.

Currently, liberalism claims the point of view of a majority, of sorts, though its representatives are mostly the well-educated, middle-class bourgeoisie, with a few token representatives of our various minority groups. Unfortunately, this officious monolithic ideology has brought us to the brink of disaster. We ignore the political subjectivity of the subordinated masses, but that does not negate their existence. As in Buñuel's surreal fantasy, wishful thinking does not alter reality no matter how well one plays their part in it. The corrupt diplomat, John Smith in Buñuel's drama, eventually faced a political coup. His haute bourgeoisie pretentions could not avoid the consequences of his drug dealing. Similarly, curricular choices do not dictate the students' work once they graduate: without incorporating real job market demands, they are nothing more than wishful thinking.

Disentangling ideological misperceptions about curricular offerings, or even embracing ideological differences among them, would only enrich law school curriculum. Moreover, exposing our students to different scholarship would only enrich future legal scholarship.

Finally, Foucauldian scholarship is one of the many ironies Marx's work has enticed. For instance, Balibar's observed that Foucault's work is a response to Marx's, and thus perhaps, without Marx, we would not have had Foucault. Balibar's remark is supported by the many references Foucault himself made about Marx when interviewed.

> Il est certain que Marx, même si on admet que Marx va disparaître maintenant, réapparaîtra un jour. Ce que je souhaite [...] ce n'est pas tellement la défalsification, la restitution d'un vrai Marx, mais, à coup sûr, l'allègement, la libération de Marx par rapport à la dogmatique de parti qui l'a à la fois enfermé, véhiculé et brandi pendant si longtemps.
> FOUCAULT 1994: 457

> It is certain that Marx, even if we admit that Marx will disappear now, will reappear one day. What I want ... is not so much the de-falsification, the restitution of a true Marx, but, certainly, the relief, the liberation of Marx from the dogmatic party that has once locked up, transported and brandished him for so long.

5 Marx's Un-American Attitude toward Religion

The general repudiation of Marx by the American intelligentsia might be also be explained by his anti-religious stance. To the extent that this is the case, his position calls for some explanation.

First, it should be noted that Marx's attitude toward religion went through various stages. During his school days, he conventionally accepted Christian ideals. As David McLellan points out (1970), one of Marx's essays for his *Abitur,* the equivalent of the baccalaureate, or graduation certificate, was on religion. It argued that Christianity was a moral necessity in the moral progress of humanity.

Then, as his studies expanded his horizon, he became interested in the role of the state in promoting religious ideas. Trevor Ling (1980) believes that this later attitude was deeply connected with Marx's legal studies, especially with "his study of the law of property and theft" (King 1980: 11), and thus the incorporation of religious thought in legal norms. Marx would recollect those debates he analyzed in 1852/53, as an editor for *Rheinische Zeitung*. Marx would credit the Debates of the Rhine Province Assembly on the theft of wood and the division of landed property as causing him to focus on "economic questions" (B [Marx] 1842).

Marx articulated his derisive position on religion quite early. In his *Introduction to a Contribution to the Critique of Hegel's Philosophy of Right*, which he wrote in 1843–44, he viewed religion as the "self-consciousness and self-esteem of a man who has either not yet won through to himself, or has already lost himself again" (1970: 131).

> Religion is the general theory of this world, its encyclopedic compendium, its logic in popular form, its spiritual point d'honneur, its enthusiasm, its moral sanction, its solemn complement, and its universal basis of consolation and justification. It is the fantastic realization of the human essence since the human essence has not acquired any true reality. [...] Religion is the sigh of the oppressed creature, the heart of a heartless world, and the soul of soulless conditions. It is the opium of the people. The abolition of religion as the illusory happiness of the people is the demand for real happiness. To call on them to give up their illusions about their conditions is to call on them to give up a condition that requires illusions. The criticism of religion is, therefore, in embryo, the criticism of that vale of tears of which religion in the halo. (Id.)

Marx's derisory position on religion could have multiple origins. Scholastically, his views on religion could have been influenced by its position that religion was an impediment to praxis, action, a tenet of his scholarship.

Marx explained the reason for taking up the issue of religion, as well as the method of engaging with religion, in an essay about man's rights. Marx was interested in Man at the intersection of history, and religion was, at the time, the all-encompassing story of that journey. In the nineteenth century, Marx's Man did not regard religion as a story to enjoy but rather as a play in which the main storyteller is also the father figure. Thus, Marx deemed that relation incestuous, or worse, cancerous. Like a night-time illusion that was dangerously slipping into daily life, religion was threatening man's potential for action, or praxis, which Marx regarded as the goal of all theoretical endeavors, religious or not. But, in a play, the beggar has a fast exit: he kisses a frog and becomes a prince. In reality, a pauper cannot leave behind his conditions that quickly.

In Marx's defense, he always perceived Man's life, the object of his theoretical endeavors, as the historical product of state and society: dynamically interconnected to the surrounding environment, manmade or otherwise. Finally, the method in which Marx analyzed and then discarded religion, "the opium of the people," is pure dialectics: it has a premise which summarizes the state of knowledge at that moment, which Marx criticizes rather than negates and then proceeds to incorporate into his conclusion, which itself becomes the basis for a new premise for another scholar. This deeply democratic engagement with religion, a human product, is indeed un-American, and perhaps explains this country's consistent reticence towards Marx and his work.

> The abolition of religion as the illusory happiness of the people is the demand for real happiness. (Id.)

The irony of this statement resides in its youthful dogmatism. Marx could not foresee the appearance of such strands of religion – like liberation theology, for instance – which were influenced by his theory and encouraged progressive social movements.

Liberation theology belongs to a different historical and geopolitical intersection. It peaked in the late 1960s and 1970s. A distinctly Latin American movement, it preached that it was not enough for the church to simply empathize and care for the poor. Instead, believers said, the church needed to be a vehicle to push for fundamental political and structural changes that would eradicate poverty, even – some believed – if it meant supporting armed struggle against oppressors (Kirchgaessner and Watts 2015).

Another irony of Marx's religious position might be seen at the moment Marx penned his disdain: In 1844, Marx was a young man, whose natural demise was decades away. Americans academia might see age, in addition to his scholarship, as a factor in Marx's religious stance. Age has been such a factor, albeit in the opposite way, for other proclaimed atheists.

For instance, Max Horkheimer, who harbored similar views of religion, and who had been described as the most influential director of the Institute for Social Research, belonging to the Marxist-flavored Frankfurt School, changed his own view on religion five years before his demise. Then, Horkheimer wrote an unexpected essay on Psalm 91:2, "In you Eternal One, alone I trust" (Goldstein 2006: 3).

6   Marx's Unshaken Belief in Human Progress

It remains difficult to ascertain the reasons for Marx's limited popularity in America. He definitely looked like a self-made hustler, the fabric of any American hero, who believed in human progress and the values of European Enlightenment. While attractive as a folk hero, he put off the academy. Perhaps he came across as too self-assured.

Marx did not seem to be acquainted with "I don't know," which American academe regards today as a mark of any advanced scientific mind. "I don't know" is the sign of a self-erected barrier against dogmatism. But what about the dogmatism of one's ignorance? How does "I don't know" fare against it? Despite whatever story we want to tell ourselves about Karl Marx's dogmatic attitude toward scholarship, perhaps it would be good to remember that he was never happy with his work, and he constantly revised it. *Grundrisse*, probably the most Marxian work, remained unknown to his friend, sponsor, and collaborator, Engels, and in manuscript form until 1937.

Jurisprudentially, skepticism, as Louis Michael Seidman (2014) shows, has deep roots in American constitutionalism. "Much of the skepticism has its roots in social contract theory itself" (id.: 9). He continues, "how exactly will words on a piece of paper stop self-interested rules [from] turning into tyrants?" (id.: 10). Hobbes gave us the answer to that worrisome question through negative capability, or "the ability to live with uncertainties, mysteries, doubts, without any irritable reaching after fact and reason" (Smith 2016: 86).

In this Hobbesian view, skepticism may well be a sign of intellectual fatigue where undesired answers to the crucial questions are ignored in favor of faith. And this is the very opposite of the type of "I don't know" skepticism. That is why perhaps, Marx needs to be re-explained: He was neither meek nor modest because he could and did deliver.

Instinctively, instead of limiting himself to a specific academic area, Marx embraced multidisciplinarianism. Early on Marx embraced philosophy, law, as well as history and economics, as he defended his studies in a letter to his father (Marx 1837). When he finished writing novels, poetry, and journalism, Marc became a scholar who continued to produce all types of scholarly literature, including a doctoral dissertation (Wheen 2000).

Marx believed that the human mind could imagine problems and fathom solutions before empirical support was available. And he proved right: every conceived thesis contained its own antithesis. To his own body of scholarship, he encouraged collaboration further encouraging diversity, such as Engels' political and empirical scholarship (Blackledge 2016). If, in the North American academic milieu, Marx's work remains marginalized like an opaque surrealist creation, it nonetheless occupies a prophetic space in some non-Western academic circles (Nogbou 2017: 60).

Ironically, whether marginalized or not, Marx's work radiates unsurpassed knowledge and affects the meaning of all scholarship production. His work continues to represent unexamined aspects of the surrounding social contingency that have yet to disappear into social irrelevance.

There are cognitive moments in human history when staying the course is not an option. Moreover, for scholarship, such as jurisprudence, whose philosophy is arguably a form of cultural politics, Marx's work is that necessary bridge to clarity. His work makes visible the structure of all social science scholarship, ergo, jurisprudence, as ideology, philosophy, and irony. The latter is evident through its significance, which is revealed through what is expressed and what is ignored, creating results rarely within the author's ability to control. If so, wouldn't a theory which makes this gambit visible help us all perceive how despotic, rarely wise, and hastily fond of jesters, all kings really are? Of course, this presumes we are all engaged in the same enterprise, to have our students fully understand the legal system, and not commit to memories a set of doctrines that will change through their career. At a minimum it exposes the frailty of our theoretical choices at this historical moment when placating tectonic social rifts with well-contained, small-impact, tribal solutions is tantamount to using band-aids to stop a brain hemorrhage.

Through Marx's work, we could gather perspective over our own act of scholarship production. In the process, we can also learn how to parse through old and new meaninglessness, paraphrasing Walter Benjamin, as well as through the folly of our times, the desire to always find ourselves in the knowing.

> "Knowledge" is the [defense] in an argument to win, [so we] may assert mastery over it. As Walter Benjamin wrote in one of his earliest essays, "the philistine, you will have noted, only rejoices in every new meaninglessness. He remains in the right."
> SUTHERLAND 2011: 111

But what if this tendency to always be accepted, to be "in the right" and thus avoid confronting the unfamiliar, is what keeps us from acknowledging that the current social cataclysm is a sign of structural oppression gone too far? Bringing attention to irony as an unavoidable, intrinsic element of scholarship should humble us and free our intellectual ambition to reach new heights: we will stumble no matter what, but paraphrasing Norman Vincent Peale, without dreaming we cannot build anything worth dreaming.

CHAPTER 2

Marxian or Marxism: Labels Differentiating Content or Fabricating Difference?

There are many reasons to study Marx's body of work. One reason is what I consider his major scholastic flaw: his lack of awareness about the impact of ideological irony, a flaw so wide-spread in the academic world. While Marx's work incorporates a non-liberal political viewpoint, Marx, arguably because he refused to label his work accordingly, seems to have missed the impact ideology exerted upon his own scholarship. Thus, despite his dialectical interdisciplinary approach to the ever-changing social reality, which enabled Marx to identify systemic social problems, lacking awareness about the ideological limitations of his scholarship impacted the solutions proposed, and his work's scholastic relevance. His lack of ideological awareness, and refusal to label his own work ideologically, ironically empowered its subsequent interpellators, who read into it unexpected layers of meaning.

Labels clarify textual meaning. Depending on their role, labels, including ideological labels, could be useful meaning-making tools in the hands of both S_1 and S_2. They help identify content and differentiate it.

Today, within the American academe, ideological self-labeling, as well as discussions about the impact of ideological biases on meaning-making, rarely receives the deserved attention. Interdisciplinarity does not cure scholars' (S_1) subjectivity. Choosing a particular research method or reasoned narrative, whether embracing pragmatism and "experiantialism" or not, does not cure meaning-making of subjectivity, especially of ideology. It does not minimize the implicit meaning-making biases which come with it. Working on expanding the scope of research while ignoring or minimizing the impact of their subjectivity, scholars do not increase the power they have over meaning-making. In fact, I argue here, text-instigators (S_1) might lose the only control they have over meaning-making: textual (T_1) clarity. This occurs, when text-instigators (S_1) avoid ideological self-labeling and thus leave subjective elements of textual meaning-making dangling. Ironically, those "hidden" elements become ammunition to be used by the text-interpellator, S_2. Leaving them unaddressed, S_1 cannot reclaim them subsequently, defending the clarity of textual meaning. Perhaps inadvertently, S_1 makes it easier for ideological irony to be awakened by S_2. Even ignored, ideology remains embedded in T_1. Avoiding ideological labels, S_1 surrenders meaning-making negotiation into the ideological hands of S_2.

Another reason for acknowledging ideological bias rests with the fact that ideological labels can be used but also misused. If S_1 does not use them for fear of boxing T_1's meaning, there is no guarantee that S_2 would not use or misuse the dormant clues to properly or improperly limit T_1's meaning.

In this context, the question I often find myself faced with is how could an entire body of sophisticated scholarship, such as Karl Marx's work, be discarded as mere ideology, or one's derided subjectivity? I struggle with this question because the near-total American ignorance of Marx's works does not make sense purely based on its content, given its metaphysical and anti-religious stance nonetheless, when so little is known of it. Neither does it make sense purely on emotions. There must be a combination of the two: something epistemological and emotional in the instinctual rejection of Marx. Paraphrasing Bryan A. Stevenson, it might be that presenting Marxian writings under the label "Marxism" keeps it intellectually unappealing.

While labels could be useful meaning-making tools, it might be of interest to follow the evolution of the qualifier of *Marxism*. For Marx, *Marxism* was

> an altogether peculiar product – so much so that Marx once said to Lafargue: 'Ce qu'il y a de certain c'est que moi, je ne suis pas Marxiste.' [If anything is certain, it is that I myself am not a Marxist].
> ENGELS 1882

Along Marx's lines, I contend that *Marxism* has stopped being a mere label. It has become a concept in itself. Friedrich Nietzsche (1999) talked about the metaphorical nature of knowledge and truth (400). Nietzsche argued that the "true" or literal meaning of a word is one to which we have become accustomed due to frequent use, not unlike a metaphor, whose metaphorical nature has been itself forgotten. With Marxism, the process is even more complex.

In 1940, when Leon Trotsky wrote about *Marxism,* he emphasized its meaning contrasting it to "petty-bourgeois opposition." For Trotsky, *Marxist* and *Marxism* denoted a particular theoretical foundation based on the works of Marx, Engels and Lenin, particular political principles of internationalism, and particular "organizational methods" of the moment (Trotsky 1965: 93). When Trotsky grouped those writers under the designation of *Marxism*, the label had already become a substitute for anti-American ethos. Since then, it has been an identifier with fluid, shifting content: a block of knowledge built on Soviet-sympathizing theory. It is an emotional metaphor used to label some highly complex, often little known, works of scholarship. Academically, *Marxism* resembled a label of geopolitical and historical origin (Eastern Europe, U.S.S.R., parts of Africa and South Asia).

Labeling is neither benign nor malign in itself. It is, in fact, a powerful epistemological practice and its result, the label, is a fundamental organizing tool of knowledge, a way to differentiate meaning. Still, because it is a lower-level abstraction, in that a mere identifier replaces the hard-to-define abstraction while it gives the audience a sense of knowledge, labels are easier to misuse. By their very definition, as Margaret Somerville (1994) explains, labels represent a different intellectual result than that of equivocations, contradictions, or ambiguities.

Audiences interacting with any label expect to quickly become enlightened, informed, edified, or educated. For instance, "right" has an ambiguous legal meaning both as a noun and adjective, but it is not necessarily a label. Labels, nouns or adjectives, clarify meaning as much as they create false assumptions, as happens when the same term is used to identify different content. Ironically, in heavily specialized intellectual areas where fluency in general knowledge is not especially valued (because it lacks), abstractions are much revered. Also, they are deemed to represent objective, superior knowledge. Labels are thus trusted and taken for granted as necessities.

Labels instill trust and quell worries because they contain an ideological disclaimer of objectivity. For example, "margarine" designates an edible spread which is not butter. In that we trust labels to identify the intrinsic quality of the product they define. No one really knows what is inside the "margarine" labeled package, except that, as the label states, it is a spread which does not contain dairy products.

Marxism has never been a mere label identifying the works of Marx. In the best of circumstance, it has included the works of Marx and Engels. Sometimes, it conveyed the idea of scholarship devoid of liberal bias. Grouping works deemed similar in content under the same descriptor has the advantage of enabling connections. Sometimes, such expediency is at the cost of accuracy and understanding. *Marxism* today lingers in the shadows of "Stalinism": emotions still substitute for reasoning, ignorance for understanding, and the conversation moves along dismissively.

When *Marxism* became a qualifier akin to "Stalinism," to literature promoting a particular anti-democratic political view, all non-liberal scholarship lost. *Marxism*, as a label, sounds worse than unpalatable; it is unpatriotic to read Marxist works. From content identifier, the label has morphed into the reason for not engaging the text, and for the rejection of Karl Marx. Rejected, his works become less and less familiar. The less familiar they are, the more unpalatable they become, and the more cognitive value the label has. The cycle grows, repeating itself at a larger level.

Marx indeed created an unapologetic theory whose critical attitude has been characterized as anti-capitalist. If Marxian is not acceptable, then, I argue that it is better to forgo expediency and use scholarly labels only by reference to the frame of thought to which they belong. In this manner, labeling would fulfill its identifying potential.

For instance, Marx, unlike Lenin, focused on history in motion, and subsequently on the transient character of capitalism. Their distinction seems as scholastically rich as their similarity. In such situations, *paraphrasing* instead of labeling might be more suited. But, as Jeremy Bentham would have explained, paraphrasing requires a high level of familiarity with the complex subject matter and its contingency so that it can be accurately summarized and reworded.

If *Marxism* needs to be used for reasons of expedience, then perhaps we should dig deeper into its American history and discuss it within the North American contingency. For instance, American *Marxism* has a multicultural history. Communists like Claudia Jones, a once-popular figure, was an active journalist and public speaker. Mentored by W.E.B. Du Bois, and a close friend of Paul and Eslanda Goode Robeson, Jones was a housemate of Lorraine Hansberry (Davies 2008). Rediscovering Claudia Jones and her work, we would rediscover the radical black female subject and bring it back into U.S. political consciousness. The ideological risk associated with integrating such eminent personalities into the canon is that, American academy would have to engage *Marx, Marxism* and its complex history instead of expediently ignoring everything.

Jones, like Robeson, dared to adopt *Marxism* in its Soviet outlook, and in the process she showed that theoretically, *Marxist* lsiterature – other than Karl Marx's work – offered a solid foundation for a critique of class oppression, imperialist aggression, and gender subordination. As Carole Boyce Davies (2007) explains, Jones proved that *Marxist* theory was far from dogmatic *and* that there was space "left" from Karl Marx (S_1) for other scholars, like her (S_2), to explore. Jones embraced a political philosophy that was anathema in the McCarthy period of the 1940s and 1950s. Her brand of *Marxism* was "anti-racist, anti-sexist, pro black community orientation" (id.: 6), and her racially and gender mixed entourage mirrored her thoughts (id.).

> Claudia Jones's position on the "superexploitation of the black woman," Marxist-Leninist in its formation, offered, for its time, the clearest analysis of the location of black women – not in essentialized, romantic, or homogenizing terms but practically, as located in U.S. and world economic

hierarchies. It thereby advanced Marxist-Leninist positions beyond their apparent limitations. To develop her argument, Jones contended that if all workers are exploited because of the usurping of the surplus value of their labor, then black women – bereft of any kind of institutional mechanism to conquer this exploitation, and often assumed to have to work uncountable hours without recompense – live a life of superexploitation beyond what Marx had identified as the workers' lot. (Id.: 2)

Claudia Jones' story is remarkable because of her vulnerability as a non-white woman and an immigrant. She reminds one of Rosa Luxembourg, herself a "non-Aryan," addressed immigrant woman engaging the world from a particular position of non-existent power (Luxembourg 1999). But, hers is not alone. Before Paul Robeson's star shone (Duberman 1989), C.L.R. James made waves by adapting Trotsky's theories to Western Europe, in the United Kingdom and later in the United States (Cripps 1997: 35).

What is common to all these thinkers of Marxian sensibility is their attempt to explain reality from a power struggle perspective. C.L.R. James considered the idea of separating the Negro power struggle from the White workers' power struggle "a step backwards" (id.). He believed that if the "white worker extends a hand to the Negro" (id.), there would have been no discussion of self-determination, but a unified front. Their work can be labeled as American *Marxism* and it would help explain its history while bringing its message into the present day.

History proved that James' failed attempt at unity was exploited by the establishment and also by the progressive forces, who believed that social and cultural difference, rather than economic sameness, needed to come to the forefront. The voices of Jones and James need to be rediscovered, as fusion is the only way to oppose a unified monied front which is on the rise.

Labels help expedite communication if they are transparent and not a metaphor taken on its own distinct meaning. They are even more necessary today, when money has monopolized knowledge and political speech to unexpected levels. One wonders whether today's have-less and have-nots still enjoy the same full democratic representation like their moneyed counterpart or whether they are fast approaching the earlier democratic experiment of 3/5s of a gentleman's voice.

Labels may also help sanitize the study of Karl Marx and North American Marxists. If universities are afraid of being perceived as legitimizing Marxian studies, labels can become a useful disclaimer. Another way to study Marx would be with a clear ideological disclaimer: Liberal Studies of Marx(ism). As such, there would be no endorsement, but a new generation of students would be able to judge for themselves a different type of scholarship. In the spirit of John Stuart Mill's free market of ideas, capitalism would be better served.

Identifiers, such as a "Liberal Critique of Marx and Marxism," would also minimize the derision of the one-word label alone, that *Marxism*, or *Marxist* tends to carry over the body of ideas. As the work of Jones shows, *Marxism* is a body of work so complex and so foreign to the evaluating frame that for everybody who employs it to do it justice, something clearer is needed.

Rather than a mere one-word label, perhaps an ideological prefix (nonliberal; a-liberal, etc.) would clarify the terms of the scholastic discourse. The evaluated *Marxist* narrative and the evaluating liberal paradigm would become equally situated and have a chance to be compared and judged on their goals, methods, and claims. In the process, for the overall benefit of knowledge, the high expediency that labeling promises would be slightly diminished.

Without ideological clarity, terminology is prone to confusion. Theories, which delight in the creation of new concepts and abstract generalities, also engage in widespread use of highly abstracted binary terminology: realism and nominalism, idealism and materialism, subjectivism and objectivism, or just and unjust. Seemingly reluctant to express their content, such abstractions function to prop each other up, giving the superficial appearance of semantic control. For Peirce (1877), *nominalism* and *realism* are a necessary terminological binary because they convey the opposite meaning. Whereas realism stands for laws and universals having a life outside the subject's mind, while nominalism stands for the opposite: "law and universals are merely products of the mind" (Forster 2011: 1). Most of the time, however, nominalism is meant to denote the mere use of labels and names.

Labels, such as "Marxism," carry meanings that go beyond the concepts they identify. Labels describe as much as they ascribe content. They are useful among the initiated, but dangerously misinforming among the rest. Unless clearly understood, a label might smear and discourage inquiry, especially when no one knows what is behind it. This makes it quite difficult to reassess the theory behind the label. How many of us are ready to accept the reassessment of something we grew up rejecting as morally evil if that entails reassessing our entire value system? It would be painful, perhaps, but demanding such a debate for Marx and his work would only benefit American jurisprudence and encourage scholars to reimagine their intellectual zone of comfort.

Jurisprudentially speaking, "naming a thing" has proven a complicated, but much-needed exercise because its object – law – has often been prone to confusion (Freeman 2008: 33). If naming or "denoting" things is hard, the answer perhaps needs to be something other than rejecting a theory of Marxian meaning.

The works of Marx and those of his followers have been insufficiently studied; otherwise misused labels could have not blemished scholars or marred politicians the way they have. Their content has rarely been clarified. Lumping them together and disregarding them for being too vague, too ambitious, or even un-American, has never required much effort, nor has it received much resistance. The body of work that Marx left behind – its philosophy, a theoretical explanation of the interaction between Man and Nature – stands apart because it is a mega-theory assimilating the history of human knowledge writ large. Marxian works incorporate Renaissance-age beliefs in the intellectual prowess of Man entrusted with never-ending human progress. It is an optimistic theory with a pragmatic edge: it aims to manipulate social evolution so we attain a decent society for all. To that end, Eastman was correct when he described Marx's work as social engineering (Eastman 1934).

This book is also an answer to improper labeling and willful or less willful scholarly confusion because it proposes both a myth-debunking (meaning is public, i.e., ideological communication actuated by irony) and a path to do it through diversity and difference. Because, if Wittgenstein was right that the meaning of a knight is given by the part it plays in the game of chess (id.), it is because the rules are known to all. Inasmuch, all the parts are taken into consideration, dialectically, and each one plays a unique role. Hence, difference ensures meaning. In a sea of liberal scholarship, embracing Marx and Marxian theory is the difference needed to give meaning.

CHAPTER 3

Textual Differences and Marx's Interdisciplinary Dialectics

The triptych structure of scholarly meaning proposed here incorporates reasoned textualism, clashing subjectivities, and their ironic outcome. The explanation relies on symbols, such as T_1 to designate reasoned narrative (Friedmann's philosophy), as well as S_1 and S_2 to identify the text-instigator and the text-interpellator, whose often divergent ideologies would clash and would ironically produce the difference of meaning between what is textually encoded and what becomes knowledge through S_2's understanding and subsequent theory production (T_2).

Here, Stuart Hall's theory of difference stems especially from the irony actuating the ideology (public subjectivity) of S_1 and S_2. S_1, T_1's instigator, sets the tone for the meaning (or reading) S_2, T_1's interpellator, will eventually ascribe T_1. That meaning-making process is the product of their ideological interaction. Its result is ironic because their difference of views, not similarity, is what gives T_1 its memorable meaning, assuring a place for T_1 in the constellation of public knowledge (K).

The method of research affects the quality of T_1's reasoned narrative, its philosophy, as labeled here. The method echoes the scholar's (S_1) abilities and often calibrates the control S_1 may exercise over the meaning of T_1.

Scholars, such as Jon Elster for instance, rely on the method of research to argue that scholarship production is an objective enterprise whose rigorous method can obscure or even eliminate the author's subjectivity. Though measurable by objective standards of logic and skill, the research method, like the entire scholarship enterprise, is never free of subjectivity.

Well before guiding the interpellator's (S_2) meaning-making efforts when engaging the text, S_1's subjectivity directs all creative effort, including the chosen method of research. As further analyzed in subsequent chapters, S_1's subjectivity covers both creative alienation and ideology. For that reason, both S_1's private and public subjectivity influence scholarship production. At a minimum, they shape the choice of scholarly interests as well as their treatment, being weaved into the choice of research method.

While not necessarily an original statement, some explaining still needs to be proffered when arguing that one's research method is harnessed by their subjectivity. S_1's education, background, cultural comfort, as well as ideology inform all scholastic choices. Again, I will rely on Karl Marx's example to explain his interdisciplinary dialectics. They are the product of Marx's education, socio-economic and historical contingency. They are both an ideological choice and outcome.

1 Dialectics and Ideology: Thinking, Researching and Incorporating Observations

Scholarship creation, I believe, comes from a moment of alienating intellectual discomfort for the scholar (S). That cognitive discomfort is an ideological moment of interpellation. S is interpellated by the existing scholarship, and in the process, S becomes S_2, a text-interpellator. Only after S_2 perceives the state of existing scholarship as inadequate and views it as an intellectual challenge, S_2 might become S_1, a text-instigator. As S_1, the scholar will reduce or eliminate that inadequacy through theory creation. If S_1 experiences this discomfort in its interconnectivity, it is very likely that S_1 will engage in interdisciplinary studies. If the discomfort is systemic, S_1 most likely will use dialectics to address reality and its representation systemically.

In another consideration, some theorists may be prone to a particular method of analysis. For instance, ironists may be predisposed toward dialectical thinking most likely because they embrace contingency and its historicity. Richard Rorty claims they do not use final vocabularies in order to limit their theoretical impact. Within this intellectual lightness, nevertheless Rorty (2001) recognized the moment of, what I call here, textual instigation as the result of "cognitive inquiry" (29). He encourages philosophers to drop the epistemological basis of thought, as well as its aspiration toward truth. Instead, he asks them to adopt a new role, that of edifier, which, in his view, would minimize the theoretical impact of any textual instigation. In doing that, Rorty does not necessarily lessen their creative starting point, as much as he invites them to consider their work as a mere connecting knot within the larger Paradigm of Knowledge. He asks them to surrender to dialectics.

> By this model, ideas and beliefs are compared and contrasted to each other within historically circumscribed "conversations" rather than in relation to any foundational form of truth.
> PETTEGREW 2000: 9

This explanatory grid is similar to Adorno's "constellar thinking." Adorno's constellar thinking incorporated dialectics to the extent that it compared and contrasted ideas as they presumably fit a larger picture.

As a method of reasoning, dialectics relies on speculative thinking focused on interconnectivity. In *Negative Dialectics*, Adorno called it "constellar thinking." He believed that there is no step by step progression into meaning-making, because concepts, as the building blocks of thinking and meaning-making, exist interconnected, into a constellation. Meaning making is thus possible because "the constellation illuminates [...] specific sides of its objects" (Adorno 1973: 162–163) unveiling them to our senses.

However, dialectics has been separated from its politics, from the scholar's ideology, probably in a desire to pretend that social sciences, as science, are not imbued with the scholar's ideology. By arguing the opposite, this book's analysis adds to the conversation.

As a method of speculative, apolitical, thinking, dialectics has been used by philosophers through history. Its attraction rests perhaps in its object of study, life itself. Life is in continual flux. From birth to death, life is a succession of accumulations and transformations until it reaches a point where it negates its specificity only to be absorbed in the larger life cycle. What better method to study it than dialectics!

As noted in previous chapters, dialectics traces back to the Greeks. It suffered a major repositioning with Hegel, then with the Right and Left ("Young") Hegelians, exemplified by Kierkegaard and Marx. By asserting "what is rational is actual; and what is actual is rational," (1952: 10), Hegel offered the central speculative link to religion, philosophy, and politics. Equating rational with actual, the Hegelian Idea became actuated into the Prussian state. The Right Hegelians built on it. The Young Hegelians rejected the reconciliation between religious and philosophical thought, which Marx interpreted as evidence of an ideological justification for the status quo, and instead used dialectics to mediate transforming reality through reasoned thought (Sinnerbrink 2014: 43):

> My dialectic method is not only different from the Hegelian, but is its direct opposite. To Hegel, the life-process of the human brain, i.e., the process of thinking, which, under the name of "the Idea," he even transforms into an independent subject, is the demiurges of the real world, and the real world is only the external, phenomenal form of "the Idea." With me, on the contrary, the ideal is nothing else than the material world reflected by the human mind, and translated into forms of thought. ... The mystification which dialectic suffers in Hegel's hands by no means prevents him from being the first to present its general form of working in a comprehensive and conscious manner. With him it is standing on its head. It must be turned right side up again, if you would discover the rational kernel within the mystical shell.
>
> QUOTING MARX; Id.: 52

Probably because they were too earnest, the Young Hegelians missed the irony in Hegel's famous incarnation of metaphysical dialectics. Ironically, Hegel's dialectics attempted to interrupt life's dynamics, which ended with the Prussian state. Marx denounced its static conception and concentrated on its dynamism.

Jurisprudentially, dialectics is suited to reflect the main component of law. According to Professors and U.S. Supreme Court Justices, Holmes and Frankfurter, law mirrors life itself. If law is messy, jurisprudence, a reflection on the state of law, cannot be ossified in a particular Regime of Truth, just because it expresses convictions or prejudices which today's legislators or judges are likely to share. Paraphrasing Justice Holmes' words in his dissent in *Lochner v. New York*, 198 U.S. 45 (1905), if our Constitution is "made for people of fundamentally differing views," (198 U.S. at 76), then jurisprudence should reflect that.

No one has ever asserted that dialectics is a simple method of research, but by considering the complexity of its object of study, life itself, it does more service to promoting knowledge than any other simpler methods. Dialectics seems best suited to account for the unaccountable (Moseley and Campbell 1997), and while it might be easily mimicked, alas, it would produce not knowledge but some mimicked version of it. If life, and its historical recount, rarely follows linear logic, then dialectical derivation might be a better match.

A few years ago, CUNY Professor Jack Jacobs shared with me how he illustrates dialectics to his students. Jacobs uses the "egg hatching" metaphor: the chick both represents evolution and revolution. The chick comes out of the egg (evolution), but in the process it destroys the egg (revolution). Dialectics, as a method, is a way to incorporate as much diverse, available information as possible, which is then analyzed and synthesized in a result that might negate its empirically verifiable premise. The author's educated imagination will bring it to a new theoretical level of expression.

2   Marxian Interdisciplinary Dialectics

Unlike his predecessors, Marx used dialectics within an interdisciplinary framework; although, like them, he believed it separate from his ideology. He delineated his intellectual interests in interdisciplinarity early in his academic career, as evidenced in the various letters he wrote to his father (Marx 1837). Through his studies in economics, law, history, and philosophy, a young Marx reconfigured dialectics, a method of analytical thinking dating back to Plato's dialogues, which visualizes the systemic and often contradictory interconnection of society. In Marx's hands, it metamorphosed, because it became the product of his education, desires, alienation, as well as his ideology. As such,

Marx's dialectics differed from Engels', whose theory popularized what many refer to as *Marxist dialectics*.

Engels promoted a three-step approach, or three basic dialectical laws, of the universe:

1. The transformation of quantity into quality and vice-versa;
2. The negation of negation; and
3. The coincidence of the opposites.
   ENGELS 1940

Marx's dialectics also diverged from its subsequent Leninist popularization (Lenin 1982). Marxian dialectics are not schematic crotches for weak minds. They sublimate contradictions into their consequences through Marx's views of contemporary history and its fundamental institutions, such as capital, which Marx described dialectically as "profit on wage labor" (Marx 1909: 282). According to Marx (1909), capital is the work of a "laborer [who himself] comes out of the process of production other than he entered" (id.: 329). Dialectically, the laborer is different, because he has lost some of his blood to the vampire's thirst for the "living blood of labor" (id.: 282). Marx's dialectics transcends abstract thinking. It sublimates the material life, and as such, it is empirically verifiable (Marx 1975: 47).

Marxian dialectics credited Hegel's dialectical method, itself traceable back to Greek philosophy. "In Plato, Hegel found the key to unlock the mystery of Being." (Windelband and Ruge 1913: 72). But, whereas Plato's dialectic worked with opposing concepts, Hegel's focused on philosophical thinking. Through the Hegelian structural lens, dialectics inherited an initial *first step* which can be described as the moment of *understanding* the data – empirical or theoretical. Having made a judgment call in favor of our ideatic world, Hegel focused on the disjunction between the real, material, surrounding world, and our world of ideas.

In his twenties, Marx wrote the *Critique of Hegel's Doctrine of the State* (1843), which focused in large part on Hegel's dialectical logic. Marx noted how Hegel inverted the world of empirical truth into reason. The finite object of study became for Hegel an idea with a universal meaning. Hegel saw a fluid duality in everything: ideas reclaimed an objectified existence only to connote a version of the Absolute Idea, of the universal. Objects existed only as embodiments of the universal Idea. Marx posited that Hegel was able to reach the conclusions he desired because he did not start from the empirically observable reality, noticing contingency in action. Instead, Marx argued, Hegel used dialectics to justify his idea of history.

> Hegel [did not start] with an actual existent [a subject], but with predicates of universal determination, and because a vehicle of these determinations must exist, the mystical Idea [became] that vehicle.
>
> MARX 1975: 80

Unlike his predecessors, Marx's dialectics starts with the study of the everyday contingency (similarly, some might say, to William James' sensuous education). Marx's work is functional, and his method focuses on scientific concepts used to explain the surrounding (material) social world. He promoted theoretical functionality as a tool to engage and to interpellate reality. For Marx, theory was a device to help humans manage, or even attempt to change their contingency, the temporary, the inevitable and uncontrollable cycles of life, rather than wait for natural changes to happen.

Although Marx never wrote a treatise on dialectics as Hegel did, Marx replaced what he viewed as Hegel's outdated scholarship. Ambitiously, he wrote:

> I shall very much want to publish two or three papers which will render the rational element of the method, which Hegel both discovered and turned into a mystery, accessible to common sense.
>
> MARX 1958

In Hegelian vocabulary, the mystery Marx alluded to was the *second step*, the *dialectical* moment of scholastic instability giving rise to the *third step*, a *speculative* moment of creation (of a new theory or solution). Unlike his predecessor, Marx was not interested in legitimizing the status quo of the Prussian state. However, in moving to the third step of dialectical analysis, ironically, Marx made the same ideological mistake as Hegel. Marx subsumed the reality of historical progression (not ideas) to his politics, to his ideology.

Marx argued Hegel's dialectics produced an apology for the existence of the Prussian state. Ironically, Marx would not be able to locate this very problem with his work, which would be read as an apology for his prescriptive recipe of historical evolution.

In *The Poverty of Philosophy* (1847), Marx set the stage for a Hegelian-like use of concepts and objects:

> Economic categories are only the theoretical expressions, the abstractions of the social relations of production.
>
> MARX 1910: 119

Marx's unsurpassed intelligence makes it highly unlikely that he was unaware of the vulnerability of his own theory. More probably, he understood that ideological irony was an unavoidable consequence of all scholarship. Somehow, he remained intentionally unwilling to surrender to it. While unable to escape the limiting bias of ideology, Marxian scholarship thrived because Marx never lost sight of the multifaceted aspect of historical contingency, as his later economic, historical, even pamphleteer work in *Capital* proved.

Marx added interdisciplinarity to dialectics. It is remarkable especially in light of the fact that it came in response to Hegel's dialectics, which was meant to unite, in the realm of thought, the dual worlds of sense and reason rather than to scientifically observe the world in its contingency and then organize its theoretical narrative. From studying history, Marx noticed the structure of each society and found patterns of social progress. Among his most perennial postulates is the undisputable role economy plays in every society, and through it, the legitimizing instruments for preserving its distributive status-quo among the members of society.

For Marx's interdisciplinary mind, the socio-economic reality had a clear legal component: it evolved around the regime of property. The object, as well as the type of property each legal system facilitated, defined history and differentiated among its eras: antiquity, feudalism, and capitalism. All three historical societies were organized around asserting private property and ownership of the means of creating what is necessary to survive for most, and then of accumulation and prosperity for the few. Marx's history mirrored the evolution of the object of private property. For most members of society, it started with the bare minimum needed to satisfy survival, such as food, clothing and shelter, and it continued to represent just that for them. Progress rested with the difference that property represented for the few.

Historically, the slave owner exerted ownership over animate and inanimate objects and provided for himself, his family and his slaves (animate objects). Additionally, he contributed to the miserable lives of the urban poor, the landless freemen, whose social value was that of producing offspring. That explains why, in antiquity, they became to be known as "proletariat." By the end of the Roman Empire, the state would soon provide for the large numbers of the proletariat.

> The Roman proletarian lived almost entirely at the expense of society.
> MARX 1887: 606

In *The Process of the Circulation of* Capital (1909) (*Capital* Vol. 2), which appeared posthumously, Marx explained slave economy in antiquity as well as in the capitalist United States:

> In a slave system, the money-capital invested in the purchase of slaves plays the role of the fixed capital in money-form, which is but gradually replaced after the expiration of the active life period of the slaves. Among the Athenians, therefore, the gain realized by a slave owner through the industrial employment of his slaves, or indirectly by hiring them out to other industrial employers (for instance mine owners), was regarded merely as an interest (with sinking fund) on the advanced money-capital, just as the industrial capitalist under capitalist production places a portion of the surplus-value plus the depreciation of his fixed capital to the account of interest and renewal of his fixed capital. This is also the rule in the case of capitalists offering fixed capital, such as houses, machinery, etc., for rent. Mere household slaves, who perform the necessary services or are kept as luxuries are not considered here. They correspond to the modern servant class. But the slave system – so long as it is the dominant form of productive labor in agriculture, manufacture, navigation, etc., as it was in the advanced states of Greece and Rome – preserves an element of natural economy. The slave market maintains its supply of labor-power by war, piracy, etc., and this rape is not promoted by a process of circulation, but by the natural appropriation of the labor-power of others by physical force. Even in the United States, after the conversion of the neutral territory between the wage labor states of the North and the slave labor states of the South into a slave breeding region for the South, where the slave thus raised for the market had become an element of annual reproduction, this method did not suffice for a long time, so that the African slave trade was continued as long as possible for the purpose of supplying the market.
>
> MARX 1909: 558–559

Moving into feudalism, the lord's ownership over the means of reproduction is not complete. The serf could produce but not enjoy the fruit of his labor because of the way society was legally organized. In Italy, emancipation provided the necessary agency for the serf to acquire property rights. Unfortunately, having the legal right to property does not equate ownership. The only agency the serf obtained was to change the landed master for the urban one: the factory owner.

> The serf was emancipated in that country [Italy] before he had acquired any prescriptive right to the soil. His emancipation at once transformed him into a free proletarian, who, moreover, found his master ready waiting for him in the towns, for the most part handed down as legacies from the Roman time.
>
> MARX 1887: 739

The former serf becomes a "free proletarian." While the Roman label continued to designate the urban poor in capitalism, Marx noted, their social role had been reversed. In the first volume of *The Process of Production of Capital* (*Capital*), Ch. 24, Section 3, fn. 3, Marx wrote:

> .... It can almost be said that modern society lives at the expense of the proletarians, on what it keeps out of the remuneration of labor.
> MARX 1887: 606

With the progression to capitalism, Marx gives a more preponderant role to specific legal systems than ever before. His work relies more and more on interdisciplinary dialectics. Marx introduced the element of contingency in his analysis. Human history was deeply conditional upon geography, politics, and culture, which had a tremendous effect on economic structure as well. As written in Marx's *Capital*, this legal explanation of primitive accumulation, as a source of private property, is dialectical and interdisciplinary. The same attention to interdisciplinary detail is given in the explanation as to how capitalism evolved in most countries. The first volume of Marx's eminent work, *Capital*, stands as irrefutable proof, and even those who have little knowledge about it have rarely attempted to refute it.

Christopher J. Arthur (2004) recently explained how dialectics worked for Marx, relying on its use in Marx's *Capital*. First, according to Arthur, Marx used both:

> [S]ystematic dialectic (a method of exhibiting the inner articulation of a given whole) and historical dialectic (a method of exhibiting the inner connection between stages of development of a temporal process).
> ARTHUR 2004: 17–18

But of what exactly does the logical development of the argument of *Capital* consist? Using dialectics, Marx explains how wholes have an internal structure, and the relations between their components are "moments of a totality" which cannot be really understood unless viewed both separately, independently and interconnected.

> [T]otality cannot be comprehended immediately; its articulation has to be exhibited. This methodological problem is not at all that of finding a pure or simple case isolated from concrete complexity; it is a matter of how to articulate a complex concept that cannot be grasped by some sort of immediate intuition. In doing so we have to make a start with some

aspect of it. But the exposition can reconstruct the whole from a particular starting point because we can move logically from one element to another along a chain of internal relations; in strict logic if the very meaning of an element is at issue (which I shall argue is the case in the value forms commodity-money-capital, each of which requires the others to complete its meaning or develop its concept), or with a fair degree of confidence if material conditions of existence are involved (as with the relation of valorization to production). (Id.: 25)

Arthur reconstructs the sequence of Marx's thought. According to him, Marx cannot start his analysis of capital, with that very concept, because, though stripped to its bare essentials it is not sufficiently simple and historically determined. Capital is as complex a concept as "self-valorization, whose immediate appearance is an increment in the reflux of money" (id.: 27). If Marx were to start with money, that concept is "an incomplete idea, having no sense except in its various relations with commodities, such as medium of their circulation" (id.). Commodity might be a better candidate for Marxian narrative, but it cannot be a suitable starting point because, according to Arthur, it fails the criteria of simplicity and historical determinacy.

In *Capital*, what is captivating is the parallel narratives which expose the system of capitalism to our understanding. Marx magisterially explains the development of the value-form and the development of the commodity-form. This parallelism made scholars of Marx, such as Jairus Banaji and Arthur, to see that

> Capital has a double starting point: the *commodity form* of the product is the analytical starting point, from which we separate out *value* [...] which forms the synthetic point of departure for developing more complex relationships [...] in the pure universal essence of the commodity. (Id.: 30)

Dialectics is a demanding method for the researcher, in part because it requires a certain sensibility, an ability to notice life in its complexity. "In our day, everything seems pregnant with its contrary," Marx wrote in 1856, and added,

> [I]nvention and progress seem to result in endowing material forces with intellectual life, and [stultify] human life into a material force. This antagonism between modern industry and science on the one hand, modern misery and dissolution on the other hand; this antagonism [...] is a fact, palpable [and] overwhelming. (Id.)

Noticing such contradictions, and using his interdisciplinary education, Marx created a form of scholarship which promoted a way for the individual to manage self-development and a life of dignity. (Berman 1999).

> Machinery gifted with the wonderful power of shortening and fructifying human labor, we behold starving and overworking it. The new-fanged sources of wealth, by some weird spell, are turned into sources of want. The victories of art seem bought by the loss of character.
> MARX 1856

Since 1856, nothing seems to have changed to prove those statements wrong. Within this antagonistic reality, Marx's analysis gave individuals the center-stage, trying to understand, adapt and eventually improve their actual conditions. Writing for this generic, although not abstract individual because viable, Marx interpellated reality in a Promethean act of actuating thinking about society into prospective action: political praxis. Marx embraced the Hegelian conception of how ideas manifested themselves, objectifying themselves through language, because concepts existed only through language: "Ego qua this particular pure ego is non-existent otherwise [than by language]" (Hegel 2003: 298). Then, he went a step further. Marx rejected the immutable nature of ideas because, as Antonio Gramsci would also later emphasize, human nature is "historically determined" by social relations (Gramsci 1971: 133), and thus it demands a method of investigation to reflect its complexity.

Marx answered the quest for complex investigation with interdisciplinary dialectics. In *The Eighteenth Brumaire of Louis Napoleon* (1852), Marx again emphasized his reliance on philosophy and history, drawing from their strengths to make his theoretical impact.

> Men make their own history, but they do not make it just as they please; they do not make it under circumstances chosen by themselves, but under circumstances directly encountered, given and transmitted from the past. The tradition of all the dead generations weighs like a nightmare on the brain of the living. And just when they seem engaged in revolutionizing themselves and things, in creating something that has never yet existed […] they anxiously conjure up the spirits of the past for their service and borrow from them names [in order] to present the new scene of world history [in] borrowed language.
> MARX 2001a: 7

Although Marx worked with Hegelian (borrowed) language, the way he connected history to politics and contingency (temporality) helped him reach a different result. Marx started his Berlin University studies only three years after Hegel ended his career there, working closely with a Hegelian thinker, Bruno Bauer. Later, though, with Bauer's dismissal, as Mah explains, Marx had to reconsider his options (Mah 1987: 180). Marx had hoped that with Bauer's help he might obtain an academic position. Maybe this lack of fortune caused or encouraged Marx to distance himself from Hegel and his followers when he chose to develop his different political views. In *German Ideology* (1845), Marx rightfully points out that his theory starts from the real conditions of human existence.

> The premises from which we begin are not arbitrary ones, not dogmas, but real premises from which abstraction can only be made in the imagination. They are the real individuals, their activity and the material conditions under which they live, both those which they find already existing and those produced by their activity. These premises can thus be verified in a purely empirical way.
> MARX and ENGELS 1998: 61

Marx's analysis of his contemporary society contains both a normative and a descriptive side. Descriptively, capitalism is presented as the historical period when people create wealth as in no other preceding epoch. Until then, people could dig gold, enslave humans (exceptionally, the United States enslaved humans during its early capitalism), and in a very limited way produce wealth from nothing: for instance, with no more than their labor, some created art. With capitalism, both wealth and survival came from labor. Wealth came from other people's labor. The laborer's means of survival were also provided by waged labor.

In *The Critique of the Gotha Program*, written in 1875 and first published in an abridged version in 1890, Marx introduced the issue of social labor as the source of social wealth. This issue will be fully presented in *Das Kapital*, whose only first volume, *Capital*, would be published during Marx's life.

Marx was able to continue the work of his predecessors and move beyond description. He demonstrated how labor is the source of wealth, and thus, private property. Through technology, capitalism deepens domination and creates satisfaction. An entire system of new desires and objects to satisfy them is conceived for mass production and consumption. In factories, workers are specially connected and individually alienated from their work products. Or better said, in factories, workers learn how to relate to their products as a source of their meek wealth: their wage obtained in exchange for the otherwise apparently worthless product of their labor.

A contemporary scholar, the German Socialist Ferdinand Lassalle gave a great explanation of waged labor conditioned to a specific socio-economic aspect: its role in the laborer's subsistence. That observation did not need to remain the prescriptive normative truth about labor in capitalism. When Marx analyzed labor both as a fountain of wealth as well as poverty, Marx challenged scholarship to do more than offer disparate, static moments of progress. Marx sensed the social continuum labor created. In its unequivocal absurdity, labor succeeds to impoverish those who work and enrich those who do not. In the process, Marx also made – once again – obvious how his (S_1) ideology affects the reasoned explanation (or what is called here, the philosophy) of all scholarship (T_1).

> [I]nstead of setting down general phrases about "labor" and "society," [scholarship should] prove concretely how in present capitalist society the material, etc., conditions have at last been created which enable and compel the workers to lift this social curse.
> MARX 2001b: 14

With *The Critique of the Gotha Program*, Marx increasingly noted omissions and discrepancies, even contradictions between what was said and what was implied across multiple disciplines. This is obvious in his following Lassallean statement incorporated in Marx's *Critique*.

> In proportion as labor develops socially, and becomes thereby a source of wealth and culture, poverty and destitution develop among the workers, and wealth and culture among the non-workers. (Id.)

Marx's political views about society and the power distribution within it, his ideology, are always on display in his narrative. For Marx, the scholar, social change appears compelling logically, and as such it was presented as the result of interdisciplinary dialectics, and politically, when change became an ideological choice. Ideologically, his political views are those of his contemporary working class: theirs produced political action, his, scholarship supporting it.

When Marx asserts that "Through history labor created wealth," he most likely means labor enabled special property relationships to be created. Wealth and its ownership became separated from the labor itself. Through his scholarship, Marx explained both the origin of wealth and the ways to change its distribution. The latter was very much connected with the reigning Rule of Law. The more distance the legal system put between the source of wealth and the owner of wealth, the less impetus the wealth creators (laborers) have to change the legal system and what Marx called "to lift this historical 'social' curse" (id.).

When people themselves were physical objects of property, as slaves, the slave-owner directed immediate ownership over the source of wealth, which was the slave. Under those conditions, slaves had clear impetus to end their subjugation: their oppressive legal status was easily understandable. When slaves became land-bound workers, they enjoyed some minimal agency. For instance, owing taxes in the French absolute monarchy, their labor became the fountain of their bondage of very limited benefits, and of the unlimited feudal wealth (Hobsbawm 1962). Their physical impossibility to move was an immediate limit to their agency and thus proved an impetus to end that bondage.

With capitalism and technology, the industrial revolution further distanced the worker from the result of his work. The alienated distance between him, as the fountain of labor, and the result of his labor proved debilitating and non-conductive of change, although the unprecedented amount of wealth produced was sufficient to be divided as capital and wages. As long as the gap between the wealth of the capitalist and the wages earned is almost impossible to trace, and if the labor receives sufficient accommodations that it finds acceptable, the enormous discrepancy between wealth and wage is no clear impetus to change the legal arrangement. The regime of property stops looking like a "social curse." And this socio-economic development Marx could not imagine. The mere possibility of refusing to lift the social curse remained incomprehensible to Marx.

Nevertheless, the method of research, his dialectics, proved the only method, paraphrasing Gayatri Spivak, able to lift the lid of appearances and show the pot of social reality in its forever boil (Mann and Wainwright 2008: 853). In the 1850s, for instance, Marx worked on his political economy scholarship and produced a manuscript that remained unknown to Engels (id.: 2). The manuscript was published almost a century later, under the name of *Grundrisse der Kritik der politischen Ökonomie (Rohentwurf)* [*Outlines for a Critique of Political Economy (Rough Draft)*] (id.: 849). What makes that manuscript special is that it contains pure Marxian thought without any guardrails (id.). His ability to view reality interconnected enabled Marx to create a new explanatory alphabet in *Grundrisse,* which would later produce the Marxian political theory encompassing economy, history, sociology, and jurisprudence.

In *Grundrisse,* for instance, Marx defined capitalism from an interdisciplinary, dialectical perspective. Marx viewed capitalism as a system of personal independence because, unlike in feudalism, waged labor was revolutionizing both the economy and the legal system regulating it. What was unique to capitalism was the appearance of equality that had never experienced before. It was an appearance that Marx debunked because he employed dialectics, rather than stay within the constraining limits of a particular academic discipline.

> Every commodity is equal (and comparable) to every other as exchange value (qualitatively: each now merely represents a quantitative plus or minus of exchange value).
>
> MARX 1973: 151

Commodities themselves unveiled their essence because Marx defined them dialectically. Specific work is invested in a specific item. But on the market, all specific work negates its specificity. On the market, specific work, i.e., specific commodities, is perceived as a new economic item, a moneyed-value commodity in an exchange transaction.

> For that reason, this equality, this unity of the commodity is distinct from its natural differentiation; and appears in money therefore as their common element as well as a third thing which confronts them both. But on one side, exchange value naturally remains at the same time an inherent quality of commodities while it simultaneously exists outside them; on the other side, when money no longer exists as a property of commodities, as a common element within them, but as an individual entity apart from them, then money itself becomes a particular commodity alongside the other commodities. (Determinable by demand and supply; splits into different kinds of money, etc.) It becomes a commodity like other commodities, and at the same time it is not a commodity like other commodities. (Id.: 151)

Capitalism can be said that it resulted from the inability of the French monarch, Louis XVI to control the existing feudal system (Hobsbawm 1962). The limited legal changes that the French aristocracy agreed upon proved insufficient for the mass of indentured rural and urban workers. Consequently, this forced all European monarchs to become involved in its defense, and eventually Napoleon legally codified the new capitalist reality. That codification became the *Code civil des Français* (1804), which recognized rights both for the pauper as well as for the wealthy, creating an appearance of fairness if not legal equality. Work became quantifiable and money became the universal standard of measuring the value of work as well as capital. Abstractly, once something is quantifiable because the standard exists (money), it is exchangeable and the illusion of equality becomes a reality.

> Despite its general character it is one exchangeable entity among other exchangeable entities. It is not only the general exchange value, but at the same time a particular exchange value alongside other particular

> exchange values. Here a new source of contradictions which make themselves felt in practice. The particular nature of money emerges again in the separation of the money business from commerce proper.
>
> MARX 1973: 151

Marxian creativity appears to have been built in stages. With the works of his youth, Marx cleared the path for the new, engaged scholarship of his mature age, when he incorporated his political agenda. While he was aware that his work was the product of his political engagement, and that his political engagement might have mired the relevance of his scholarship, he never stopped.

In his *Critique of Hegel's Philosophy of Right*, Marx wrote that Germany's underdeveloped political life had resulted in an overdeveloped and overly abstract intellectual life, which included his work (Mah: 222). Nevertheless, Marx ignored (perhaps out of necessity) the irony of his own scholarship production – irony which I argue is the only way to keep scholarship from being born irrelevant or becoming dogmatic. Marx seemed to have ignored the implications of his interdisciplinary dialectics – that progress is contingent on technology, a Pandora's box for our times, whose development, and especially, its consequences, remain highly unpredictable. For instance, technology both satisfies old wants and creates new ones in a vicious circle whose end perhaps depends on taming the human nature. The unpredictable development of technology, as well as Marx's political views, limited the normative value of his work, but never its explanatory power.

Ideology does not affect one's body of scholarship uniformly. Its impact depends on the text-instigators' awareness as well as their choice of managing it, such as the method of research. First, when text-instigators are aware of their ideology, their analysis is presented as such, i.e., a liberal view of the Rule of Law. Sometimes ideology may co-opt their work as if it were pure propaganda, or, depending on the sophistication of the research method employed, it may act as a barrier between relevance and irrelevance, transforming the scholarship into a perennially valuable historical example of scholarship. When they are unaware of their ideology, their biases often come through as a matter of accidental irony, or as mere propaganda.

Marx's writings were differently affected by his system of political beliefs. But, what saved them all from immediate irrelevance, I believe, was his wide breadth of expertise, his interdisciplinary dialectics, as well as his refreshing intellectual honesty. An "author, if he pursues his research, cannot literally publish what he has written six months previously," Marx wrote in 1846 (McLellan 1971: 14).

That Marx favored a political solution that imposed a predictable historical evolution is ironic in its simplicity, especially in light of his interdisciplinary dialectics. It could also be viewed as a political choice based on endless simplifications. Perhaps he was unaware that he bent his reasoning to fit his ideology. Perhaps he thought the gambit worthy. In the process, Marx, ironically, opened his scholarship to both political ridicule and endless misreading. By avoiding to ideologically label his own scholarship, Marx enabled subsequent interpellators to cannibalize it and use it within their own label. Much-reviled Soviet propaganda did just that, which might explain the continuing resistance to incorporate Marx within the academic canon.

3 Dialectics and Post-Marxian Scholarship

Like all acts of (societal) scholarship, Marx's work mirrors his methods of research (interdisciplinary dialectics) and his subjectivity, identified as "imagination" in *German Ideology*. For Marx, history actuates meaning (the "premises" of imagination). Ironically, meaning reflects both what S_1 chose to express, the "abstraction," but also S_1's omissions. Through the filter of that moment's meaning-making contingency or "premises," S_1 builds abstractions out of past theories (rejected dogmas) and present subjectivity: "imagination."

> The premises from which we begin are not arbitrary ones, not dogmas, but real premises from which abstraction can only be made in the imagination.
>
> MARX and ENGELS 1998: 61

There is so much space for Marxian criticism (applying Marx to Marx) and needed discussion to find the current best theoretical paradigm to fit our new social and economic reality, which has changed so much since those early nineteenth-century days of capitalism. Technology has only increased the distance between the source of wealth and its enjoyment, though some form of labor remains the origin of both. Labor contributes to social wealth in ways hardly fitting the Marxian paradigm of factory-based capitalist exploitation. Today, freelancers work from the comfort of their home, fandom provides script lines without any remuneration or recognition, and temp workers do menial work with no expectations of benefits or minimal recurrent employment. At the time Marx wrote his opus, capitalism was massively investing in infrastructure and means of production, making it easy to notice and to correctly equate economic wealth with ownership of the means of production. While money has continued to offer the illusion of quantifiable equality, as

John Rawls noted, it has become increasingly opaque to connect the decision makers from those they exploit (Rawls 2007: 323).

This Rawlsian stage of social development of capitalism needs interdisciplinary dialectics as the prevalent method of research even more than its previous eras. Ideologically-transparent systemic approaches to knowledge production are so needed especially now when the liberal academia is imbued with various ideologically-neutered shams of technocratic methods of research.

Unfortunately, as explained earlier, there is a lot of academic resistance to embrace Marxian dialectics. Briefly, Marx has produced some apologists, but mostly vile detractors. The Western extremes lay between Max Eastman, in his Marxist phase, when tried to explain that Marx never stated that economy stands in a causal relationship with the political and legal structure but in a determinant role (Eastman 1955), and the likes of F.A. Hayek or Leszeck Kolakowski. Building on what Hegel omitted due to his ideology and historical contingency, the irony is that in the same way Marx is the ironic answer to Hegel's scholarship, the post-Marxian scholarship, including today's socio-economic and legal scholarship, is the liberal ironic answer to Marx.

For instance, his neo-liberal detractors, such as Wilhelm Roepke, F.A. Hayek, and Ludwig von Mises, never challenged the foundational role of economics. Their assumption has been that democracy rests on private ownership and the utopian free market. Or, as Eastman (1955) misguidedly or naively said,

> You cannot dodge this issue by talking about a 'mixed economy.' (30–31)

Unfortunately, Eastman ignored the fact that his scholarship was blinded by his (new) ideology. That lack of awareness perhaps can be blamed for his lack of imagination. Today, China proves Eastman wrong. China's "planned" mixed economy is ruling that immense economy and dominating the world economy.

Columbia University's Jon Elster and Oxford College's Leszeck Kolakowski wrote brilliant tomes about the work of Marx in attempts to minimize his scholastic contributions or simply vilify them. Whereas Elster, the objective liberal scholar, made a still-life portrait of his work, Kolakowski never stopped blaming Marx for the loss of Eastern Europe to Soviet Russia (others may want to blame geography, e.g., Malta).

In an interesting take on Marx, at a time when the Internet had not yet revolutionized how people built their financial and social capital, Elster (1985) described Marxism as a specific type of social criticism (87 et seq.). He viewed it, not necessarily as addressing the capitalist economic inequity, which is what Marx defined as economic alienation. Instead, Elster described it as aimed at the unilateral material dimension of capitalism, which generated few subjectively perceived needs and even fewer satisfactions (id.: 79–86). While these needs are hard to pinpoint, they are central for the alienation experienced as he "feels outside himself" in his work (id.: 74). In other words, Elster credits Marx for being able to perceive capitalism as causing a "lack of a sense of meaning" and as responsible for "the experience of one's self and life as empty" (id.: 74–75).

When feeling generous, Kolakowski saw Marx not as an academic writer but as a humanist in the Renaissance-sense of the term:

> [Marx's] mind was concerned with the totality of human affairs, and his vision of social liberation embraced, as an interdependent whole, all the major problems with which humanity is faced. (1983: 5–6)

Kolakowski identified one of the main obstacles to studying Marxism, one to which he contributed himself. Kolakowski deemed Marx responsible for "the ideological tradition on which Communism is based" (id.: 1). For instance, in a discussion about human rights, Kolakowski found a causal connection between Marx's quest for a better society for everybody and the Soviet state's project of "extinction of personal life, reducing human beings to perfectly exchangeable units of productive processes" (id.: 92). Similar to that of Eastman and Michel Henry, Kolakowski's take on Marxian scholarship is continued by the likes of Martin Amis, who views it as symptomatic of "wastelands called Never Has Been, Never Could Be and Never Should Be" (Amis 2017).

Marx's critics seem to forget that what they criticize is a Paradigm of Knowledge they reject, and even that criticism is not objective, but ideological. They do not necessarily criticize something empirically verifiable, such as Marx's method of research, but his ideology. Foes and epigones seem to forget to apply Marx to Marx and reconsider why they embrace or reject Marx.

However, as improbable as it may be, Western scholarship builds on the shoulders of giants, and it would never progress if it were to only be involved in salvaging establishment scholarship. Thus, it is refreshing (and expected) to note that whether Marxian or not, a systemic paradigm versus a technocratic one is at work in today's jurisprudence.

In a groundbreaking recent article, "Working Themselves Impure: A Life Cycle Theory of Legal Theories" (2016), Columbia Law School Professors Jeremy K. Kessler and David E. Pozen proposed a systemic analysis of prescriptive legal theories. Kessler and Pozen explicitly refuse to label their analysis as dialectics.

> We submit that the prescriptive legal theories that have gained the broadest support in public law fields over the past several decades have shared these features of abstraction and proceduralism, together with a common life cycle.
> KESSLER and POZEN 2016: 1892

Instead, they talk about a life cycle that builds on the work of Harvard Law School's Duncan Kennedy. Kennedy also avoids the dialectical cycle of jurisprudence, apparently preferring to explain the decline of the liberal legal worldview "as such" (Kennedy 1982).

> Whereas Kennedy sought to explain what he took to be the decline of the liberal legal worldview as such, our life cycle theory aims to explain the divergent fates of contemporary prescriptive legal theories – all of which operate within the tenets of the liberal legal worldview, however "decrepit" those tenets might appear from other perspectives.
> KESSLER and POZEN 2016: 1892

Nevertheless, Kessler and Pozen engage Kennedy's work dialectically. They present its "invariant sequence of six stages ... from robust good health to utter decrepitude," as flawed. Critically they separate themselves from Kennedy by choosing to focus "on a different set of transformations and a different set of external factors" (id.). As shown below, their approach is a much clearer dialectical approach than Kennedy's. Theirs starts with the birth of a theory (T_1) and ends with the negation of that theory, which is never absolute and therefore the adulterated presence of the primary theory.

> Birth – At T_1, the theory introduces a decision procedure or criterion for judgment that seeks to resolve a highly politicized legal conflict in terms that are relatively alien to the main points of political contention; in so doing, the theory differentiates itself from preexisting legal theories used to negotiate the conflict.
> Critique – At T_2, critics of the theory highlight its failure to secure certain values that gave rise to the conflict in the first place.
> Reformulation – At T_3, the theory responds to these critiques by *internalizing* them – supplementing or modifying its approach so as to better serve the initially ignored values. As a result, the theory's constituency expands, but at the price of normative and conceptual purity.
> Iteration – At T_4, this process of criticism and response recurs.

Maturity – At T_5, the theory has come to reflect the conflict-ridden political and theoretical field it had promised to transcend. To the extent the theory ever posed a direct threat to particular participants in the underlying conflict, that danger has dwindled.

Death or Adulterated Persistence – At T_6, the theory either falls out of favor with mainstream legal actors, at least for the time being, or persists in substantially adulterated form. (Id.: 1822–1823)

Interdisciplinary dialectics is not a Marxian invention. Students of pragmatism, so influential in American academia, have known it for a long time. For instance, Charles Peirce's method of inquiry can be described as a struggle for answers that is born out of the dissatisfaction caused by doubt about the existing state of theoretical explanation, and as such it has dialectical connotations (Peirce 1877). Peirce's rational inquiry implies that there is such a thing as truth, and that it is attainable through subjective, inquisitive struggle. His method of inquiry is not limited to a narrow slice of reality.

Like Peirce, Marx viewed reality as comprehensible through all-encompassing human investigation. Marx's dialectics focus on the contingency of each historical moment, and his scholarship, as well as that which he inspired, may as well be the precursor to today's interdisciplinary studies. Marx used political economy, history, and sociology to understand humanity.

•••

No one will ever know if some people are born with Marx's capacity to notice the intricacies of human societies and the empathy to root for the underdog. No one will ever know how some scholars identify discrepancies in the existing theoretical paradigms and then forge them into new theories meant to guide progressive human action. Similarly, no one will ever know what caused Marx's intellectual curiosity, or his ideological layer: his intellectual genius or his moral compass. Harold Mah (1987) almost surprisingly noted that Marx chose journalism "as an alternative career" (180). But despite its origins, his intellectual curiosity ensured his interdisciplinary studies, which in turn, ensured his ease with conceptual thinking and empirical observations making it easy to avoid the pitfalls of mere generalizations. Rawls noted in one of his last lectures Marx's study of jurisprudence, philosophy, and economics, and described his interdisciplinary approach as a remarkable achievement (Rawls 2007: 319).

As such, Marx was singularly positioned to avoid ideatic postulations. "Above all we must avoid postulating 'society' [...] as an abstraction *vis-à-vis* the individual" Marx would write in *Economic and Philosophical Manuscripts*

(1848). Whether it was his research method or his subjectivity, we would never know what liberated his own creative forces. But, it seems possible that his interdisciplinary perspective enabled him to make the cultural leap to notice that alienated labor was the result of a lack of *Bildung* – the education necessary for a life of self-fulfillment.

While Marx explained how creative forces depended on labor to stop being alienated through the demands of daily subsistence, he did not address the alienation caused by creation, although he alluded to it. For instance, Marx experienced creative alienation. In January 1845, Marx signed a publishing contract for a *Critique of Politics and Economics*, McLellan (1971) tells us, although he did little to fulfill it, Engels encouraged his friend's decision to publish urging him to ignore his doubts (4). The manuscript had been with Marx for a long time. Probably Marx, the text-instigator, was unable to easily separate himself from his creation. This alienation, part of the author's, S_1, subjectivity, I believe has an important role in meaning-making. It colors S_1's creativity, leaving areas of meaning unexplored, whether accidentally or willingly. These areas would subsequently be filled with the text-interpellator's, S_2, meaning, colored by their own subjectivity, and thus further completing the unaccounted ironic aspect of the meaning-making process.

CHAPTER 4

Private Subjectivity – Alienation and Theory Production

Textually, T_1 represents a reasoned narrative (Friedmann's philosophy), which reflects S_1's subjectivity as incorporated in their research methodology. However, T_1's meaning is the result of a rather complex process, which, I argue here, has an ideological ironic component. Irony is actuated by S_2's ideology when interpellating T_1. Thus, if the structure of scholarship includes philosophy, ideology, and irony, why raise any additional issues? Alienation is not an additional issue. It belongs to S_1's subjectivity and it affects S_1's research method, and as such, T_1. As S_1's private subjectivity, alienation affects and is affected by S_1's ideology. Finally, as reified subjectivity, alienation is present in T_1's latent irony.

Scholarship, T_1, situates specific academic understanding within the larger academic frame of knowledge (K) according to the existing Regime of Truth. S_1, the text-instigator, usually creates T_1 in a private space, experiencing what I call here "creative alienation," which comes with a sense of loss or elation. The creative process incorporates S_1's set of beliefs, desires, interests, feelings, cultural background and emotions to such an extent that T_1 sublimates and objectifies them. To produce T_1, S_1 engages in a process of objectifying knowledge, private experience, and desires. As shown in Figure 3, creative alienation, which, despite the common belief of fulfillment, incorporates all types of negative feelings produced by social and individual alienation (Zhanga et al. 2016), is an integral part of knowledge production.

Some feelings of despondency may be caused, for instance, by the imposition that the creative process puts on the scholar's family or even on other professional commitments. Knowledge production requires scholarly investment of sustained effort in generating it, as well as a sustained effort in promoting, and communicating it. Scholarly communication can be viewed as the second stage of scholarship meaning-making, a highly structured space, where meaning becomes negotiated between S_1 and S_2 (the text-interpellator). The anxiety produced by how the scholarly community perceives T_1 adds to the creative alienation S_1 experiences and implicitly shapes how S_1 perceives her public position, her ideology.

Scholarship production, T_1, as shown in Figure 4 below, manifests itself in reasoned narrative (called here philosophy) and incorporates and transforms

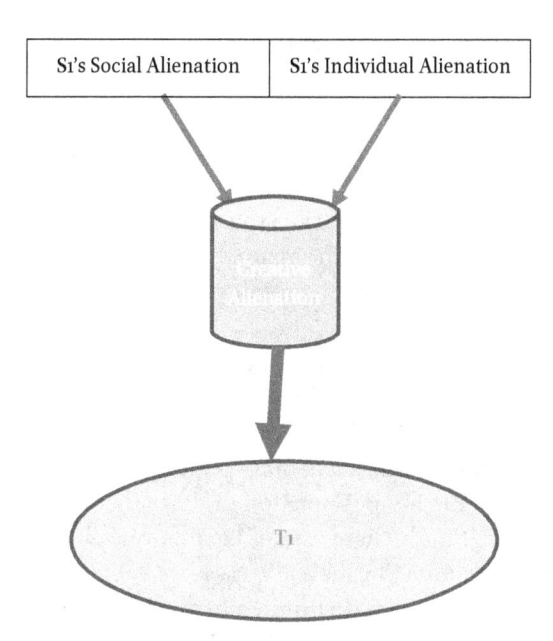

FIGURE 3   S₁'s alienation and its role in Theory Production, T₁
SOURCE: CREATED BY AUTHOR

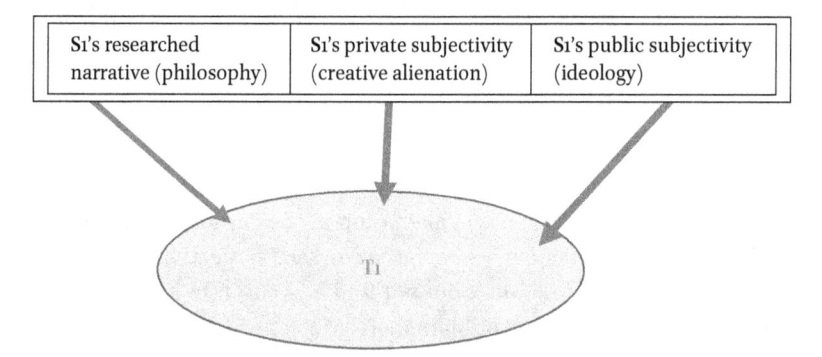

FIGURE 4   T₁'s theory production = $f_{[S_1\text{'s Research, Alienation and ideology}]}$
SOURCE: CREATED BY AUTHOR

the scholar's subjectivity. Whether creativity is the genesis of alienation or alienation encourages creativity, it is hard to pinpoint. In a certain manner, it reminds one of the dilemmas surrounding the capitalist factory-based mode of production: whether the capitalist mode of production is behind the factory discipline and alienation, or whether, as Michel Foucault explained, the factory is the consequence of the social order and discipline of the alienation and obedience implemented by a centralized power system (Dardot et al. 2007: 163).

The mental and psychological costs of being creative – the alienation involved – may be dependent on the position S_1 occupies on the hierarchy of knowledge production. Not all theories are born equal, and not all of them will have the same role in the production of knowledge at a specific historical moment. Alienation does not necessarily represent the amount of creative work. Like menial work, intellectual work can also be the result of a highly skilled alienated individual.

Studying academic alienation requires much more attention than what I could offer the subject here. My interest in alienation comes from its creative presence. Alienation, as objectification of the S_1's persona, is present in every theory production. My contention, thus, is that alienation, connected to theory production, partially explains academic irony. Alienation explains the latent, dormant irony, which is nascent within T_1. There cannot be a universally encompassing T_1. Even at the personal, individual level, S_1 uses her knowledge, emotions, desires, etc., partially in every single T_1. Irony embeds what is omitted, ignored, left unsaid, unobserved, or discarded. When T_1 interpellates its readers, the process actuates irony. From a corollary of potential meaning, irony escapes its potentiality, when S_2 engages T_1 and starts negotiating the meaning of T_1. With social theory, I contend that it is the reader's S_2's ideology unveiling T_1's irony.

1   Alienation as Creative Reification

Marx discussed human reification and alienation in the context of his theory of value. Marx did not distinguish between the worker's subjectivity along the spaces where it is experienced. Marx did not find alienation to belong to the private sphere and ideology to the public sphere. Moreover, he did not analyze their interconnectivity. Nevertheless, Marx consistently addressed alienation.

Beginning with his early writings in the *Economic and Philosophical Manuscripts*, and continuing through his so-called transitory writings, including *Grundrisse*, and again in his later masterpiece, the multi-volume *Das Kapital*, Marx addressed alienation as the private impact the capitalist economy had on the individual. Individual alienation is the fruit of an unfairly structured market place, holding the labor at the bottom of the capitalist pyramid.

For the pyramid to exist, capitalism has to be overinclusive and highly structured, while enabling the masses to willingly occupy the bottom of the system. As explained in the *Communist Manifesto* (1848), capitalism proved itself sufficiently attractive to draw all nations into "civilization" (Marx and Engels 2012: 77).

> The bourgeoisie, by the rapid improvement of all instruments of production, by the immensely facilitated means of communication, draws all nations, even the most barbarian, into civilization. The cheap prices of its commodities are the heavy artillery with which it batters down all Chinese walls, with which it forces the barbarians' intensely obstinate hatred of foreigners to capitulate. It compels all nations, on pain of extinction, to adopt the bourgeois mode of production; it compels them to introduce what it calls civilization into their midst, i.e., to become bourgeois themselves. In one word, it creates a world after its own image. (Id.: 77–78)

Alienation, the opposite of happy participation, appears as a better choice than rejection. Alienation also appears as a better choice than the "Idiotismus [idiocy] of rural life" (id.) (the original translation was Idiotismus as opposed to "idiocy").

> The bourgeoisie has subjected the country to the rule of the towns. It has created enormous cities, has greatly increased the urban population as compared with the rural, and has thus rescued a considerable part of the population from the idiocy of rural life. (Id.)

Alienation as a "state of subjection," or economic dependency, is a capitalist by-product for Marx. Nevertheless, this state of subjection is complemented by gratitude from having been rescued from rural idiocy.

Alienation appears in many Marxian works, constituting a basic element of his linguistic arsenal of social criticism of capitalism. For instance, it appears in the first nine chapters of *Capital* (1887), where Marx focused on commodity fetishism. Georg Lukács and Kenneth Smith would argue that Marx's concept of commodity fetishism is about alienation, about the question of "false consciousness" (Smith 2012: 156).

Marx described commodity fetishism in a few passages. This passage seems to support both Lukács and Smith's opposite contentions:

> A commodity is therefore a mysterious thing, simply because in it the social character of men's labor appears to them as an objective character stamped upon the product of that labor; because the relation of the producers to the sum total of their own labor is presented to them as a social

> relation, existing not between themselves, but between the products of their labor. This is the reason why the products of labor become commodities, social things whose qualities are at the same time perceptible and imperceptible by the senses ... It is [only] a definite social relation between men that assumes, in their eyes, the fantastic form of a relation between things. (Id.)

Marx's reification is about transforming the real, the social– the human labor– into abstractions. In this aspect, his theory of alienation seems to correspond to what scholars experience as creative alienation. For instance, fetishism, as Smith points out, attributes social existence to things, but also to symbols, to abstractions (id.). Symbolically, fetishism connects T to S by objectifying S.

The Marxian reification theory, as expected, is mixed with his ideology. Thus, his theory is connected to the workers' false consciousness. Smith, though, is not convinced that reification needs to be connected to false consciousness and class ideology.

> The labor of the individual asserts itself as part of the labor of society, only by means of the relations which the act of exchange establishes directly between the products, and indirectly, through them, between the producers. To the latter, therefore, the relations connecting the labor of one individual with that of the rest appear, not as direct social relations between individuals at work, but as what they really are, material relations between persons and social relations between things.
> QUOTING MARX; Id.: 159

There is nothing in Marxian theory which negates the possibility for alienation to be experienced privately. Whether it is material or emotional dissatisfaction, Marxian alienation is a result of market place inequality. It could be experienced independently of any political power structure or cultural system. For the scholar-for-hire, for instance, Marxian alienation would be determined by one's desires, interests, emotions, etc., within their sphere of privacy, which often is culturally determined.

Here I differentiate alienation from ideology based on the sphere where the scholar experiences them. Ideology springs out of the subject's position in society. Ideology interpellates the subject publicly, making them aware of the surrounding power structure, making them aware of their position into that public structure. Alienation, while a consequence of one's ideology, defines the subject privately. Alienation impacts the creative process in many ways. One of them is due to the text-instigator's loss in creative sublimation. For S_1, it is alienating to know that the moment T_1 is publicly communicated its meaning becomes the result of an open-ended negotiation with any number of text-interpellators. That knowledge of loss represents a source of creative alienation.

As Marx noted, not only does "conscious life-activity directly distinguish man from animal life-activity," but as "Conscious Beings," humans treat their own lives as if they were an object (Marx 2007: 75). Text-instigators do just that with their emotions, feelings, interests, or desires. Scholars internalize them in a manner that separates them from the mundane in order to engage the observed phenomena and create the symbolic translation of the observed into a theory That text is communicated and constitutes the foundation of scholastic meaning-making, T_1. The act of scholarly creation rests on S_1's alienation from their emotions, desires, and interests. Through that act of creative reification, the scholar's thinking becomes available to the scholarly community, through the theory itself, T_1.

In *Making Sense of Marx* (1985), Elster discussed alienation as a lack of self-actualization or spiritual alienation. Elster's view of Marx's alienation is reification as in "the power that the products of man may acquire over their creators" (74). It manifested itself either as "a lack of sense of meaning, or as a sense of a lack of meaning" (Elster 1985: 74). Similarly, Gerald A. Cohen explains spiritual alienation as "human self-estrangement," (Cohen 2018: 211).

Building on Marx's *Economic and Philosophical Manuscripts*, Elster views alienation as discrepancy between potential and reality. For Elster, alienation is the result of the work not being intrinsic to the nature of the worker,

> What then constitutes the alienation of labor? First, the fact that labor is external to the worker, i.e. it does not belong to his nature, that in his work, therefore, he does not affirm himself, but denies himself, does not feel content, but unhappy, does not develop freely his physical and mental energy, but mortifies his body and ruins his mind.
> MARX 1975: 274

Along these lines, scholarship production as an employment prerequisite certainly appears to engender creative alienation. In the academe, for instance, scholarship production can easily rise to the level of work one is hired to produce. As such, it must certainly affect the scholar's output. Cohen mentioned spiritual alienation as the soul-destroying effects of laboring (id.). Scholars surely experience creative alienation knowing that their academic destiny depends on how their work is received by their peers. Once published, T_1 takes on a life outside their control and is eventually ignored or incorporated within the

Paradigm of Knowledge, according to the ideological views of its subsequent interpellators.

The scholars' subjectivity, including their alienation, is intrinsic to their scholarship, as shown above in Figure 4. The goal of all scholarship production is sharing it with the scholarly community. Published, T_1 takes precedence over S_1, or T_1's publication constitutes S_1's reification. As a result of that, T_1's meaning takes on a life of its own in the public sphere and becomes a variable dependent on many factors; S_1's creative alienation having been displaced by S_1's and S_2's ideology.

2   Alienation and Ideological Resistance to Power Structures

The concept of alienation has always attracted thinkers, and its meaning looms large within the realm of philosophic inquiry. While I differentiate here between creative alienation as being experienced privately, and ideology, as the hallmark establishing the scholar as public subject, alienation has been connected to the power structure historically.

In *Phenomenology of Mind* (1807), Hegel saw alienation akin to false consciousness. Deplete of any negative connotation, alienation is a fundamental aspect of the consciousness's development into the Absolute Knowing. In its pursuit to reach Absolute Knowledge, consciousness has to overcome alienation from itself.

> [Consciousness wins] its truth only when it finds itself utterly torn asunder. It is this mighty power, not by being a positive which turns away from the negative, as when we say of anything it is nothing or it is false, and, being then done with it, pass off to something else; on the contrary, mind is this power only by looking the negative in the face, and dwelling with it.
> HEGEL 2003: 18–19

Ludwig Feuerbach (1855), likewise, describes alienation as merely intellectual or cognitive, as a kind of false consciousness. The difference is that Feuerbach attaches a negative connotation to it. Alienation becomes a weakness in the individual's attempt to overcome religion. Ideologically, alienation amasses a negative connotation; it becomes the hook religion has on the individual.

For Marx, on the other hand, alienation escapes the realm of thought to move into reality. Later, Hannah Arendt would also talk about alienation as phenomenologically grounded in the experience of actual events, conditions, and systems. Arendt further explains,

> World alienation, and not self-alienation as Marx thought, has been the hallmark of the modern age.
> ARENDT 1998: 254

Marxian theory builds toward one conclusion: mass revolt. If ideology is the way to engage the labor in the public sphere and guide their actions, something is needed to work on that transformation privately within the realm of desires. The concept is Marxian alienation.

For Marx, alienation starts the labor's resistance to the power structure because it is the result of generalized want. Interestingly, neither his dialectics nor his interdisciplinarity opened Marxian imagination to discuss technology other than a tool that deepens alienation. Through technology, Marx thought, labor develops more needs that cannot be satisfied, therefore deepening the resentment between laborer and bourgeoisie. In *German Ideology*, Marx pinpointed the connection between technology, the expansion of needs, and the satisfaction of those needs, discussing the rising demand for clothing, the division of labor, and increased productivity through technology, which is further developed in *Economic and Philosophical Manuscripts*. Marx explained his theory that technology deepens alienation because technology empowers and impoverishes, because "the worker is related to the product of his labor as to an alien object" (Marx 1959: 29).

> [E]very new product represents a new potentiality of mutual swindling and mutual plundering. Man becomes ever poorer as man, his need for money becomes ever greater if he wants to master [his needs]. (Id.: 306)

For Marx, alienation could only be experienced as despondency, as a failure to satisfy our needs, as increased unhappiness, and perhaps as alienation from society, or what Arendt would later call "world alienation." Seen as a dynamic negative force, alienation can be viewed as the beginning of any social revolt.

Because alienation fit so well into Marx's theory of history, he lost sight that perhaps there was more to it than its economic fact. In 1985, in an interesting take on Marxian work, Jon Elster described it as a specific type of social criticism (Elster 1985: 74–78). According to Elster, Marx viewed it aimed at the unilateral material dimension of capitalism that generated few subjectively perceived needs and even fewer satisfactions. Elster developed alienation as a "lack of a sense of meaning," or "the experience of one's self and life as empty" (id.). This interpretation may seem simplistic today, but it germinated my thoughts of alienation: neutralizing the needs to manage alienation. Elster addressed Marx's alienation as a two-headed beast: a spiritual as well as a material alienation (id.). Elster identified spiritual alienation as the negative feelings of despondency created by the mere fact of being a wage-earner. Elster discussed material alienation, a process caused by what Marx called the "one-sided, crippled development," produced by a society which emphasizes a thirst for money at the expense of a more complex human development (id.: 78).

Building on Elster's analysis, I addressed how technology changed the commodity paradigm between the worker and the capitalist. Contradicting Marx, who believed that technology would only deepen alienation, somewhere else I demonstrated how technology has become the most important tool of alienation management.

> Technology has made it possible for capitalists to pay workers "in status" (think about interns or Wikipedia "experts") rather than "in money" in exchange for the profit they receive. Technology has enhanced the complexity of the workforce/capitalist equation. Technology has also changed the workforce identity. There are instances when the workforce cannot perceive itself as a workforce but as some type of co-contributor to the final product. When the workforce brings in the social and knowledge capital – their network of friends or online acquaintances that co-produce the final product – they cannot perceive themselves in a position of inferiority or even dependence. In exchange for their involvement, they receive the satisfaction of a job well-done – think crowdsourcing, which allows users to vote up and down your product – satisfaction that is often anonymous to the masses, who end up paying for the product or using it. In a very interesting twist, perhaps the most long-lasting Marxist lesson is that we need to understand humanity as very complex, with individual and collective multi-facets that explain how we experience alienation and when we choose to attempt to end it.
> NEACŞU 2014: 162

Furthermore, technology has blurred the distinction between leisure time and time spent performing labor. Technology has achieved the incredible feat of taking the wage out of discussing inequality.

> [Technology] has enabled individuals to work and enrich capitalists whom they do not perceive as capitalists, because the latter do not hire and thus do not financially compensate these individuals. In a perverse way, technology puts the Marxist capitalist/worker inequality concept on its head, and makes this relationship appear equal because technology erases one economic facet: the capitalist does not pay for the work he

> receives, the wage Marx analyzed in *The Capital*. In classical capitalism, the capitalist had to pay the workforce their subsistence in exchange for profit: "The value of labor-power is determined by the value of the necessaries of life habitually required by the average laborer." However, capitalists today can make a profit without paying any workforce – the workforce engages in work as leisure. WIKIPEDIA, for example, "makes" money for its foundation, WIKIMEDIA, along with its attorneys, broadband managers, and ninety-five employees. WIKIPEDIA's content is free of advertisement; its excellence attracts donors to finance the foundation, its founders, and employees. The content is exclusively created by users/editors who engage in anonymous work. The users/editors likely avoid thinking about themselves as a workforce because they engage in work in the comfort of their homes, during their leisure time. Thus, technology has created the illusion of freedom and capitalist power.
>
> NEACȘU 2014: 166

Technology has a complex relationship with creative alienation. Its impact on knowledge production is far from uniform. By enabling mechanized productivity, technology has produced both the scholar's estrangement from the creative process, by encouraging routine production, and personal fulfillment, sometimes in spite of that. Scholastic alienation aside, nevertheless, technology seems to have insulated scholars from facing their own ideology, and especially from reckoning with it during theory production. Otherwise, I cannot explain the rise of technocratic empiricism and other quantitative methodologies as something other than a false apostle of objectivity, unattainable as long as knowledge rests on meaning-making negotiated by text-instigators and interpellators.

3 Alienation and Scholastic Needs

In Marx's use of binary terminology, alienation is the result of unsatisfied needs. Marx is aware of needs which are either "real or false," as well as, "actual" or "imaginary." In the *Economic and Philosophical Manuscripts of 1844*, he writes about needs in connection to alienated labor. As soon as people are no longer forced to sell their labor to satisfy their drives and needs, such as hunger, they avoid it like the plague. In *Capital*, a commodity is described as any object which satisfies a need – any need.

In 2005, I noted the lack of Marxian theory in the elite law school curricula. That curricular omission, I was arguing, had a negative impact on the law school graduates' abilities to deliberate "upon the full range of issues which might appear directly or indirectly on a less impoverished [contemporary] political agenda" (Neacşu 2005a: 252). Elite law schools, usually associated with elite universities, pride themselves in offering a liberal legal education. They mold their offerings after John Stuart Mill's nineteenth-century principle of "free market of ideas." Only a content-rich curriculum could ensure that Mill's fear of "the peculiar evil of silencing the expression of an opinion" did not occur (Mill 1947: 24). Such a curriculum would only promote Justice Holmes views in *Abrams v. United States*, 250 U.S. 616, 630 (1919), as he expressed it in his dissenting opinion:

> Expounding the marketplace of ideas theory stands for individual choice of which ideas and beliefs deserve expression based on their availability on the free market of ideas. (Id.)

From the point of view of meaning-making production, the battle for elite law schools' curricula matters because elite law schools produce legal knowledge, legitimize the ideologies behind that knowledge, and school tomorrow's leaders. First, elite law schools create legal scholarship and implicitly legitimize the ideologies behind that knowledge. They do so through academic legal articles published in their own student-edited journals. Any other curricular decision would be offensive to Mill's view because it would be

> robbing the human race; posterity as well as the existing generation; those who dissent from the opinion, still more than those who hold it.
> MILL 1947: 24

Then, I was arguing that omitting Marx's writings was not an innocuous curricular reduction. If theories are subjective constructs and "academic elites make theories in their own image," then a curriculum stripped of a theory that emphasizes a different perspective about legal phenomena risks being perceived as a mere exercise in cultural hegemony (Neacşu 2005a: 252). No elite law school wanted to be perceived as a factory of duped, status-quo-defenders and white-collar workers.

My 2005 argument was two-pronged. In addition to promoting a curricular diversity to impart knowledge, it also touched on knowledge production. Every law school, A.B.A. accredited or not, has a few law journals. Thus, the hundreds of law journals published by law school students represent the vast majority of legal scholarship. Theoretically, all those journals establish both the Knowledge Paradigm in jurisprudence and the Regime of Truth. But, it is common knowledge that the odds for a law review article to be persuasive and cause any (legal) stir are significantly better if it is published by the elite law schools' students. Further, difference exists between the elite journal of each law school – called that school's "law review" or "law journal" – and their sleuth of specialty journals (Closen and Dzielak 1996). The five most cited journals, and thus those with the most scholarly impact, are the main law reviews/journals from Harvard, Yale, Columbia, Stanford, and Michigan, as shown in Table below.

Additionally, the elite law schools' main journals publish mostly articles authored by their own faculty or faculty from other similarly positioned schools (S_1). To make matters more ideologically monolithic, the published faculties (S_1) are the elite law schools' graduates too, as browsing any AALS *Directory of Law Teachers* makes it apparent. Thus, what S_1 professors from elite schools teach and publish (usually in their own law reviews) becomes the authority within legal academia more than mere legal scholarship (T_1). It becomes the Paradigm of Knowledge and the Regime of Truth. Accordingly, it influences not only their own students but also law professors (S_2), and, through them, students from lower tier schools. Thus, the content of the elite schools' legal curricula shapes more than their own students' legal knowledge and beliefs: it establishes the Regime of Truth and it shapes the Knowledge Paradigm.

But maybe the premise of my 2005 argument was wrong, and its lack of traction supports that conclusion. My argument started from Mill's perspective and regarded ideological difference within the academe as a desired value. Instead, maybe, it should have noted the want of Marxian theory and attributed it to the absence of academic needs and a lack of academic alienation. There were no Marx-based courses because there was no need for his interdisciplinary dialectical perspective. Those aught years represented the culmination of Fukuyama's end of history, first predicted in 1992 and reprinted with a new afterword in 2006.

TABLE 1   Most-cited legal periodicals: U.S. and selected non-U.S

	Name of Journals	1996–2003	1995–2002
1	*Harvard Law Review*	6682	6557
2	*Yale Law Journal*	5582	5716
3	*Columbia Law Review*	4742	5057
4	*Stanford Law Review*	4262	4400
5	*Michigan Law Review*	4065	4173

SOURCE: HTTP://LAW2.WLU.EDU/LIBRARY/MOSTCITED/METHOD.ASP

Today, there is a different historic contingency, and Marxian writings, much like Buñuel's characters, have cachet. Whatever was happening in American academia in the early part of the twenty-first century is no longer here. That intellectual "pork chops tribalism," paraphrasing Huey Newton, seems gone. Nevertheless, alienation is not only the product of unsatisfied needs, alienation is also the product of a lack of choice, an inability to express one's needs. For that reason, Marx's writings remain relevant. In the process of engaging them, we might become aware of our scholastic biases and limitations and open the doors of the academia to a multitude of viewpoints, even if they seem to be superfluous in the moment.

• • •

A quarter-century ago, Michel Foucault prophesized that Marx would make a comeback; that his work would be liberated from the burden of the ideological Soviet lens his detractors imposed on it.

> Il est certain que Marx, même si on admet que Marx va disparaître maintenant, réapparaîtra un jour. Ce que je souhaite [...] ce n'est pas tellement la défalsification, la restitution d'un vrai Marx, mais, à coup sûr, l'allègement, la libération de Marx par rapport à la dogmatique de parti qui l'a à la fois enfermé, véhiculé et brandi pendant si longtemps.
> FOUCAULT 1994: 457

> It is certain that Marx, even if we admit that Marx will disappear now, will reappear one day. What I want ... is not so much the defalsification, the restitution of a true Marx, but, certainly, the relief, the liberation of Marx from the dogmatic party that has once locked up, carried and brandished for so long.

These days the prophesized comeback seems closer than ever. Marxian work seems poised to be perceived as profoundly pragmatic and clearly not un-American. The substance, the philosophy of his writings, using Friedmann's terminology, seems ready to prevail over the existent scholastic prejudice, a condition perhaps of the social alienation of the American academy. Moreover, its ideology, more than its dialectical methodology, might even become more relevant in this sea of monolithic (neo)liberalism.

CHAPTER 5

Ideology as Public (Political) Subjectivity

The scholarly meaning proposed here starts with the publication (public communication) of scholarship, T_1, and it represents the result of the symbolic negotiation between the text-instigator, S_1 and the text-interpellator, S_2. The meaning-making process reveals the scholars' public subjectivity, and as a result has an ideological irony component, because it often denotes something totally different, or even opposed to the literal intention of S_1 as expressed in T_1.

Ideology, like irony, is as ambiguous as it is multifaceted. When it comes to scholastic meaning-making, irony becomes deeply ideological, and ideology becomes ironic. Controversial, both concepts are mistakenly misperceived as adulterating meaning. In that interpretation, meaning is regarded as a textual add-on, controlled by S_1's intellectual prowess as they transpire through the chosen method of research. But as shown earlier, S_1's intellectual prowess is deeply subjective, tainted by creative alienation and as revealed below, hegemonic attitudes about the contingent power structure. Furthermore, once T_1 is published, S_1 shares control over its meaning-making with S_2. Their ideology becomes imbedded in meaning.

I view ideology as political subjectivity. It does not determine the truth a theory holds, thus it is not necessarily reality-distorting. However, ideology affects meaning-making, whether S_1 ignores it or acts as if unaware of it. S_1's political views would be interpreted by subsequent text-interpellators like S_2, because they imbue the textual narrative. When ideology is honestly expressed and assumed by the text-instigator (S_1), the text-interpellator (S_2) will treat it according to S_1's guidance. Then, S_1's ideology in S_2's interpretation would promote a meaningless ironic than otherwise, when S_2 would have more control over its interpretation. Thus, whether reflecting S_1's or S_2's subjectivity, ideology adds a layer not of distortion, but of meaning. In the process of determining T_1's knowledge clout, ideology and irony actuate each other.

Ideology colors all scholarly investigation of social reality. Propelled by our private feelings of alienation, it is that subjectivity which brings us into the public forum. Through it, scholars interpellate reality and engage it.

Ideological encounters with reality often appear ironic to another public observer. When aware of it, one's creativity may be playful or even meteorically inspiring. When unaware of it, one's creativity risks becoming easily dogmatic or irrelevant when engaged in theory production.

Jurisprudentially, ideology colors all discussions, from hefty concepts to specific issues. Whether the topic is liberty as a human right or the liberty to enter into a contract, all analysis of liberty is bound to be ideological. For instance, liberty as a human right would touch upon liberty belonging to the individual as a monad, or to the individual as a community member, and whatever path is chosen, liberty would have to be connected to civil and political rights or to socio-economic rights, according to the scholar's ideology.

> Those who know the normal life of the poor ... will realize well enough that, without economic security, liberty is not worth having.
> EASTMAN 1955: 60

1 Ideology through the Ages

Ideology may denote many things, but there is no arguing that it does not belong to the animal kingdom. Animals identify themselves with their life-like activities (eating, mating, nesting, etc.). They do not engage in any conceptual representation of those activities for their own private benefit or for the benefit of the others. Humans, on the other hand, can and often do make their life-activity (eating, mating, etc.) the object of their will and consciousness, and when they reify it publicly, their ideology attaches to that symbolism.

Ideology, as a concept and as a theory about that concept, has a very political birthdate. Ideology was first defined as a science of ideas by Antoine Destutt de Tracy, an educated nobleman (a count) and a political revolutionary who supported the French Revolution of 1789. Interestingly, de Tracy identified it as a type of "specialized" knowledge ("true") belonging to the rarefied sphere of intellectuals, or savants, to whom the 1795 Convention entrusted the management of the newly founded *Institut de France* (de Tracy 1817).

> Ideology represented "true knowledge" aiming to discover the sources of what we know. Ideology belonged to the first level of knowledge, ontology, if we were to oppose it to other forms of specialized knowledge production, such as epistemology, knowledge about knowledge.
> KEKRŠYTĖ 2017: 503

Decades later, Marx also studied ideology. His position on this topic vacillated, but it never lost its defining qualifier: ideology reflected the subject's political values, which set it apart from other systems of belief, such as religion or ethics. In *German Ideology* (1846), Marx addressed ideology in a multifaceted way.

> The production of ideas, of conceptions, of consciousness, is at first directly interwoven with the material activity and the material intercourse of men, the language of real life. Conceiving, thinking, the mental intercourse of men, appear at this stage as the direct efflux of their material behavior. The same applies to mental production as expressed in the language of politics, laws, morality, religion, metaphysics, etc. of a people. Men are the producers of their conceptions, ideas, etc. – real, active men, as they are conditioned by a definite development of their productive forces and of the intercourse corresponding to these, up to its furthest forms. Consciousness can never be anything else than conscious existence, and the existence of men is their actual life-process. If in all ideology men and their circumstances appear upside-down as in a camera obscura, this phenomenon arises just as much from their historical life-process as the inversion of objects on the retina does from their physical life-process.
> MARX and ENGELS 1998: 68

From this passage alone, one could argue that Marx clearly saw ideology in the vein of Destutt de Tracy, epistemologically, or using Clifford Geertz's vocabulary, as a cultural add-on determined by the *material intercourse of men*. From Marx's use of the term "camera obscura," ideology appeared akin to an optical illusion, as a distortion of truth. As false class consciousness, ideology could have one function individually and a different one socially.

While the latter position may not necessarily be representative of his work, it certainly unified the epistemological toil of his detractors and epigones alike. Contrary to most of them, I regard Marx's position on ideology not as truth-related but as an add-on influenced by a myriad of material and subjective factors. Furthermore, in light of Marx's enthusiasm for technology and technological metaphors, before we agree that his use of *camera obscura* supports his view of ideology as a value-ridden distortion, we should remember that our eyesight is the result of our cornea, iris, and retina working as a *camera obscura*. Simultaneously, we should remember that when we have good vision, because our cornea, iris, and retina are working properly, what we see is what exists, rather than that what we imagine seeing. However, when we do not accept various disabilities, such as myopia, distortion occurs, like it did for Edgar Alan Poe's (1903) character Mr. Froissart, in "The Spectacles." His pride and ignorant prejudice against eyeglasses delayed Froissart's acknowledgment of his malfunctioning *camera obscura*.

More telling for his view of ideology is how Marx's ideology transpired in his analysis of specific social phenomena. Because Marx engaged in practical philosophy, a guide to social action, his ideology is always on display, although, I contend here, he might not have been aware of its scholastic meaning-making value.

As a historian, Marx described and analyzed socio-economic phenomena and their legal institutions. For him, progress required wealth. Always interested in the process, he studied both the creation of wealth and its legitimation. For Marx, in capitalism, wealth is the product of a laborer's work and not the product of land, feudal property.

> Just as landed property is the first form of private property, with industry at first confronting it historically merely as a special kind of property – or, rather, as landed property's liberated slave – so this process repeats itself at the level of the scientific comprehension of the subjective essence of private property, labor. Labor appears at first only as agricultural labor; but then asserts itself as labor in general.
> MARX 2007: 97

Wealth, legitimized by private property, is inherently boundless. It accumulates and creates capital.

> All wealth has become industrial wealth, the wealth of labor; and industry is accomplished labor, just as the factory-system is the essence of industry – of labor – brought to its maturity, and just as industrial capital is the accomplished objective form of private property. (Id.)

When Marx talks about the meaning of private property he displays his particular views on the topic. He denigrates private property. For him, partly because he never enjoyed it, and partly because his political views aligned with those of labor, private property is never presented as a fundamental freedom or liberty. Marx's analysis of property shows how property legitimizes possession; nothing more. "By possessing the property of buying everything, by possessing the property of appropriating all objects, money is thus the object of eminent possession," Marx instills in our perception about money, his (Marx 2007: 137).

Thus, Marx's applied ideology most tellingly imparts his views on ideology. Analyzing it like this, it appears that for Marx ideology expresses the individual's idea about their position vis-à-vis others within the market place. Elster (1985) developed this Marxian angle when he contended that ideology is a reflection on human alienation, whether material or intellectual. I add to Elster's take that ideology reflects on the individual's alienation within the societal web of power.

Marx's position on ideology has been widely misinterpreted (Barrett 1991). John Torrance (1995) put together an illustrative list of thirteen prominent propositions about ideology that have been wrongly attributed to Marx, indicating to whom each view should be credited:

(1) Ideology is a psychological process, not a theoretical product (Engels).
(2) Ideology is an effect of false consciousness, i.e. ignorance of the real class motives that determine personal motivation (Engels).
(3) Ideology is the "top tier" in a model of historical determination of superstructures by the economic base; or alternatively, the entire superstructure is "ideological," but has two levels, the political and the religious, philosophical, etc. or else one level of institutions and another of ideas (Engels, Plekhanov, Kautsky, Althusser, etc.).
(4) Whether or not the ideas of a class are ideological depends on whether its ascendancy is functional or dysfunctional for the further development of the productive forces (Kautsky).
(5) Ideology is not a critical concept. Ideologies are not distinguished from other non-scientific ideas by the false beliefs they contain, and socialism and Marxism are proletarian ideologies. The working-class movement demonstrates the inferiority of bourgeois ideology either by its ethical superiority (Bernstein) or by its historical success (Lenin).
(6) The character of ideology present in a society is explained by its function of promoting interests, and in a class society is explained by the state of the class struggle (Lenin).
(7) Class consciousness is explained primarily by the power of the ideologies required by the state of the class struggle (Lenin).
(8) False consciousness is class consciousness that does not correspond to the ideology required by a class's historical role (Lenin, Lukács).
(9) Socialist ideology is developed by revolutionary intellectuals quite independently of the development of the working-class movement (Lenin).
(10) The truth of historical materialism is not to be judged by epistemological criteria modeled on the methods of natural science, which

are superstructural phenomena reflecting reified consciousness or bourgeois ideology, but it can be vindicated within a dialectical philosophy of praxis (Lukács, Gramsci).

(11) The dominant ideology thesis: the stability of a class society can be explained primarily by the effects of ideology (Gramsci, Marcuse, Althusser).

(12) Ideology, like the economy, may or may not be the dominant structure level in a society, and thus secures its social cohesion depending on economic conditions (Althusser).

(13) Ideology is both defective and necessary in any human society, even a communist one, to sustain the illusion that the individual "bearers" of social structures are the "subjects" of social action (Althusser).

TORRANCE 1995: 27–28

The issues of subjectivity continued to occupy much of late twentieth-century academic writing, including that of Michèle Barrett, Terry Eagleton, Stuart Hall, Ernesto Laclau, and Chantal Mouffe, and of course, Michel Foucault. In fact, there are variations within the position of the same author vis-à-vis its meaning. Most postmodern scholars view ideology as a subjective representation of reality colored by the subject's political and cultural identity – what Hans Georg Gadamer called meta-knowledge (1986).

Louis Althusser (1971) famously stated that "Man is an ideological animal by nature" (171), and further developed the Marxian meaning of ideology (1971, 1984). Althusser noted how ideology works in everyday life, and how it transforms individuals into specific social and historical subjects through "interpellation." When individuals engage their surrounding cultural environment, reality is mentally reproduced and appropriated in accordance with the dominant relations of production. This is not a mechanical process. In the process, we engage our willingness, pleasure, and intellectual abilities; we create our own ideological semantics. Sometimes, we might even become aware of our social and political condition: the condition of being duped, lied to, and taken for granted.

Michel Foucault integrated subjectivity into his theoretical explanation, making it an integral part of it and classifying its textual outcome as "discourse." The label of "discourse" indicates a narrative whose truth is its very "justification." This somehow circular reinterpretation of political subjectivity does little to clarify Foucault's position on this issue, other than his desire to distance himself from Marx. However, even when Foucault addresses jurisprudence, he remains indebted to Marx because he views the role of jurisprudence, as legitimizing and preserving the status quo of the power structure. For instance,

Foucault criticizes jurisprudence for having abandoned its ambiguous justificatory idealism as a theory of justice, in favor of the quantifiable and "externally guaranteed" truth. However, the concreteness of "truth," Foucault contends, does not make it any more satisfactory; both concepts – justice and truth – share the same legitimizing function.

Foucault embraced the idea that a theory's ideology marks its role in the Paradigm of Knowledge, endorsing thus the political value of scholarship, its public subjectivity. Foucault connected a theory's system of truth with the existing theoretical paradigm to argue that if it accorded with the societal system of truth, then the theory became part of the public discourse. This appears to be a highly pragmatic way of demystifying theory production at a specific historical moment. Decades earlier, Dewey explained how a theory's transparent subjectivity affects its hierarchy of truth, and how the theoretical framework defining a theory marks its utility in the larger human pantheon of ideas. However, Dewey, never keen on irony, did not seem concerned by the means to correct situations in which a theory did not conform to the existing paradigm, or how a paradigm which had outlived its usefulness could be replaced.

Foucault, hardly keen on irony himself, discusses epistemological truth in opposition to Marx's concept of ideology, which he calls "the economics of untruth" (Barrett 1991: 155). Using the triad of *Truth, Discourse* and *Power*, Foucault persuasively asserts that truth was the goal of discourse, but that power could corrupt it, and that it could be achieved only when facts were presented from multitudinous points of view. Foucault both raised and answered the question of who is served by such discourse. He acknowledged that behind any public discourse ("the posing of the question"), lay socio-political power. By allowing only certain questions to be posed, Foucault explained, the receiver was encouraged to assume that they were the important questions (Foucault 1980: 116–133).

For Foucault, the entire public discourse at one moment in time represented that society's "régime of truth." While his description of the régime of truth may be debatable, he magisterially summarized its function. According to Foucault, the régime of truth – meaning institutionalized truth, or institutionalized knowledge – installs and legitimizes a political regime. For him, the régime of truth was "not merely ideological or superstructural; it was a condition of the formation and development of capitalism" (id.). Conceptually, Foucault politicizes subjectivity. While for cultural studies scholars like Stuart Hall, for instance, authorship is embedded in the cultural matrix of the author, much in line with Dewey's logic, for Foucault, authorship is in the service of "truth," whose ultimate purpose is ideologic, legitimizing a power structure.

Brendon Edgeworth shied away from pointing to the Marxian heritage in Foucault's *Power/Knowledge*. Nevertheless, that pedigree is evident in Foucault's thesis on mainstream understanding of legal theories. For Foucault, a theory becomes part of the public discourse, Edgeworth noted, only to the extent it can be legitimized with the stamp of "power-knowledge" (Edgeworth 2003). That happens when the public subjectivity incorporated in a theory does not threaten but fits the Paradigm of Knowledge. In the process, mainstream knowledge subjugates other alternative "knowledges" and identities (id.). Ironically, this is how Foucault's theory replaces the vacuum created in the American academe by its rejection of Marx.

Ira Katzenelson (1998) noted two decades ago, that ideologically speaking there was one remaining ideology in America: liberalism. While not a self-evident term, especially for Americans, Katzenelson continued, liberalism reached the hegemonic meta-ideology status. Liberalism became, he noted, "the primary constitutive grammar of political thought, in what [has been called] the globe's single time zone of the imaginary" (17).

Liberalism today is, indeed, the basis of moral and instrumental political reason. But what if we pass this historical moment? What happens if the academe take a stance against scholarship soaked in this "one-dimensional political thought" (id.). If liberalism, a once-embattled ideology "against religious intolerance, prescientific ways of knowing, feudalism and its legacies and visions" (id.) is to remain a progressive ideatic badge, then it needs to express its views not dogmatically, as the hegemonic ideology, but in a free exchange of ideas.

Katznelson himself mentioned the possibility of other non-threatening ideologies: socialism, liberalism, and pluralism. Katzneslon's list is not exhaustive, but illustrative. His three options excluded Marxian thought with its conviction in the role of a civil society whose individuals are self-aware of the alienation capital accumulation creates. Marxian ideology promotes individual freedoms not in the abstract, but in a manner protective of community and totality, understood as humanity, and not as factory shanty-towns or Google's employee community (Burchell and Robin 2011).

Among other possible ideologies American scholars can embrace is also Bertrand Russell's. Russell's political subjectivity promotes an industrial humane society. Its power structure has the following four prerequisites:

(1) the maximizing of production;
(2) justice in distribution;
(3) a tolerable existence for producers; and
(4) "the greatest possible freedom and stimulus to vitality and progress".
ATKINSON and HUGHES 1972: 17

As shown here, ideology is as complex a concept as are theories about ideology. In this book, ideology is inherent to knowledge production and especially to the meaning-making process. It reveals the scholar's conceptual relation to power. Using Foucault's vocabulary, ideology transforms writing into discourse and designates its position within the existing hierarchy of truth. Foucault's "hierarchy of truth" metaphor explains how a particular statement fits the historical network of meaning (Barrett 1991: 126). And this is as good an answer as any to Foucault's rather famous question:

> How is it that one particular statement appeared rather than the other?
> FOUCAULT 1972: 27

The Italian Marxist Antonio Negri (2006) further developed Althusser's view of ideology. For him, ideology duplicates the real world within the borders imposed by the juridical and political image of the moment. Within this paradigm, legal and political information is inherently ideological. It both socializes us within a political image and actuates that political image for us with concrete information on the events of the day.

Gunther Anders' views on technology best help us to understand, more than previous philosophers, the myriad ways in which ideology slips into our theoretical perception of reality. Within the current process of reification – wherein the devices we have created to distract us do so with incessant flows of information, while also transmitting our "likes" and "dislikes" to corporations, who use that data both to determine what to sell us next and to sell our privacy to the highest bidder – ideology has undergone a radical transformation. It is hailed as the symbol of "participatory culture," comprising user-generated content.

Technology has relegated the engagement of political information to an antiquated mode of action. Christian Fuchs (2016) calls this the ideology of the post-ideology using Anders' vocabulary (2017). To the extent that ideology is also another term of art for designating a particular position on the map of political power, social media can be viewed as leveling the playing field, as it gives the false perception that all opinions can be posted and all content can be assessed and commented on equally according to their merit. As Fuchs explains, "the asymmetry of visibility and attention in the flood of information," in addition to the simple obstruction of critical voices, result in differences becoming increasingly difficult to notice (2017). Briefly, this is the technological embrace of ideology: within the current power structure, content at the top of the visibility scheme is that which matters.

Ideology may remain a concept ripe for further studies, but most importantly, as public subjectivity, ideology is an inherent limit to all scholarship, and when ignored it often cripples the text-instigator's (S_1) meaning-making position. Marx ignored taking into account the impact of his own ideology in his normative theory, although his ideology was always on display.

For instance, he wrote about ways to better society while addressing individual alienation. From a Marxian perspective, ideology is the set of beliefs we develop within the process of alienation. However, human alienation is more complex than what Marx chose to emphasize. It is dissatisfaction with one's life and it encroaches both the private and public sphere of all, irrespective of gender, age, or even employment. Today, it is further compounded, as technology destroyed all public/private boundaries. Since the times when Marx studied the alienating impact of technology, technology today has caused further causes while creating the perception of fulfillment through the appearance of abundance. Through technology, almost everybody has something: a digital space to lose any established sense of self in favor of a fluid appreciation of infinite possibilities.

Notably, Marx limited alienation to the adult male. Marxian alienation was caused by the market place but it followed the individual in his private sphere as well. Ironically, this perspective, which was viewed as well-encompassing at the time, proved to be rather limited, perhaps due to its political subjectivity. But, as Adorno said (1973), "No theory escapes the marketplace" (4). Thus, perhaps more needs to be done to explain the interconnection between alienation and ideology, but that goes beyond the scope of this book. From a meaning-making position, I only argue that ideological awareness and transparence would only encourage more diverse scholarship, and with it a Paradigm of Knowledge better equipped to help us understand our complex reality, because,

> Each one is offered as a possibility among competing opinions; all are put up for choice; all are swallowed. (Id.)

2 The Case against (Academic) Ideological Purges

Not enough is said about the correlation between democracy and mass-spread socio-economic prosperity, and even less about the latter's impact on a vibrant political discourse, which is indispensable to a functional democracy. Political discourse is as diverse as the political views of its participating players, and the participants' views are shaped through education, whose core takes place in institutions of education.

In 2010, Vincent Lyon-Callo noted the decline of education in public schools and the passive acceptance of a neoliberal curriculum under budgetary constraints. While baffled by the trends in education, because they did not reflect its historical contingency, he explained them persuasively. Lynn-Callo (2010) linked the trends in K-12 and higher education to the leadership's neoliberal corporatist ideology and to a deep-seated interest to preserve the status-quo.

Schools, through their curricula, shape both our public debate and our system of republican government. For instance, in 1960, "only 22 percent of voters had been to college; now more than 52 percent have" (Neacșu 2005a: 227). As more and more voters are college graduates, more and more leaders are too. Consequently, the percentage of law school graduates in the government is only deemed to increase as well.

Of course, many of those college-educated attend state and city schools. But, as the absolute number of undergraduates has steadily increased, from 935,140 in 1980–1901 to 1,244,171 in 2000–2001, similarly has the number of those from elite schools. "[T]he top 26 universities and colleges represent ... 1% of these students." The increase in the number of such graduates has only cemented their significant leadership role (id.).

The relationship between the growth in the nation's number of college graduates and its effect on this nation's future, on one hand, and the need for exposing college students to a wide array of ideas, on the other hand, was succinctly intimated to by Justice Powell twenty-five years ago when he delivered the Supreme Court's decision in *Regents of University of California v. Bakke*, 438 U.S. 265 (1978). Justice Powell observed that the "nation's future depends upon leaders trained through wide exposure to ... ideas" (id.: 313).

More recently, Justice O'Connor in *Grutter v. Bollinger*, 539 U.S. 306 (2003), summarized the leadership role played by law school graduates – especially those graduating from elite law schools. Justice O'Connor expressly identified only one type of leadership role played by the graduates of the "handful" of highly coveted law schools (the Ivy League and other elite schools): that of molding our judicial system. Nevertheless, their other roles as prominent members of the legislative and executive body can easily be inferred from her mentioning the role played by all law school graduates.

> [U]niversities, and in particular, law schools, represent the training ground for a large number of our Nation's leaders. [...] Individuals with law degrees occupy roughly half the state governorships, more than half the seats in the United States Senate, and more than a third of the seats in the United States House of Representatives. [...] The pattern is even

more striking when it comes to highly selective law schools. A handful of these schools accounts for 25 of the 100 United States Senators, 74 United States Courts of Appeals judges, and nearly 200 of the more than 600 United States District Court judges. (Id.: 332)

This trend will continue, chiefly for graduates from elite schools, because they, more than any other graduates, are brought up to have a certain self-image – that "of a strong likelihood of succeeding in the practice of law and contributing in diverse ways to the well-being of others" (id.: 332). Recent past Presidents (Bill Clinton, George W. Bush, Barack Obama), as well as the current one, are all products of Ivy League education.

Most agree that schooling shapes us emotionally, and economically. Schools and universities are sources of knowledge production and ideological relations. Educational institutions reflect, reinforce, and produce particular ways of thinking and being. Historically, education played a particularly important role in both the popular imagination about possibilities and possibilities for upward mobility in the U.S., as well as the actual ones. And few would dispute the correlation between educational achievement and lifetime earnings.

Similarly, there is little to be debated about the fact that more education equates with social mobility and economic affluence. Thus, the lack of curricular options for Marxian scholarship might be understandable in elite schools, if Marxian scholarship stands for Soviet propaganda. But, the crux of my argument is that while scholarship is deeply ideological, when actuated, ideological meaning is ironic.

Furthermore, a diverse education of our future guardians of the law is vital. At the higher echelons of our higher education, curricular uniformity has been unsettling, especially if John Stuart Mill's values are to be upheld. Here I argue that political subjectivity is embedded in scholastic meaning. To dismantle politically uniform meaning-making seems thus to require a less uniform theory production, which comes from a less uniform (legal) education. One way to achieve this goal is through a curriculum which incorporates a variety of scholastic political views.

Thus, the elite schools' graduates represent this "Nation's leaders" (*Grutter v. Bollinger*, 539 U.S. at 308) and its guardians. Moreover, the elite law schools' graduates are charged with protecting what Thomas Paine (1922) called the jewel of the crown of our American King, our Rule of Law. Knowing that their beliefs are shaped significantly during their higher education, it only makes sense that university discourse and its curriculum should be as inclusive as possible and incorporate alternative theories that only forge one's better understanding of the world. In a representative democracy, leaders are expected to represent all their constituents including the poor, although many of them have lost their right to vote. Moreover, in our democracy with global extensions, our leaders are also expected to understand the rest of the world – the billions of have-less and have-nots. At a minimum, Marx, through its focus on economic factors would force us to take their interests into account.

In 2005, I noticed the scarcity of legal courses that taught Marxian ideas about social and political hierarchies in the market place, hierarchies Marx describes as determined by ownership of the means of production. From my perspective, it looked "as if the raging right-wing forces [had] successfully shaped and manipulated our collective fantasies" (229). That article remained obscure and unread, and the legal academe as unfazed as it has always been on this topic. If there has ever been an Ivy League curricular debate over Marxian teachings, then that debate must have started somberly, paraphrasing Shakespeare's foreboding words spoken by Hamlet in his famous soliloquy.

> To be, or not to be, – that is the question
> Whether 'tis nobler in the mind to suffer
> The slings and arrows of outrageous fortune,
> Or to take arms against a sea of troubles
> And by opposing end them? To die, – to sleep, –
> (SHAKESPEARE 1906: 95)

Today, such potential debate brings to mind a different version of Hamlet's soliloquy, the one the "duke" taught the "king" in *Adventures of Huckleberry Finn*:

> To be, or not to be; that is the bare bodkin
> That makes calamity *of* so long life.
> TWAIN 1917: 190; emphasis in the original

If Columbia University (CU) and its course bulletins are an example, elite schools need to readdress their curriculum both at the undergraduate and graduate level. As shown in Columbia University Bulletin 1961/62 through 1994/1995 ("Bulletin"), the number of CU courses using Marx's readings or even the word "Marxism" in their course description has steadily decreased since the mid-1990s (Neacşu 2005a: 252). From the 1960s through the early 1990s, there were scores of CU courses whose readings covered Marxian works. They were taught within the *Contemporary Civilization Program*, and those of *Philosophy, Government* (then *Political Science*), and *Sociology*. After more than two decades, its only course dedicated to Marxism ceased being listed in the CU Bulletin (id.).

At CU, for the last two decades, the realm of Marxian thought seems to have been delegated to one of the undergraduate core courses: *Introduction to Contemporary Civilization*. Interestingly, if every writer on the reading list has a particular work assigned for students to read, Marx has "selections from the Marx-Engels Reader," as the *Reading List* (https://perma.cc/3A2B-JARW) for 2017–18 shows. The only reasonable way to explain this intellectual penury is to paraphrase Foucault in *Discipline and Punish* (identified on that reading list): Columbia University, as an example of Ivy League education, seems to feel that acknowledging specific titles by Marx would potentially enable students to remember them and perhaps seek to (re)read them in depth. An off-hand mention to anonymous "selections" by a couple of writers and the rubric "Marx" sounds detached and clearly not endorsed by the institution.

Interestingly, if Yale University used to offer no course on Marx, it currently offers *Critical Race Theory*, a course which incorporates topics on "race and Marxian social relations" as *Bulletin of Yale University*, Series 113, Number 10, on August 10, 2017 indicated.

More aligned with this disregard for anything non-liberal is the Columbia University Law School's curriculum, which has no course required readings from Marx. As said earlier, if only skimmed, Marxian writings do appear as belonging to a bygone era.

Similarly, among the other Ivy League Law Schools (Harvard, Yale, Stanford, Cornell, and University of Pennsylvania), Marx's work has been carefully omitted, too. If 15 years ago, "University of Pennsylvania Law School offered a course in Jurisprudence which mentioned the word 'Marxists' in its description" (id.), such a course is no longer offered. Or, if it exists, it is not proudly advertised to attract students. Yale Law School, perhaps in part because it once had a Marxian thought-friendly curriculum – when David Trubek taught property when John F. Kennedy was a student there, Becca Heller was involved in Critical Marxism (id.) – still has a course requiring Marxian readings.

In 2005, Harvard Law School mentioned two courses whose descriptions require their students to read Marx: *Central Ideas of Contemporary Law and Legal Thought, Social Theory* and *Political Philosophy Now: Seminar*. Taught by renowned Critical Legal scholar, Professor Roberto Mangabeira Unger, they both covered readings from Marx's works (id.). However, they were not offered every year. For Spring 2019, Professor Mangabeira offers four courses which potentially might cover Marxian works, but none has the readings available on the school's website.

A decade ago, I was writing that the University of Michigan Law School was in a class of its own. It offered a course entitled "Idea of Equality," but its online description omitted Marxist readings: "[r]eadings will be drawn almost exclusively from non-legal sources, works of philosophy, literature, and sociology. Among the readings: John Locke, Jean-Jacques Rousseau Edmund Burke, Mary Wollstonecraft; Alexis De Tocqueville; W.E.B. Du Bois; Edith Wharton; Yevgeny Zamiatin, Simone DeBeauvoir; Zora Neale Hurston and John Rawls" (id.). Today, there are no readings mentioned in the course description.

The case for Mill's free market of ideas cannot be thus made in most elite law schools and the majority of the Ivy Leagues. Marx's writings are not among the readings, if any, or if there are, they are not advertised to their students (present, alumni or prospective) or their parents. Worse, their curricula do not include such readings either in support of a socio-economic identity (rather than gender, race, or social orientation) or in a critique of the rights theory. To the extent that all theories are subjective interpellations of reality, incorporating the author's subjectivity (ideological irony), and philosophy – rationally descriptive following various methods of research and recording the findings – I posit that the main reason for this persisting rejection of Marx's work is his subjectivity, and especially his ideology.

Unfortunately, this ideological fight for our students' minds, the minds of the future guardians of our King, the Rule of Law, is fraught with unpredictable, hardly manageable, results. Today, the marketplace of ideas, whose seeds are planted through education, is easily apparent in cyberspace. Public subjectivity is mediated by technology through a myriad of platforms that have transformed the physicality of the classic (Habermasian) public forum, where the exchange of ideas required one's physical presence. This new format has perhaps emboldened preaching instead of dialogue. Symptomatic of this new reality is the political discourse in the higher echelons of U.S. power, which is mostly a monologue as can be easily assessed in the case of the United States President via Donald J. Trump's Twitter feed.

Rather than using the inherited power structure in the confines of social media – i.e., the official (@POTUS) account – President Donald J. Trump uses a personal account (@realDonaldTrump) to conduct presidential affairs. Because he uses an alias that would typically indicate a private account to exercise duties associated with his presidential role, Trump attempts to achieve the proverbial position of having his cake and eating it too. As a "fake" private person who can enjoy exposing his ideological statements publicly, he chooses to block followers from commenting on his presidential speeches as if he were a private Twitter user who can block followers whose ideology he dislikes. He uses labels to hide the ideological and political role of the President. Lawyers representing some of the blocked users made this point clear, as they stated in a recent letter,

> This Twitter account operates as a 'designated public forum' for First Amendment purposes, and accordingly the viewpoint-based blocking of our clients is unconstitutional. ...Though the architects of the Constitution surely didn't contemplate presidential Twitter accounts, they understood that the president must not be allowed to banish views from public discourse simply because he finds them objectionable." ... "Having opened this forum to all comers, the president can't exclude people from it merely because he dislikes what they're saying."
> SAVAGE 2017

Despite these thorough academic purges, Marxian theory fits intrinsically the Ivies' curricular teachings. As shown here, Marx's work revels in German philosophy, English political economy, and French Socialism, all highly abstract knowledge products. Furthermore, Marx was never an intellectual outcast, which should only add to his unthreatening bourgeois charm. Marx was expelled from France and Germany, but his work "was profoundly integrated within the German and European culture of his age" (Lichtheim 1967: 212), Not Marx's but Lenin's and even Leon Trotsky's work represent something marginal and unconventional, as it transpired from *The Case of Leon Trotsky* (1937), for instance.

Teaching Marx is long overdue in our Ivy League (law) schools. And his work is pertinent to many undergraduate as well as graduate courses, including as a theory of social development, or in various courses on gender and sexual orientation studies or identity politics.

At first glance, it may seem that identity politics and Marxian subjectivity have very little in common. Of course, "if you lick my nipple," as Michael Warner (1996) remarked (43), "the world suddenly seems comparatively insignificant" (Morton 1996: 35), and with it any macro socio-economic analysis. Identity becomes central and more than a cultural trait; it becomes "the performance of desire" (id.). It becomes a place of "ideological and material contestation over need" (id.); in other words, an ideology that demands legitimacy for its desire.

However, Marx too talked about desire, albeit as the result of the never-ending production of commodities. As an identity theory, for example, it might even highlight socio-economic distinctions among members from different minority groups. In that instance, Marxian thought would bring in a second level of ideological analysis, which might open up the otherwise apparently ossified micro-social discussion.

Socio-economic identity is more than cultural ornament. It is more than an innocuous quaint parallel reality because "cultural divisions," Elster (1985) demonstrated, "are never class neutral" (392). It is invariably the case that classes are distributed "non-randomly over cultural groups" (id.). And, one may add, over minority groups, too. Additionally, Marxian theory offers an identity to the millions of have-less and have-nots, the many more that struggle to pay their mortgages and get their children off to college, and also to the few that don't understand either poverty or struggle.

In terms of subjectivity, Marxian scholarship is about the "economically other," but instead of addressing it in terms of personal failure it views it as a societal ailment. For instance, during the last ten years, the American middle class has been declining. This systemic impoverishment cannot be satisfactorily explained as a massive failure at a personal level. Still, little is done to educate future scholars in a structural approach to addressing this problem. As such, the education system refuses to mirror reality with matching classes. Students remain unexposed to concepts about wealth distribution as a means to prevent the increasing economic inequality.

When Marx noted the plight of workers, his tolerance and compassion were as much on display as it was his sense of observation. Indeed, Marx did not differentiate among labor, and he overlooked the hardship of female and children's work in the household. Because he stood for labor in the market place and demanded his readers do the same, his theory has been regarded as essentialist, in a denigrating manner. His ideology informed his theory. Marxian individuals were classified according to their means of subsistence. They sold their workforce for wages or they accumulated and re-invested capital. Have these identifiers outstayed their usefulness? Can they still find a referential place alongside non-economic identifiers such as gender and race?

Academically, gender and race seem to have become distinctions drawn to enable the appearance of more academic disciplines. This curricular development inadvertently might have caused the theoretical disappearance of totality, or better yet, borrowing Georg Lukács' (1971) vocabulary (35), the loss of "the problem of totality in the interests of greater specialization" (id.). This overspecializing might be perceived as mindless speculation at the academic level – speculation which alienates the subjects involved in it when it is perceived as lacking any possibility of bringing real-life changes or solutions.

What if, instead of creating academic subjects as imagined by scholars, we start by observing what questions are meaningful today to various social segments and, as Lukács would suggest, we address them based on their social distribution. Then we examine the social significance of their answers. If real problems are inverted and discussed to exhaustion to the point that they become superfluous theoretically, while unaddressed at their practical level, we address the curriculum accordingly. From this perspective, I would say, it would become apparent that the academy addresses gender and race as ideological constructs, or more exactly, as liberal constructs. Their ideological nature is twice destructive. They seem to be used to dismantle the idea of social unity, making it a problem, while achieving the liberal goal of disrupting the Marxian unity of a single theory and praxis. Once we understand the limitations imposed by such an academic approach, we might want to refocus the debate on non-liberal concepts of gender and race, which in turn might foster social change and unity.

This is not a call to replace courses. To the contrary, it is a call to stop academic purges, acknowledge inadequate teachings, and improve them. Employing dialectics, we could contradict the traditional norms of adequacy. Paraphrasing Adorno, we pushed the depth of our research and discover a bottomless abyss. Such a dialectical and interdisciplinary perspective would allow comprehensive research into human alienation. The irony of this endeavor is the author's inevitable ideology, which would direct his gaze for solutions. Whether ideological or not, Marx promoted the dichotomy of exploited masses and exploiting bourgeoisie. As such, this binary fomented a separation of the powerful from the oppressed. The oppressed could aim to elbow their way into the power in small numbers. The terminology of "oppressed minorities" is a way of distinguishing among the oppressed masses by criteria than their mere oppression, such as gender and oppression, race and oppression, sexual orientation and oppression, or a multitude of such identifiers, as Kimberlé Crenshaw (2008) suggested with the concept of "intersectionality."

Subordination is a social problem, which is compounded by gender and racial vulnerability. The hyper-exploitation of immigrant, black and Latina working-class women is as much a reality today as it was a century ago when Claudia Jones, a deported immigrant, created opposition in the United States of America (Davies 2008).

Jones dared to adopt Marxian thought in its Soviet outlook. In the process, she showed that theoretically, it offered a solid foundation for a critique of class oppression, imperialist aggression, and gender subordination. As Carole Boyce Davies (2008) explains, Jones proved that Marxian theory was far from dogmatic and that there is space "left" of Karl Marx. Jones embraced a political philosophy that was anathema in the McCarthy period of the 1940s and 1950s. Her brand of Marxian thought was "anti-racist, antisexist, pro-black community orientation" (id.: 6). But she "constantly explained the issues of gender in terms of their connection to class struggle, anti-imperialism, and the battle of peace" (id.: 31). Through her writings, Jones engaged in a hierarchy of thought and action to reach the ultimate communitarian anti-imperialist goal.

From this perspective, both the historicity and social connectedness of gender and race, to use Lukács' and West's vocabulary, become obvious. Subordinated to a liberal ideology, race and gender, the same non-economic social constructions, do not seem to encourage unity of action in the sense of a total social transformation. It seems that their ideological epistemological code defines their usefulness. They lack mass appeal because, while they focus on features that all humans have, they empower only certain groups with certain features.

Within the liberal meta-ideology of liberalism, the isolating coding of race and gender seems unaddressed in the academy. As Lukács (1971) reminded us, Rosa Luxembourg would have said that most social changes on racial and gender grounds are still "exploding like pistol shots" (id.: 40). Thus, every four years, during presidential elections, for instance, we are witnessing the impossibility of presenting them as social changes benefiting all the people in spite of their various differences. Perhaps a different intellectual identifier, which would transcend insularity for the good of broad, mass-accepted legitimate social changes, would work better to ensure connectedness in a specific historical contingency. For me, that would be a Marxian ideology.

Whatever antagonism race and gender create within our society, that antagonism is conceptualized as integral to the general societal harmony. Rather than organically incorporated into a more societal strategy for social change, race riots, no matter how traumatic, end up being remembered like the excesses of the French Revolution. Disavowed, they are eventually forgotten. Again, using Lukács' words, the disruptions gender and race produce, and the identity of their interests, begets no general community, or "no national unity and no political organization." As such, their problems and their solutions lack legitimacy and broad acceptance, running the risk to be dismantled with each following change in the federal legislative body or presidential election.

How is this lack of unity possible? Lukács (1971) would say gender and race-united communities lack unifying interests (61). Also, to the extent that we can identify gender-based and race-based communities, there is no unifying ideology, or conceptual representation of their interests, even if there is a communion of interests. The lack of unity and the antagonism between interests and their representation is not monolithic. It has a dialectical aspect in its connectedness, being influenced by the existing historical circumstances. The larger, societal implications of these problems might combine so that they become the problems of the society at large. But, that presentation is an ideological undertaking, and the recipients – the body of all people – have to be susceptible to that explanation. Or, have experienced it or witnessed it at some point and can identify with that set of problems.

From a non-liberal perspective, one might argue against isolating social problems and presenting them as belonging to a specific minority, gender or race, and against demanding solutions targeting that specific minority. But too much specificity walls off problems and solutions.

Because ideology often dictates what we can see as a social problem, or what is in need of a political solution, perhaps students should understand that everything taught to them is deeply ideological. If educators acknowledge their biases and still taught academic subjects in an academic manner, students would be less inclined to behave differently when engaging each other in public spaces.

State-sponsored ideologies are dangerous because they are propaganda and they determine the Regime of Truth. Today, scholarship is in danger of becoming propaganda because there is little debate. There is one particular view promoted, and that is unsatisfactory. When Ivy League institutions promote a monolithic ideology such as liberalism, be it a feminist, corporate or critical liberalism, their solutions become limited to the problems they could possibly solve. And if we were to look at the distribution of those problems and their social value, we would see that they reflect a small societal segment.

Let's think about property for a minute and see how it could be addressed so the solutions envisaged would benefit the most. For instance, Karl Marx described capital in *The Communist Manifesto* as a social power (Marx and Engels 2012: 86). There are many ways in which this statement could be interpreted. A more orthodox Marxian view would be that capital is a collection of individual interests which want to maximize their share of the capital, and thus we can talk about a social class; ergo capital is a social force. Whether we call them shareholders or not, their actions have a social character corresponding to a specific social identity – that of a shareholder.

Going back to the Enlightenment era, capital accumulation was regarded as a form of freedom of consciousness, and as a form of increased freedom, or as a progressive type of freedom – freedom from religion. Wise and able men were seen as the architects of their own lives and fortunes, or as Thomas Jefferson liked to say, "faber suae quisque fortunae" (Gay 1969: 7). Capital accumulation rewards those who have access to capital. Furthermore, capital, unlike landed property which was hereditary, theoretically, is available to everybody. This means, academically speaking, everybody can accumulate capital. Accordingly, classes and class interests, as well as the ideology correlated to this perception of social structure, must be flawed.

But, what is the reality? For instance, Initial Public Offerings (IPOs) are the first time that the stock of a private company is offered to the public. The IPO for Facebook was the biggest in technology and one of the biggest in Internet history. But how many benefited from it, in addition to the company's leadership? Those who had (a lot of) money to invest in FB shares.

Similarly, the system of credit has been employed to mask the lack of capital. Lukács (1971) called it a "façade" which organizes the entire society according to the interests of Big Capital. Capital has its own ideology which sells capitalists the story that only Big Capital is worth aspiring to.

In other words, capital does not want any ideological explanation which would focus on the totality, but single organisms, whose actions act as chain reactions more than individual, well insulated moments. Nevertheless, despite attempts to present the liberal ideology as promoting the Rule of Law of the capital and its minority interests, the dominant ideology has been able to define the terms of its criticism. In this context, they focus on further destroying the totality with specific minority-based identities. Also, it is done by tarring the value of any anti-liberal ideology as fascist or communist, where communism is a label which stands for Soviet, or more recently Russian, imperialism.

Lukács (1971) believed that the lack of organization of the capital-controlling class was a sign of weakness and capitulation of the class consciousness of the bourgeoisie (67). Writing this statement today is laughable. It seems obvious that only the weak need organizing. But, what remains relevant is Lukács' explanation of how social stability is ensured through hegemony:

> [H]egemony is exercised not merely by a minority but in the interest of that minority, so the need to deceive the other classes and to ensure that their class consciousness remains amorphous is inescapable for a bourgeois regime. (Consider here the theory of the state that stands "above" class antagonisms, or the notion of an "impartial" system of justice). (66)

Ideology, or the manner of representing any situation with a public component, is crucial, because, attitudes are as important as realities. Going back to the Enlightenment era, when capital was created, philosophers were the ideologues of the newly found confidence in technology and progress. Locke was promoting the mind of man as well, fit for creating knowledge for "the use and advantage of men" (Gay 1969: 6). Kant, in his *Critique of Pure Reason*, wrote that Reason, with its principles in one hand and experiment in the other, approaches nature not like a pupil but for answers to questions it has already formulated (id.: 7–8). Though they do it within the accepted Regime of Truth, which is liberal ideology, scholars continue to use ideology to legitimize pursuits within the public sphere.

Why does it matter? Let's return for a moment to *The Communist Manifesto's* description of capital: "Capital is, therefore, not a personal, it is a social, power." (Marx and Engels 2012: 86). In that statement on Capital, Marx referenced modern bourgeois private property, as opposed to hard-won, self-acquired, self-earned property of the artisan, artist, or the farmer. Thus, his analysis was limited to specific social relations of property, whose owners had similar interests. Their class of capitalists was defined by their wealth based on the work of others. Capital was the product of waged labor, and gave capitalists power over waged laborers. From identifying capital as power (or lack thereof), it was treated as a social differentiator as important as gender and race is a small step; especially today when gender and race are fluid social constructs.

However, this analysis is ignored by the current property law textbooks because it does not promote an individualist liberal ideology. The scholars' (S_1) ideology marks their analysis, reasoned explanation, the T_1's philosophy. T_1 is a function of S_1's ideology because what is outside S_1's set of public, political set of beliefs cannot and does not shape S_1's analysis. To further argue, one cannot describe the taste of lobster as lobster without having tasted it before. It can only be compared to that of tofu if tofu is all she has been exposed to. T_1 is also a function of S_2's ideology because by the same token, what is outside S_2's set of beliefs will not shape the negotiating meaning-making S_2 would propose for T_1. Plus, when S_1's ideology clashes with that of S_2, as argued here, irony takes center-stage in negotiating T_1's meaning-making process.

While most scholars make the case that it is hard to observe their ideology (Bond et al. 2015), this book, using Marx's work as an example, contends differently. Their position is understandable, especially if they regard ideology like Mr. Froissart regarded spectacles in Edgar Allan Poe's (1903) story with the same title. However, as public subjectivity, ideology is currently experiencing a novel phase due in large part to cyberspace. Technology of communication has made it possible for individuals to freely embrace their political subjectivity under the veil of physical privacy. While easily visualized in the process of communication due to the complex technological progress we witness, ideology has become a new badge of group identity. As such, perhaps ideology deserves its own curricular subject.

3 Mass Media – Technology Actuating Ideology

Here, ideology represents an individual's beliefs about their position within the public sphere, whether it is the job market, civil society or the government.

In light of this, technology breaks the barrier of privacy, thus, ideology is often actuated through mass media communication as stimulated by social media.

Technology has enabled every willing soul to become a self-portraitist and enjoy individual exhibits on digital spaces such as Instagram or Facebook. However, this is just mere appearance. In the process of exposing one's needs, the individual feels further alienated in ways never imagined by Marx: alienation transferred from the devalued workspace and time to the devalued leisure space and time. Under the guise of further fulfilling old wants individuals discovered new wants even more ephemeral and out of reach. Technology touts the ability to be rich and famous through unlimited social media exposure, but these new wants are unreachable: the intrinsic quality of the rich and famous is scarcity.

From this feeling of dissatisfaction, ideology rises as the individual's understanding of her position within the power structure. It is not the structure of power within one's family except that often family structure, and its paternalistic organization, mirrors the societal power structure. To that extent, gender and age start becoming added centers of powerlessness and impact one's ideology.

Social media materializes imagination. Its world is well structured. When participants sign up, they must submit themselves to the structure of the digital space. They must follow the rules or else, get banned. To participate in social media, one has to accept an autonomous space organized for a particular purpose. It requires submission and an abandonment of any criticism of its structure. Wherein domination is encouraged, this is a closed universe of open competitiveness.

Ideology is present both in the process and in the content of the communications. The process simulates relationships which are highly structured by the number of followers or the number of likes. Contextually, social media provides a hostile environment where liberty of expression is an illusion. First, the inequality of status understood in terms of communication skills and evidenced by the number of followers, for instance, has a clear impact on the content of the communication. Then the environment of social media, with its emphasis on individual fame and self-satisfaction as the final goal, postulates that everyone is their own master, thus promoting the clearer libertarian value (Mauco 2009).

As a concept, mass media has always integrated technology – from content conception to content delivery. Mediated content through the newly emerged technologies has reshaped the experience of politics, as well as the politics of education, and thus, all ideological endeavors. As with ideology, media came out of the technological progress from the Enlightenment Era.

During that time, it became obvious that political progress could happen only if the overpowering presence of the illiterate masses would be first tamed. In the absence of the habit of individual autonomy and absent any freedom of conscience or thought, political progress was limited. The path to individual autonomy of thought, Peter Gay explained, was connected to the freedom of commerce. Exercising it daily as a freedom of choice, it developed in freedom of thought, which the times' thinkers took upon to encourage with political information. Political discourse and newspapers soon incorporated the thinkers' ideological account of their political goals. In the process, the informed (or misinformed), built what has been called public opinion, that mysterious power which makes and breaks rulers. Through information, political thinkers were able to observe and base their observations then propose ways to achieve their goals of government. In his *Contract Social*, Diderot wrote:

> One over the greatest disasters that could befall a free nation would be two or three consecutive reigns of a just and enlightened despot. [Such despots, were they the best of men would] would habituate the nation to blind obedience; in their reigns the people would forget their inalienable rights; they would fall into a fit of trust and apathy; they would no longer experience that continual uneasiness that is the necessary guardian of liberty. [Such despots where like good shepherds who reduce their subjects to animals; they would] secure them a happiness of ten years for which they would pay with twenty centuries of misery.
> TOURNEUX 1899: 144

One may ask what makes servility misery if the life provided by a despot is comfortable. For the researcher, it is a matter of perspective, and certainly of values. If civic involvement for the public good is a value that society agrees to promote, then civic disobedience has equal merit because it acts as a corrector for individual and institutional excesses in the discharge of public functions. This discussion thus requires mass education and a mass media to spread these ideas, in order to create a public opinion that power creates leaders and dismantles their career as well.

In 2008, John Pavlik defined public media to include all media that produce, deliver, and package content and communications for the public rather than private consumption (2008). But without adding more, that definition is misleading. Because of digital media, "the systems of public communication, the systems of content production and distribution, and the computer and network-based technologies that support and shape them" (id.: 8). Mass media today include all traditional media of mass communication containing newspapers, radio, television. In addition, it also involves the online accessed media which, although, originally limited to private networks, extended beyond the interpersonal. Finally, it made it into the public arena to become part of the mediated public communication. More than Facebook, this is the case of another politicized platform, Twitter.

The Enlightenment, also known as the Age of Reason, witnessed the development of highly rationalist theories that approached knowledge as a purely mental representation of the world. While highly reasoned knowledge was produced by a few privileged individuals versed in the arts and sciences, rich folk traditions within the masses continued and at times overlapped.

Today, we can talk about human knowledge as an empirical abstract that embodies physical experience. We have come to understand that knowledge is not the mere sum of empirical observations and rational thought. Rather, knowledge is integrated. Right now, the simplest task of integrated learning can start with reading a map on a smartphone for instance.

> The user needs directions or location information [and] this interaction can also support user social and entertainment activities texting the social media communication such as tweeting status updates are our applications which enhance users' understanding of their environment but also cause them to reflect on the complex mediation network of sensors, transmitters, analytical tools and displays involved in their experience. Thus, engagement in the digital part of this experience increases and the result is a generation of a true hybrid physical digital knowledge.
> LEHRER, RIKAKIS, KELLIHER 2013: 48

The example above described is mostly utilitarian. But, technologies have created multifunctional platforms. For instance, technology first allowed users to choose content, such as choosing Netflix movies, or selecting music from the Pandora station, or even organizing pictures in iPhoto. Through a variety of digital delivery components, users started to customize their entertainment consumption.

Next, technology enabled users to create and publish content. Flickr and YouTube, for instance, incentivized casual creativity, utility, and content sharing. It made it easier to grow the supply of user-generated content. These opportunities to create and publicize content have changed the generated and collective knowledge within the digital community. In the process, it has also blurred the private/public distinction. Through this knowledge, users felt emboldened to enrich social media and to contribute to the growth of social media platforms. As such, beyond being a way to share interest stories, events and photos, Facebook was primarily a mechanism for constructing and experiencing a digital community. In this process, participants became significantly involved with computational facets, including issues of complex computer networks, recommendation mechanisms, and conductivity.

Finding the platforms so satisfying, users spend an inordinate amount of time involved with them. As such, they necessarily limit their exposure to news and civic information mediated through online social networks (Bakshy et al. 2015).

But even if ideology is easily discernible from Facebook data analysis, one still needs to do the work and look for signs even if the platform aggregates the likes of particular political personalities or political postings. Though, I contend that the trend is to make that ideological identifier even easier to spot than by finding likes of particular pages results in transforming the Facebook user into a "fan" of that page. Fandom translates with access to "the content published on that page in their news feed" (Bond et al. 2015: 65). Of course, Facebook employees know their users' ideology, based on the pages that users "like," or endorse (id.). Facebook users need to cursorily investigate the page of a particular user and see who they choose to endorse in their own profile, and reliably estimate the user's ideology.

Snapchat, Instagram and Twitter offer a sneak preview into anybody's politics of experience. Social media has broken the private/public barrier by making it easier to be surveilled and trolled. Also, by making it easier to gauge meaning-making. The impact of the visual signals on what makes us public subjects in the Althusserian mold of interpellation, has been unprecedented lately, adding yet another layer of ironic meaning.

For instance, the U.S. 2016 presidential elections are a case in point when it comes to the role ideological visualization has played. How much could we blame the Democrats' loss on Hillary's old woman face as opposed to Donald's old man's appearance? How much does the Democrats' loss owe to Trump's minimalist, aggressive, and vindictive tweets, reminiscent of verbal barks?

Twitter has introduced a visual approach to communication tantamount to using words as emoticons. In fact, the backlash created by the increase of characters allowed in a tweet for appearance reasons further supports my idea that today's McLuhan's medium is the message has become the visual is the message. Furthermore, the more minimal is the visual appearance of the message, the more masculine and conservative, ergo, the more authoritative, and easier its acceptance. But such role-playing with unclear rules is tantamount to accepting an ideological label which may be more prescriptive than descriptive, and thus misleading.

Under these circumstances, resisting the mold social media impose on us is to resist a pre-determined way of alienation. Such a stance requires reimagining our frame of reference.

Within this hybrid, and ever-evolving space, binary may not be sufficient to explain reality, but perhaps integrating their value might be a better approach than discarding them. The binary powerful/oppressed might easily identify Marxian imaginary while, the qualifier "oppressed minorities" is a liberal identifier. Now, that we know their origins, let's use them as building bloks of more relevant knowledge, within today's contingency.

It is beyond debate that our individuality is a function of our society. Strong societies often built strong individuals while weak societies rarely do so. As Max Eastman correctly noted, Karl Marx's work is built on the binary individual/society, where individuals can actuate their potential only within the larger society. That is why both feminism and identity politics, as liberal theories positioning specific groups – gendered or racially identified – against the larger society, seem unable to inculcate larger societal alliances. To the extent that all narratives are propelled by circumstances, they are also limited by the very contingency which made them possible. For instance, identity politics first appeared as an American middle-class intellectual phenomenon, different or even opposed to the Black Freedom Movements of the 1960s, whose terminology never used "identity politics." As recounted by (Angela) Davis, Shakur, and Brown, their narrative about the Movement is a narrative about the interplay between gender and racial dynamics in a "resistance struggle," viewed as part and parcel of a larger struggle for individual and group self-determination within the dominant liberal culture (Perkins 2011). Their Movement was not a desire to emulate the surrounding white liberalism. Their Movement was not intent on placing representatives at the liberal negotiating table where few are victorious and the toiling masses are ignored. From this perspective, today's identity politics appear to be a white middle-class movement.

Maybe, white America, having reached a level of economic comfort as a majority, felt unthreatened, and it could sympathetically imagine the lives of minorities. Also, in 1970, that empathy was mostly highfaluting and probably self-aggrandizing. At the time, only one in four white children lived in neighborhoods with a 10% poverty rate, making poverty and minorities both foreign and manageable (Williams 2017: 3). Somehow, poverty transformed within whites' imagination as being non-white. It was a minority problem of black or brown.

While that transformation was taking over the middle-class imaginary, something else was taking place: the white working class was becoming invisible. As Joan C. Williams explained, during the following decades, impoverishment continued. By 2000, one in four white children lived in neighborhoods with a 40% poverty rate (id.: 5). During this time, between 1993 and 2013, the death rate of the white working class, men and women, aged 45–54 "increased substantially" (id.). As such, poverty was reconfigured as a minority stereotype, a segregated phenomenon, and became addressed only in terms of identity politics. It suited white elites to contain the poor and disadvantaged in groups identified by color, gender, or age. Also, it allowed white elites to maintain their liberal position in the face of social disintegration. Consequently, poor whites became the invisible, generic, face. Following suit, those in the academe and political class who were products of liberal (Ivy League) education, ignored the white working class and attacked all their union-driven benefits.

This trend continued unchecked until we reached a point where the three wealthiest Americans own more wealth than that the bottom half of U.S. residents. Now, income and wealth inequality are worse than at any time since the 1920s. Inasmuch, the privileged/oppressed dichotomy is making an academic comeback. Thus, there is a new connectedness, using Cornel West's vocabulary, or better yet, a lack of it. Also, there is value in adopting a Marxian interdisciplinary, dialectical position, asking for what Yvon Quiniou called a Marxian culture, "une culture marxienne" (Quiniou 2013: 151). It is an alternative to the currently morally bankrupt, liberal subjectivity.

The current dichotomy is reminiscent of the nineteenth-century dichotomy between urban capitalists and their urban counterpart – the proletariat. At that time, Karl Marx offered the most relevant social theory. That was the result of many factors, including his dialectical understanding of how society works. Today, a dialectical interdisciplinary approach to data would show that there are no exploited masses in the United States that reorganized by the industry they occupied. It is fairer to talk about crushed communities. They are marginalized, exploited communities; some are forced to go underground for fear of deportation; some are forced to go underground for fear of incarceration.

Having been ignored for so long, the academe, in its self-imposed liberal impotence, has minced the oppressed in various liberal-minded minority groups. However, no such group has been empowered outside the few lucky individuals promoted as "success stories." In this vacuum of hegemonic (liberal) legitimacy, why not build a narrative which does not favor any specific oppressed group? Why not try to incorporate a political subjectivity which aims for "social equality, not for some groups, but for all groups?" (Williams 2017: 5).

∴

Ideology has been around for a while, clearly as long as scholarship produced theory for public communication. Ideology is something that both S_1 and S_2 possess and express in theory production and meaning-making negotiation where they address the power structure. Jurisprudence, perhaps even more so, is ideological because it plays a very subtle role engaging in criticism and status quo approval. But even within a monolithically liberal ideology, which I argue is nefarious for a creative, relevant, and especially engaged academia, there is a difference of views, and that is where irony comes into play.

4 Ideological Meaning-Making

From a meaning-making perspective, ideology matters because it represents the scholars' perception of their cultural and political position within the surrounding power structure. From this perspective, there should be little discussion on whether ideology affects scholarly production, and more on how, or to what extent. First, the text-instigator, S_1, is a public person and as such is exposed to the prevalent ideology. Second, T_1 is meant for public consumption and not for some private drawer. Finally, the scholarly meaning-making process takes place in public, where power is visible: S_1 publicly communicates T_1, which then interpellates S_2 at public conferences, or other public presentations, from the classroom, during coffee breaks, to institutional hallways.

Ideology colors meaning and adds input, which is rarely axiological. Ideology has meaning-making value not due to its potential impact on theoretical veracity, but because it represents bias. Ideology is inherent to knowledge production. Acknowledging it should be something scholars do automatically, so their theoretical relevance has a greater chance to persist through subsequent theoretical development.

All explanations about how ideology affects meaning depend on the scholar's own ideology and understanding of the concept. My view of ideology does not contradict Althusser's supra-historical cultural definition, and neither Clifford Geertz's cultural system (Geertz 1973). Ideology is a symbolic individual system of translating power, which denotes both the subjects' S_1, S_2, etc., knowledge and awareness of power, as well as their situation within that system.

Ideology has come to incorporates individuals' beliefs about their position within the public sphere, whether it is the job market, civil society or the government. As described by Georg Lukács' *History and Class Consciousness: Studies in Marxist Dialectics* (1923), and subsequently explained by Cornel West's *The Ethical Dimensions of Marxist Thought* (1991), ideology makes transparent human interaction, West's "connectedness," within the public sphere.

Ideological meaning making rests on my view of ideology as the scholar's awareness of their position within the public sphere. The public sphere is conceived as broadly as possible, whether it is the Habermasian public space shaping participatory democracy, or our Twitter and Instagram cyberspace where most of our public exchanges take place now (Fernback 2002: 36).

While limited to the human realm, ideology is a recent addition to scholarship. Its birth is related to intellectuals engaging in public life activities, in what Peter Gay (1969) called "the politics of experience," when scholars objectify their public persona (448) for cognitive reasons. The representation of their public lives occurs during the process of alienation from whatever they experience, and representing their experience, scholars incorporate their ideology.

Ideology does not affect private intellectual pursuits in any specificity, whether they are science or philosophy. Ideology is different from that mysterious power, *public opinion,* which, according to John Lukacs, makes and breaks rulers, as well as morals, and truths, though it informs it, or more recently it misinforms it (1968). Conceptually, ideology is representational, a concept about perception, about a set of beliefs about power and how the individual fits within the momentary power web.

Let's think about story telling. Both historians and novelists engage in storytelling, as a way to objectify experience. But, if facts separate historians from novelists, then ideology unites them both. How facts are perceived and then represented is a matter of the author's ideology, or more precisely of the text-instigator's ideology. Ideology affects all public representational intellectual pursuits, and especially those which are linguistically formulated in a theory.

Those representations are connected to the beginning of the "open" society, where court thinkers metamorphosed their work from the king's private entertainment to legitimizing the government in the eyes of the masses. That change of purpose, borrowing Gay's words (id.), represented a political will, which some described as "obstructing" pure thinking. But no writing was ever "pure." It was always the product of economic patronage, only during the Age of Enlightenment, thinkers (Gay's philosophies) added a representational layer of purpose to their writing. Their work incorporated a set of ideas, the ideological "add-on" element of meaning, which differentiated between representations of the world for the benefit of the king's chamber and those for the benefit of the king's survival in that chamber: the latter were meant for public consumption.

> [During Enlightenment], perception was obstructed by sheer novelty; the kind of politics the philosophes' thought implied, in fact demanded, was only in its rudimentary stage in the eighteenth century. The men of

the Enlightenment sensed that they could realize their social ideals only by political means, and, with their verbal facility, with their partisan pamphlets, tendentious histories, and semi-public letters, they set the stage from the kind of politics they needed. As professional men of the word, the philosophes did more than feed political discussion; in some countries they did nothing else than to bring it into being. (Id.: 448–449)

Gay's philosophes thus experienced public life, objectified it, and represented it in order to achieve their newly found goal of public importance, which formed the beginning of a class consciousness of sorts for public thinkers or establishment intellectuals. Their writing would have great importance in legitimizing a particular set of ideas, as well as in legitimizing their ideology as the acceptable frame of thinking.

The Enlightenment Age produced a public consciousness among theorists. Philosophes encompassed ideology when they reflected on government. Legal theorists engaged in ideological theoretical pursuits as well. In our country, the Enlightenment produced a very successful political uprising, the American Revolution, which, in turn, ended with the creation of the American Republic. During those years, Alexander Hamilton, together with James Madison and John Jay, engaged in political writings for a particular goal: making the republican revolution palatable to the masses. That required making the republican ideology familiar and non-threatening.

As a strategy, they incorporated a lot of British and French writings. For instance, they looked at Thomas Hobbs and John Locke's writings and saw them as appeasing the monarchal fears of the masses in the aftermath of the bloody revolution lead by Oliver Cromwell. From this perspective, both the Hobbesian and Lockean natural law explanation of the British public order, the original "social compact," becomes a political, and thus a highly ideological choice.

They are not alone in their choice of natural law for political reasons. Starting with the 17th century, natural law became secularized in an attempt to both correct the imperfect positive or civil laws and add authority to them. Even when those thinkers referred to God as the author of natural law, and as its source of authority, as Peter Gay reminded us citing Diderot's Dec. 6, 1768, Correspondence, "they all derived its origin and binding quality from the nature of man, [from] the infallible general will of men" (Gay 1969: 457). But this ideology proved limited in its usefulness, perhaps because Montesquieu was wrong when he said: "though we might be freed from the yoke of religion, we should never be free from the yoke of equity [and justice]" (Montesquieu 1758: 169–170). Soon afterward, the accepted ideology became less lofty with ideals and more functional. The grounds for legitimizing the public order stopped being fatalistic, of the Lockean type of "this is the humanly best order available." The justification for any public order became the security of life of the newly propertied bourgeoisie, whose numbers proved to be relatively fast increasing and far exceeded the landed class. So, when in 1776, Jeremy Bentham wrote in *Fragment on Government* that the measure of right and wrong for any government was its ability to provide the greatest happiness for the greatest number, he meant it in a relative way, as determined by the existing historical circumstances. More directly, he regarded his views to be royalist in London and republican in Paris (Gay 1969: 461).

Some areas of scholarship are more ideological than others. Political theory or "the science of politics," as Alexander Hamilton wrote in 1787, in *The Federalist*, No. 9, is such an ideological endeavor. Its ideology was on display from the beginning, under what Gay (1969) called "differences of opinion," due to the thinkers' different "political experience at home and abroad," and their "idiosyncratic manner of interpreting their [political] experience" (448). Ideology was a novel representational ingredient because the element of public consciousness, of purpose and will, first appeared during the Enlightenment years. If philosophers had always dealt with the big questions of life only in the Age of Enlightenment they added a sense of purpose into their theories. Then, technology opened-up the decision-making process to outsiders, allowing the formulation of public opinion, and thus loosening up the authorship control to outsiders' interpretation. Using Althusserian vocabulary authors become text-instigators, and their audiences, text-interpellators.

Liberalism, the ideology of a mobile, relatively open society, built outside clerical and aristocratic domination, influenced our Founding Fathers to the extent they were both students of the Enlightenment, and in contact with the American institutions of their time – all of British import. In their writing, liberalism evolved. Alexander Hamilton, for instance, in *The Federalist Paper No. 1*, imparted his reflections on liberally oriented, public debate:

> It seems to have been reserved to the people of this country [...] to decide the important question whether societies of men are really capable or not, of establishing good government from reflection and choice, or whether they are forever destined to depend, for their political constitutions, on accident and force.
> HAMILTON 1787: 21

Hamilton's "choice" reflects his liberal ideology, whose elements are further developed in the other *Federalist Papers*. But, what it is of import is that this ideology is legitimized and seemingly indestructible. While it preached the good of all men, it only delivered that for a particularly propertied, gendered, age limited, racial minority. It did that by focusing the attention away from the identifiers of the controlling minority: property, gender, age, and race, to the vices and virtues of all men. Government became essential because vices overbalance virtues. "If men were angels, no government would be necessary," (Gay 1969: 565), Madison apparently explained the need for a republican government to protect private rights and public happiness.

The words were so appealing, that the ideology behind them remained inscribed in the fabric of the American mind. However, when those words are interpellated with a different ideology, their meaning becomes ironic. Whether those words were ever meant to deliver more than what the British monarchy had done in England, we will never know. However, ironically, their meaning has changed in time.

CHAPTER 6

The Irony of Scholarship Production

The previous chapters map out the first two elements of scholarly meaning: reasoned narrative and ideology within general meaning-making geography as it pertains to Marxian work. Marx (S_1) employed dialectics to understand and explain social reality in its flux. Taking into consideration the history, and evolution of knowledge, his theory explored myriads of interconnected components. His work, the product of his own objectification and alienation, sublimated his observations and emotions as well as his cultural baggage and view of the world. Published, it became T_1. Ironically, it fit within the existing and subsequent Knowledge Paradigm (K), probably because his objectified subjectivity never alienated all scholars (S_2). Scholastic irony, deeply ideological, is the third element of our geography of meaning-making which actuates meaning and shapes understating. Its scholarly neglect may be due to the fact that irony does comes with no cartography.

T_1 interpellates scholars (S_2) in various, unexpected, encoded ways. All the while, S_1's ideology shapes T_1's interpellating value through what is contained in the text and what is omitted. During communication, which starts the meaning-making negotiation, irony as meaning is the result of theory production as much as the result of textual interpellation.

Buñuel's 1972 movie is a tale about the perils of ignoring one's given circumstances: the *haute bourgeoisie* ought not to mingle with the thugs. Buñuel's *Discreet Charm* dispatches irony. Buñuel's movie appears to focus on an upper-class sextet whose lives revolve around lunches and dinners. While they are supposed to be scheduled irrespective of their surrounding circumstances, as if they could happen by the power of habit, they prove to be badly timed and impossible to happen. The reasons their false attempts to feast keep failing are a vaudevillian mixture of events both supposedly actual and imagined (the death of a restaurateur or a drug deal gone awry), but which nevertheless could have been managed.

The story is about an ostentatious bourgeoisie, the opposite of its nineteenth-century embodiment during the time of Marx, when the bourgeoisie was the new class of haves – brash, uncultured, and uneducated: all welcomed attributes of the youth if the youth is inclined to improve. But in the twentieth century, the time of Buñuel's classic, the bourgeoisie was expected to have aristocratic charm, which the movie proves as lacking.

That is why, in addition to being ironic, Buñuel's title is also mordantly sardonic. It mocks and criticizes what by then has become yet another parasitic social class akin to aristocracy. The fears of missing opportunities makes the haute bourgeoisie, a pillar of twentieth-century capitalist society, act thuggishly, one might say, true to its roots.

Similarly, scholarship could take into consideration the surrounding reality in a systemic or incremental way, while accepting limited impact: immediately or at a later date. But, instead, it goes unmanaged, as the plans in Buñuel's movie do. Relying on what was relevant at a given moment in specific conditions makes one vulnerable to missing the moment of transition into irrelevance. Reality produces knowledge and knowledge can be applied to understand, manage, or even change, reality. Scholarship is rarely a match for reality, which develops and changes incessantly; its parts interconnect, and it demands too much skill, knowledge, and determination to keep up with its pace. Furthermore, a human product of reflection and reproduction, it reflects human subjectivity embedded in the text and expressed in meaning-making, whose outcome is both ideologic and ironic.

1 Encoded Irony in T_1

Earlier, I described meaning-making as dependent on public subjectivity, recognizing how partial and blinkered we all are and how little scholars (S_1) control their published ideas (T_1) and their subsequent knowledge value. By way of explanation, I used Marx, the author with a high degree of mastery and ambition, a comprehensive theorist whose biggest theoretical mistake was not to acknowledge ideology as a scholastic bias. That very omission contains the seeds of (Marx's) any T_1's ideological irony. Those dormant seeds will germinate into meaning when T_1 interpellates S_2, and S_2 interacts with S_1's textually embedded ideology.

S_1's reign is limited to the process of textual production, when S_1, as text-instigator dictates the guiding terms for the subsequent process of textual interpellation. When S_1 acknowledges her subjective biases, then S_2, trusting S_1's intentions and impressed with S_1's intellectual rigor, will most likely accept S_1's guidance to T_1's interpellation. Thus, S_1 eliminates unintentional ideological irony, and will exercise more control over T_1's meaning-making process.

Irony is an ambiguous concept. It has many meanings (Lear 2011). Whereas, American jurisprudence mostly uses it in its etymological meaning of *eirōneia*, "simulated ignorance," others use it in its Rortyan encapsulation of specificity that is a particular type of intellectual enterprise standing in opposition to philosophy. While there is irony as a lifestyle and irony as criticism, no one has considered ideological irony embedded in the scholastic meaning-making process.

From this point of view, irony has nothing to do with falsehood or morality. Subjective like ideology, irony exists to various degrees in all meaning-making processes. All textual instigations contain a residue of implicit statements, caused by voluntary or involuntary omissions, whose meaning is subsequently activated by text-interpellators. In legal terms, irony is the reason that the United States Supreme Court engages in statutory interpretation to explain statutory meaning, and subsequently, lower courts strive to find new reasons to divagate from that constitutional significance.

Irony is the unforeseen element of meaning-making which is embedded in any conceptual scholarship relying on language, rather than mathematical symbols. It is actuated when text-interpellators engage the text of scholarship. Thereby, its prevalence has increased with the diminishing role of authorship, and the increased role of audiences as text-interpellators.

Irony can be blamed for this imbalance.

The irony of scholarship, the meaning outside the letter of the text, has been noticed by scholars though from a different angle. At times, it has been identified in terms of the confluence between a Master and an Agent discourse (Zwart 2017). Others identified it as the dynamic imposed by the Aristotelian way of addressing the contingency of human life, itself variable. Discussing the dichotomy between contingency and necessity, Kolakowski reminds one of Stuart Hall's theory of meaning:

> [T]he expression "contingent" is only meaningful in opposition to the expression "necessary." Hume's position is that the world is what it is, and the antithesis between contingency and necessity has no basis in experience. The universe, for Hume, is contingent in exactly the same sense as it is for Sartre: it is not founded on any "reason" and does not authorize us to seek for any.
> KOLAKOWSKI 1978: 42–44

Textually, irony is embedded in meaning through what Edward Said (1975) called the "intentional production of meaning" (5). S_2's ideology actuates T_1's dormant irony. Like with ideology, erroneously, scholars may see the role irony *adulterating* T_1's meaning. That is because irony is seen as happenstance. To the contrary, irony is perceived here as "encoded" meaning actuated by S_2's public subjectivity (ideology). Following the communication of T_1 and during the meaning-making negotiation between S_1 and S_2, ideology activates T_1's encoded irony in light of the body of social, political, and legal scholarship at the specific historical moment of textual interpretation.

Irrespective its breath, no scholarship can neutralize the irony within. When communicated, T_1 might be read to mean the opposite. For instance, young Marx (1837) showed early on, an inclination for metaphors, as the excerpt from his short humoristic novel *Scorpion and Felix* indicates:

> Every giant ... presupposes a dwarf, every genius a hidebound philistine, and every storm at sea – mud, and as soon as the first disappear the latter begin, sit down at the table, sprawling out their long legs arrogantly. (https://www.marxists.org/archive/marx/works/1837-pre/verse/verse41.htm)

Through those metaphors, Marx presents himself as a work in process. He employs both temporal (subsequent) and spatial (interwoven) contextualism. For Marx, every storm at sea presupposes other, qualitatively different elements: as soon as the storm disappears, the mud appears "sprawling out their long legs arrogantly." What becomes apparent is what defines Marxian work: his attention to the large structure as well as to detail.

Read alone, the paragraph above has one meaning. However, read in the context of Marx's entire body, it reads like a precursor to his dialectical research method. During the larger context of meaning-making, its embedded dormant irony awakens according to the cultural baggage of the scholar engaging the text.

Generally speaking, the Marxian body of work remains a useful tool because its reading changed so much in time. For instance, Marx discarded the impact of the private sphere production from the capitalist production, when in fact it has always been an integral part. Even in the nineteenth century, the workforce relied on the work of unpaid family members for unwavering material and spiritual comfort. That omission has been read as a voluntary reductionist approach to the Marxian social criticism. I believe it is the result of Marx's own creative process, the social and individual alienation experienced, and the cultural history of the moment when he produced his work. The irony is that Marx can be presented both as a misogynist and a dated historian or just engaged in structurally limited social critique. The encoded irony is in the text for the ages. Nonetheless, each reading will activate one particular irony.

Examples about embedded irony abound if we care to look for them. For instance, Walter Benjamin wrote that "irony is the condition of possibility for history." Coupled with ideology, irony actuates meaning, elevating it from the realm of possibility.

> In short [...] irony is the condition of possibility for history. That is what Walter Benjamin has taught us by reading the concept of irony in German romanticism and then extending that reading in all directions through his study of allegory in both the baroque Trauerspiel and Baudelaire's poetry.
>
> NEWMARK 2012: 11

Irony is always present in the text, but it does not need to be willfully encoded, as Barbe (1995) suggests. Whether specific signals are present in each occurrence of irony or not, irony is actuated in the process of T_1 communication and the subsequent meaning-making progression. Sometimes S_1 is in the habit of signaling such occurrences, as Marx was.

Marx used food terminology to define social-economic and legal terms – such as *Gallerte* (gelatin) – to explain work as an element of profit, wages, and capital. *Gallerte* is embedded irony. When he talks about work as *Gallerte*, Marx directs our gaze from abstract to visual concepts. In the process, he guides our meaning-making with a specific viewpoint about the social value of work. *Gallerte* indicates subsistence for the lower classes and repulsive frowning by the upper social echelons.

> Abstrakt menschliche Arbeit [is a] bloße *Gallerte* unterschiedsloser menschlicher Arbeit.
>
> Human labor in the abstract [is a] mere *congelation* of human labor.
>
> SUTHERLAND 2011: 39; emphasis added

However, Marx's encoded irony challenges any subsequent scholar to understand it. Not only does *Gallerte* require the scholar's awareness of German cuisine, but it also demands S_2's artistic sensibility to see how a visual clue would work better than any abstract concept to convey the Marxian meaning of labor. Finally, S_2 would benefit from a thorough familiarity with Marx's rejection of abstractions, generally. The latter point is magisterially made by Bhikhu C. Parekh (1982) when he explains why Marx rejected any discussion of "property as such." As Parekh explains, such an "empty phrase" would have been an illogical choice for Marx, because of its lack of socio-economic specificity. "Property as such" cannot be an object of Marxian investigation.

From this perspective, it appears that Marx had to choose *Gallerte* as a conceptual reference for labor. A meat-based gelatin, which could be eaten as an appetizer similar to jellied pork legs, *Gallerte* is best situated to express the transformation of labor. In English, perhaps *spam* (*Special Processed American Meat*) would have been an adequate food-related term to reflect what all commodities contain: "the same sort of labor, human labor in the abstract" (Marx 1887: 5).

As scholars have pointed out, the English translation of the German vocabulary, *Gallerte*, lost its precise sensorial meaning for the benefit of a sanitized translation, politely replete with vagaries (Sutherland 2011). By way of warning, many of the philosophical roots of American jurisprudence, which come from foreign minds, have often become *Gallerte,* lost in translations. Another reason for Marx and his American counterparts (scholars) to read different meanings in their common intellectual roots might also be the underlying Regime of Truth, and which often acts as a colander or sifter of all scholarship (T_1) (Figure 1).

Philosophy, as a discipline, has particularly impacted American jurisprudence, perhaps as much as to support Derrida's belief that jurists are the twenty-first century philosophers. But, the survey of philosophical ideas presented here has an additional role. It will promote my argument that meaning-making is a negotiation between S_1 and S_2 having T_1 as a starting point. When S_1 and S_2 have different ideologies – where ideology is that ideatic component, which transubstantiates private individuals into public subjects – the same philosophical political thought might give rise to different meanings.

Irony can be encoded in many ways, including visually. For instance, Hobbes' *Leviathan* (1651), focuses on the role of the government to enforce an original compact or social contract. Hobbes' contract reflected "the mutual transferring of rights," between the masses of people and a ruler.

The textual meaning of Hobbes' *Leviathan* derives from the literal exposition of his reasoning, and his particular type of monarchic ideology. His text is encoded with both the literal and the meaningfully omitted. In the subsequent process of decoding, or interpellating his text, readers arrive at Hobbes' governing solution. He favors the social contract on the premise that survival is only possible in exchange for total submission to the authority of an absolute – undivided and unlimited – sovereign power. Scholars have pointed out that, although religious, Hobbes situates the suzerain above God to the extent that without the suzerain there is no order, hence, without order there is no space to worship God.

> [I]n Leviathan chapters 14 and 15 Hobbes engages in natural law discourse. There he suggests that natural laws as such have no obligatory force. Obligation can derive only from the word of God, but the word of God requires sovereign authorization, as we know from book two of Leviathan. Therefore, natural law, like the word of God, obliges only by the power of the magistrate [suzerain].
> SPRINGBORG 2008: 682

FIGURE 5   Hobbes' *Leviathan*
SOURCE: *LEVIATHAN*, ENGRAVED TITLE PAGE (LONDON, 1651)

However, the engraved title page of the 1651 edition of Hobbes' *Leviathan* tells a different story, as Figure 5 shows.

> There is broad agreement that the print underscores Hobbes's conception of a dominant and radical sovereignty encompassing civil and ecclesiastical jurisdictions. Much attention has been devoted to the significance of the composite figure: the looming 'Leviathan' is made up of all sorts of figures – gentlemen, women, priests in a skull cap and Geneva bands, workmen and soldiers.
> CHAMPION 2010: 259

Additionally, that title page is ironic. The visual elements of the title-page to *Leviathan* present more than the book's gist about the consensual origins of a unitary civil sovereignty: church and state. The two sets of panels – left and right on the lower half – tell a more complex, different, even an opposite story.

> Here the elements of civil and ecclesiastical power and authority are contrasted in facing columns which echo the sword and the crosier wielded in the sovereign's left and right hands. Representing civil and religious institutions (and functions) the 'Castle' is ranged against, and contrasted with, the 'Church.' (Id.)

There is nothing consensual in the origins of the civil sovereignty: it is just submission. This visual irony adulterates the meaning of Hobbes' *Leviathan* (T_1) and its understanding. It can also be viewed as the basis of future writings (T_2), such as Locke's *Second Treatise of Government*.

Perhaps in response to Hobbes' paradoxes, Locke writes in his letters that all the freedom he can wish is to "enjoy the protection of those laws which the prudence and providence or our ancestors established, and the happy return of his Majesty has restored" (King 1864: 8). Nevertheless, Locke (1884) resists in his *Second Treatise of Government*, the arbitrary power of an absolute sovereign. Still, the only way to make sense of their work is to put the works of the two authors in context and be open to their ironic meaning, the meaning beyond their face value.

2 Dormant Irony as T_1's Textual Omissions

The irony residing in both Locke and Hobbes' work is apparent. It is also visible from what is not encoded, from its textual omissions. Engaging their work, subsequent text-interpellators fill in the space of those omissions, an actuating meaning. As Richard Rorty (2009) pointed out about Locke and all seventeenth-century writers, (and by extension Hobbes), they

> did not think of knowledge as justified true belief. This was because they did not think of knowledge as a relation between a person and a proposition, [but rather as a relation between persons and objects].
> RORTY 2009: 141

Rorty's observation may seem obscure especially if we start with a modern view of social studies in the Weberian vein, which suppose legal studies as studies of particular social structures allowing social solidarity to exist (Cotterrell 2006). Knowledge becomes propositional, according to various sets of beliefs: private and public (or ideological).

Rorty further muddies the waters of knowledge with multiple layers of subjectivity when he introduces the larger epistemological problem of true belief and knowledge. I view irony by omission coming out of these murky waters.

Irony by omission colors Marx's work. He does that when in his theoretical treatment of property through history. When Marx talks about bourgeois property, for instance, he uses metaphors, a figure of speech that makes an implicit, implied, or hidden comparison.

> Modern bourgeois society with its relations of production, of exchange and of property, a society that has conjured up such gigantic means of production and of exchange, is like the sorcerer who is no longer able to control the powers of the nether world whom he has called up by his spells.
> MARX 2001: 15–16

Are we supposed to read something ironic? What? Marx reverts to specificity when in the *Communist Manifesto* he discusses progress and using the regime of property, especially property over the means of production, as a tool to mark it. For capitalism to make inroads, for instance, property had to change from feudal (immovable) property into a different (movable) type of property. Is progress unclear?

> For many a decade past the history of industry and commerce is but the history of the revolt of modern productive forces against modern conditions of production, against the property relations that are the conditions for the existence of the bourgeoisie and of its rule. [...] The productive forces at the disposal of society no longer tend to further the development of the conditions of bourgeois property; on the contrary, they have

become too powerful for these conditions, by which they are fettered, and no sooner do they overcome these fetters than they bring disorder with the whole of bourgeois society, endanger the existence of bourgeois property.
MARX and ENGELS 2012: 79

Again, I raise the same questions: Are we supposed to read something ironic in his ideas of progress? What? Marx's historical progress is different than Plato's. In Plato's *Republic*, for instance, the highest social honor was becoming a property-less city leader, who was a guardian. In capitalism, to the contrary, the highest social honor does not need to be the highest form of social order. Plato's guardianship position came with a unique prerequisite, incomprehensible in our liberal democracy: the guardian was expected "to give up all other [private] crafts and very precisely be craftsmen of the city's freedom and practice." This political suggestion is interesting in light of the fact that Plato himself was a scion of a wealthy family. Most likely the pupil of an often-unpaid philosophy teacher, Socrates, Plato had noticed the nefarious effect of unbridled private wealth. As such, Plato must have reached the conclusion that wealth rather than poverty was destructive of the very fabric of his utopian republic. Plato's subjective distrust of private wealth in public office became an ethical choice.

But, is Marx's view of bourgeois property the result of a justified belief, or some accurate objective piece of knowledge? Is it dependent on "the productive forces at the disposal of society," or is it more resilient? If we look at Marx's work on property from a Rortian position, then its value is based on his statements about property, whether they are synthesized from existing scholarship on property or whether he authors them. However, they are not without irony – a component of all forms of scholarship interpreting social relations. In Marx's work, irony exists irrespective of his (text-instigator, S_1) intentions to incorporate it textually through literary tools, such as metaphors, or explicit omissions of certain topics (e.g., the type of property the most of us enjoy). Even when dormant in T_1, irony magnifies knowledge to areas S_1 might not have even imagined, when the text interpellates S_2 et al and through the meaning-making process expands that body scholarship, according to how T_1 is understood and further open for subsequent communication.

3 Textual Irony and Rorty's Intellectual Ironist

Richard Rorty philosophized about irony (lesser level intellectual enterprise), ironically, using the "final" vocabulary of philosophes, whom he derided.

I doubt that Rorty saw the irony of his serious work on irony, but he "encoded" it like any S_1 would do with their T_1.

Rorty focused on irony in relation to philosophy, itself viewed, not as the reasoned narrative included in the body of all scholarship, but as a specific type of scholarly production. Like philosophy, Rorty's irony, too, is a type of scholarship. Ironically, Michael Williams (1989) noted in the Introduction to the thirtieth anniversary edition, of Rorty's *Contingency, Irony, and Solidarity*, Rorty rebelled against the very idea of "a professionalized discipline with a distinctive subject matter" (xv). Philosophy holds in absolute regard, and almost mythical, universal truths. Rorty's irony, different, it is a professionalized discipline. Philosophers were intellectuals whose "central beliefs" (id.) refer back to "something beyond the reach of time and chance" (id.). Richard Rorty explained. To the contrary, for Rorty, ironists had no such beliefs (though they too could belong to a professionalized discipline).

Rorty's ironists do not believe "in an order beyond time and change which both determines the point of human existence and establishes a hierarchy of responsibilities" (id.). The crux of Rorty's "ironism" is that there is nothing "beyond the reach of time and chance" (id.) or outside historical contingency. However, Rorty wrote about irony as a philosopher, opening his work to my ironic reading.

When Rorty states that ironists are intellectuals, but not philosophers, he limits philosophy to Enlightenment rationalism. His ironists do not believe humans possess "anything deep" which could be transferred into the public sphere, which could be used for some progressive structural project. For him, there is no other public endeavor to imagine. As such, the most a government can achieve is John Stuart Mill's liberal project, which constituted of optimizing the balance between leaving people's private lives alone and preventing suffering (Rorty 1989: 63). Once the structure is in place, there is no need for philosophers. Then, the only utopia is a liberal ironist's utopia, the existing reality. The ironists are the only intellectuals deeply aware of their derivative position, that of "describing," not making, reality. Alas, Rorty and himself was not an ironist. He was a philosopher.

From a static position, that of his work, Rorty was able to offer a very perceptive critique of reality. Reality is not static. It changes, but not structurally, only in a managerial, technocratic way. For Rorty, only the ironists' perception of reality was susceptible to change. Ironists are "always aware of the contingency and fragility of their final vocabularies and thus of their selves" (id.: 73–74). It remains unclear whether that *is* the case, or whether Rorty hoped for it to be the case. Ironically, Rorty noticed everything an ironist could while being a philosopher.

For Rorty, irony dabbles in transient situations, and the ironist does not make the mistake of using final vocabularies, abundant in generic multisemantic concepts. The ironist is disciplined and uses specific vocabularies, limited to the present circumstances. In other words, Rorty paints his liberal ironist as being disdainful of grand theories and distrustful of revolutions; she is a light-hearted, good-humored minimalist. Moreover, Rorty's ironist will never attempt to change the world, or even tell general truths, because this ironist does not believe in final principles of universal application. The truth is temporal and local. For Rorty's ironists,

> what matters is not a consensus about what is desirable for the universal humanity, but a consensus about the desirability of any topic of discussion. (Id.: 84)

Using Foucault's vocabulary, if the universal intellectual, the philosopher, is one who views herself as "the consciousness/conscience of us all," then Rorty's ironist qualifies as a "specific" intellectual. If we continue Foucault's premise negating the very existence of the universal intellectual, then all scholars become Rorty's ironists, at least potentially. Foucault believed that all intellectuals were "specific" by virtue of being in the service of the "State or Capital" as technicians, magistrates, or teachers (Sheridan 1980). From that position, the specific intellectual contributes to truth-creation, according to the "ensemble of rules" that establish what is true (id.). Then, according to Foucault, the main issue becomes that of the battle to promote a certain type of truth for economic and political reasons.

Rorty's ironist could be added to the list of intellectuals in the service of legitimizing a system of power. The ironists understand that "anything can be made to look good or bad by being redescribed" (Rorty 1989: 73). For ironists, truth is a temporary construct which ensures social stability at a specific moment. Both would also agree that vocabulary, and the employment of vocabulary, give shape to our minds: concepts often come with assumed abstract meaning, as well as meaning given by the contingency offered by the moment at which the vocabulary is used. The refusal to enlarge it with additional words and other contingent connections is a rejection of any possibility of change. Ironically, as in a rite of passage, no specific intellectual could aspire to become a philosopher or a "public intellectual" without realizing the irony of small, finite vocabularies, so fragile and so easily replaced (Hauser 2006; Selemeneva 2007). The same is true for a legal theorist, as is further discussed below.

Ironically and unexpectedly, Rorty employs what he calls "final vocabulary" when he discusses the essence of irony. His vocabulary is deeply political, as he describes irony as deeply liberal, and filled with anti-communitarian values.

From a meaning-making point of view, it is unfortunate that I cannot expect Rorty's comments to my take on his work on irony – neither in generally nor, especially, on the irony of his work on irony. From my position as S_2, his work (T_1) is ironic because, while it preaches contingency, it reads like what Rorty derided most: philosophy. Rorty did not seem to have understood his position as a liberal philosopher of irony. He repositioned irony to fit his ideology. In the process, like Marx, he missed his one ideological bias. While applauding his irrational belief in the goodness of man (Rorty 1989: 153), Rorty's lack of self-awareness makes it hard for me to criticize or approve much of it. Like all the other examples, Rorty's work is only another instance of encoded irony by omission, whose meaning became actualized through subsequent interpellation (S_2).

CHAPTER 7

Ideological Irony – S_2's Ideology Actuating T_1's Irony

Karl Marx, like all scholars before and after, interpellated the existing Knowledge Paradigm before he engaged in theory production. Before he became a text-instigator, Marx noted ironic discrepancies in the work of many, such as Hegel, Lassalle, Ricardo, and addressed them. Conversely, Marx's work is prone to ironic meaning according to its interpellator's subjectivity. For instance, Leonard P. Wessell, Jr., (1979) interpreted Karl Marx's work as romantic mythopoeic writings. That Wessell understands Marx's vocabulary poetically, only supports my claim about the role of textual interpellation in the meaning-making process, and in the production of scholarly understanding.

As explained earlier, S_1's ideology shapes T_1's interpellating value through what is contained in the text and what is omitted. S_2 engages T_1 when T_1 is communicated. In that process, meaning-making is negotiated. The negotiation is ironic because its result is unexpected: it could be the opposite of what S_1 laid down as T_1's philosophy (reasoned narration). Ideology actuates the private individual into a public persona. S_1 produces T_1 in her privacy facing her own creative discomfort. When S_1 communicates T_1 to the scholarly community, S_1 enters the public sphere, ideologically positioning herself within the power structure. That happens whether S_1 is aware of her ideology, embraces it, ignores it, or denies it. This is how the layer of ideological irony originates, though no one can predict its thickness or how much of T_1's meaning making it will occupy.

Textual interpellation depends on scholarly communication, and as such, it can happen simultaneously with the process of communication or subsequently, upon publication. For instance, at faculty lunches or conferences, the text-instigator shares her work to those present during interpersonal communications. The co-orientation model developed by McLeod and Chaffee (1973), as well as Kessler and Pozen's (2016) vocabulary when needed, provide the framework for identifying the relationships between the text-instigator, S_1, which is behind the *birth* of T_1, and the text-interpellator, S_2. In turn, the scholarship community engages the text, T_1, which produces the *critique*, their view of T_1's meaning. I extrapolate those observations for the remote, subsequent communication process, where S_2 engages the text on their own outside any direct interaction with the S_1.

The McLeod and Chaffee theory remains as valuable now as it was in the early 1970s. The co-orientation theory functions on the assumption that communication, a type of human behavior, is a function of both "private cognitive construction of the world" and of the perception of the others' cognition.

> [A] person's behavior is not based simply upon his private cognitive construction of his world; it is also a function of his perception of the orientations held by others around him and of his orientation to them.
> MCLEOD and CHAFFEE 1973: 470

Understanding the meaning of T_1 comes as a function of communication, which is an extension of the interaction between the text-instigator's and the text-interpellator's subjectivity. The text T_1 connects the scholar and the scholarly community. Paraphrasing Marshall McLuhan's (1964) "medium is the message," T_1's meaning is the scholars' (S_1 and S_2) subjectivity. Compared to the literal text, that meaning is inherently ironic. S_1 extending her private self into the social, attaining a public self, and the scholarly community (S_2) engaging that extension when interpellating T_1. Irony interferes with the socialization of the self. At the meaning-making level, S_1 writes making particular choices from an entire field of scholarship and presents them as a text (T_1) using specific research methods according to her cultural background, education, and ideological inclinations. The text, T_1, denotes literal meaning from what is specifically explained. Additional meaning is designated from what is omitted. Unlike the literal, expressed, meaning, dormant meaning is open-ended. Each subsequent interpellator activates it according to their material and subjective contingency. That dormant meaning is fodder for irony.

Meaning could be visualized as a sphere of meaning surrounding a text of scholarship. The sphere of textual meaning of Theory 1, T_1, becomes, Figure 6.

Meaning is a variable, a function of the scholar's system of thinking, "philosophy," shaped by the method or research and ideology, as well as irony, as Figure 7 below indicates. Irony, dormant at the moment of *birth*, is a function of the finite nature of the vocabulary scholarship uses, and also of the limits of any method of research, irrespective its breath. Irony becomes alive in the process of communicating T_1, when textual interpellation happens and T_1 enters its social existence. Its understanding, and ascent into the Knowledge Paradigm, if any, has thus begun.

In the same way S_1's ideology positions the scholar's writing within the political spectrum, irony layers the meaning of those ideological choices. Each ideological meaning is compounded by irony. What the academy identifies as Marxism is only a body of scholarship whose authors' subjectivity is not liberal.

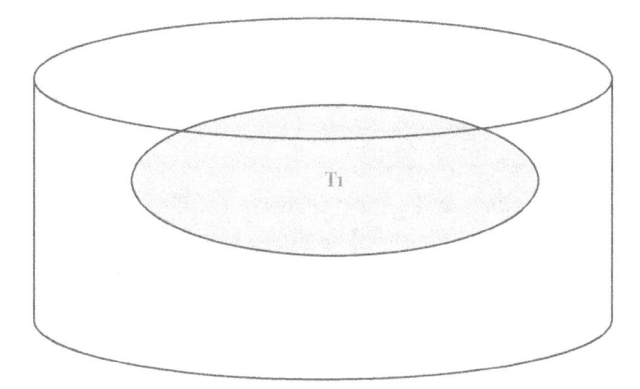

FIGURE 6 T_1's meaning $f_{[T_1]}$
SOURCE: CREATED BY AUTHOR

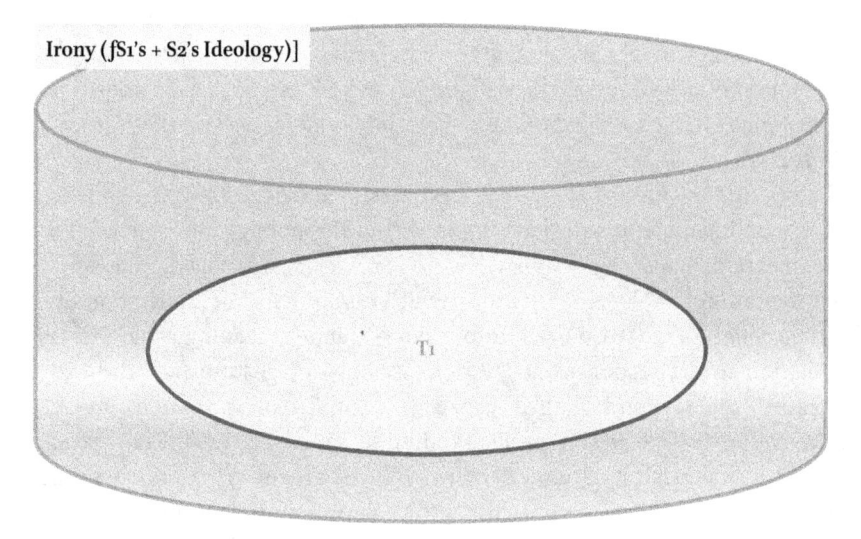

FIGURE 7 T_1's meaning $= f_{[T_1 + \text{Irony}\,(fS_1\text{'s} + S_2\text{'s Ideology})]}$
SOURCE: CREATED BY AUTHOR

Similarly, within a liberal ideology, there are a multitude of spectral choices which might clash or complement the author's scholarly writings. Irony colors all of them.

Meaning-making engages S_2 with what I call understanding. If we were to visualize meaning-making and understanding, we could visualize them having no connection to each other, being opposite, or having some overlap. However, we are talking about scholarship production and communication, so T_1 is the connector between the two steps of the meaning-making process. As a result, I define meaning as a function of the instigating text, T_1, which can be described as $T_1 f(S_1)$ and understanding, as a function of T_1's interpellator, S_2, $T_1 f(S_2)$.

In basic communication models, the emphasis is on the message (T_1) sent from a source (S_1) through a specific medium to a receiver (S_2) (Shannon and Weaver 1949). In the co-orientation model used here, the emphasis is on the role of cognition in the communication process: identifying that a specific problem exists T_1, and identifying how to understand T_1. Chaffe's method is best suited to describe meaning-making as a two-step process: T_1 meaning and T_1 understanding. As such, T_1 orientates both S_1 in her meaning-making attempt and the scholarly community (S_2) in their understanding attempt. The orientation becomes thus a function of S_1's ideology, but also of S_1 vocabulary, which creates literal and ironical meaning. It also becomes a consequence of the surrounding contingency at the moment of interpellation. That contingency is determined by S_2's own body of scholarship, S_2's prevalent ideology at the moment of actuating of interpellating T_1, as well as S_2's ironic disposition. For instance, Rorty's ironists would certainly note it easier than Rorty's philosophers.

S_1's orientation toward the others becomes ideological irony. It expresses both S_1's political views and positioning within the public sphere, as well as S_1's own experience of contingency, the irony of her own scholastic existence. The orientation held by S_2 is the irony which comes with the understanding, the interpellation of T_1. Co-orientation theory defines meaning as relational, "in relation to the response [i.e., understanding] the gesture [i.e., the text] generates" (McLeod and Chaffee 1973: 473). For this reason, there cannot be any meaning to T_1 without understanding T_1 and vice-versa. The textual meaning is instigated by S_1, and becomes $f(S_1)$. Therefore, T_1's understanding is the result of S_2's engagement with $T_1, f(S_2)$. Between production and meaning-making, T_1 becomes $T_1 f(S_1) \& f(S_2)$. Ironical ideology is the result of this socialization of textual meaning into public understanding and eventually knowledge (K).

Ideological irony actuates meaning when T_1 is communicated and S_2 notices it due to the textual clues that S_1 left behind intentionally or not. Often the process of communication may come with its own supply of irony, but in terms of localizing it, irony rests with the self, at the intersection of S_1's and S_2's private and public subjectivity. More than control, by acknowledging the impact ironic ideology has on meaning, S_1 makes the first move in the game of meaning-making chess with S_2.

1 Irony and Direct Scholastic Criticism

When communication happens interpersonally, for instance, at conferences, meaning, criticism and understanding temporarily overlap. In terms of scholarship production, T_1 criticism sets up the stage for the textual production of T_2. When both the text-instigator and the text-interpellator face each other, irony becomes more prevalent. In addition to the ways it affects scholarship explained above, irony is often used to keep open conflict at bay.

During interpersonal communication, at conferences for instance, where scholars present their findings to an audience of peers, the participants experience irony. Any speaker, whether the text-instigator or the text-interpellator, takes turns as "producer[s] of irony" (Bajerski 2016: 236). Bajerski tells us that the etymology of irony is "pretended ignorance," and it is often employed as a teaching tool. In this situation, the producer of irony often styles himself as the teacher who uses irony literally, as "pretended ignorance."

Socrates embodied this concept of irony. In his study of Socrates' irony, Søren Kierkegaard (1965) cogently summarized the Greek philosopher's communication style:

> He was not a like a philosopher lecturing upon his views [...]; on the contrary, what Socrates said meant something "other."
> KIERKEGAARD 1965: 50

Socrates' use of irony was experiential. Whether he used it scholastically in his writing remains a mystery because he left no writings. We can only speculate why he chose this outcome. Maybe he was aware of the role of irony in scholarship. Or maybe Socrates resigned to the fact that, in time, all scholarship "is apprehended through an integral calculation" (id.) beyond the author's control, as Kierkegaard tells us.

Nevertheless, we have access to the writings of two of his contemporaries, Aristophanes and Plato. Both apparently were able to grasp Socrates' irony. While Aristophanes is often perceived as criticizing the master, Plato appears as an adoring fan. In *The Clouds*, according to Piotr Nowak (2014), subsequent scholars, including Hegel and Kierkegaard, read Aristophanes' satire as the result of his annoyance with Socrates' behavioral irony, with his "sophistic gift of turning everything inside out." (Nowak: 15).

To the contrary, in *Dialogues*, Plato describes that gift euphorically. In fact, Plato supplied the foundation of our understanding of the *Socratic Method* of eliciting truth through raising questions whose answers Socrates pretends not to know. Plato introduces us to this method when he describes how Socrates lectured the Sophists for understanding how *to discourse* but not how *to converse*. Socrates makes the Sophists realize how they only attempt to show off (discourse) in conversation so long as they refrain from engaging in questions and answers (converse).

An admirer of both philosophers, Kierkegaard points out that Socrates is sincere in his criticism of the Sophists. However, while favoring dialogue, Socrates is convinced that they both have a limited utility. Metaphorically speaking, for Socrates, whether conversing or discoursing, the mystery of life (deity) is not revealed.

> [For Socrates], the significance of the dialogue ... is symbolic of the relation between man and deity. Although this relationship has reciprocity it contains no moment of unity.
> KIERKEGAARD 1965: 73

Despite Kierkegaard's poetic take on Socrates' method of teaching, known as the Socratic Method of teaching law, it is still frequently utilized in our law school classrooms. In this prosaic approach, it is used to elicit answers on case law: their factual and legal issues, as well as their implications. Its irony focuses on its verbal, interpersonal aspect when the producer of irony and its recipient are spatially and temporarily connected: they are both in the same classroom.

Similarly, there are myriad other instances where irony is interpersonal. Reyes, Rosso, and Veale (2013) cogently summarized such situations. Let us consider three examples of verbal irony these authors found in everyday situations:

1. Going to your car in the morning, you notice that one of your tires is completely flat. A friendly neighbor chimes in with: "Looks like you've got a flat". Marveling at his powers of observation, you reply "Ya think?".
2. When having breakfast in a greasy-spoon cafe, you hungrily polish off everything on your plate. Seeing your totally clean plate, your waitress quips: "Well, that must have been terrible". "Yes", you reply, "absolutely awful".
3. A professor explains and re-explains Hegel's theory of the State to his class of undergraduates. "Is it clear now", he asks. "Clear as mud," a student replies.

> These examples suggest that pretense plays a key role in irony: speakers craft utterances in spite of what has just happened, not because of it. The pretense in each case alludes to, or echoes, an expectation that has been violated, such as the expectation that others behave in a civil fashion, [not consume every single speck of food on their plate, or] speak meaningfully and with clarity. This pretense may seem roundabout and illogical, but it offers a sharply effective and concise mode of communication.
> REYES, ROSSO AND VEALE 2013: 241

Reyes, Rosso, and Veale point out that irony is ambivalent. In interpersonal communication, it becomes a tool of criticism. It manages open conflict or, what I could call, scholastic passive-aggressive behavior.

Experienced irony has also an emotional component. For instance, Bryan Stevenson (2014) noted that irony, as used in the Socratic Method, makes students aware of their ignorance because it humiliates them. Studies show that the use of irony carries a risk of excessive criticism, thus hurting the interlocutor (Bajerski 2016: 236). On the positive side, it encourages those unscathed by humiliation to excel.

From interpersonal communication, irony brings to scholarly communication a sharp eye for what is crooked, wry, distorted, for what is erroneous. Irony mediates idea and actuality because it "points out the contradictions" (Kierkegaard 1965: 141). This irony is what I claim to be the very reason for all scholarship.

2   Scholarship as (Ironic) Polite Criticism

In interpersonal communication, irony appears as a great tool for speakers to be impolite while appearing polite, which fits so well into the mold of the adversarial common law system. As part of S_2's solitary interpellation of T_1, irony becomes a form of polite criticism.

All theory production comes out of a major subjective tension between the scholar's surrounding reality and the theory, or the conceptual framework available to S_1. When the state of theory at a specific point does not convey reality as S_1 perceives it, or as is desired, that tension reaches a point of instability which incites scholarship production. The scholar (S_1) becomes a text-instigator, producing scholarship to be communicated.

As soon as it is publicly imparted, published for solitary interpellation, or presented at conferences for interpersonal interpellation, scholarship becomes theory, T_1. T_1 takes on a life of itself as the object of meaning-making processes whose outcomes vary with the text-interpellator and the surrounding contingency. During that process, irony actuates meaning which shapes theoretical understanding.

Earlier I argued that when the text-instigator, S_1, acknowledges their subjectivity and the impact it has on meaning-making, S_1 is able to exercise a larger control over the meaning-making negotiation. That is because sometimes S_1 is able to recognize the difference between the appearance of meaning, which ascribed during textual production and the production of meaning, which appears during T_1's subsequent interpellation. That meaning-making control appears when S_1 anticipates the polite (criticism) irony S_2 might use in their critique of T_1. The more aware of the changing nature of the contingency surrounding meaning-making, the better situated is S_1 to manage the tension between the textual appearance of meaning, and the subsequent meanings and understanding of T_1.

In this instance, irony, as polite criticism, is connected to understanding and meaning-making. It unites the text-instigator as the originator of meaning, and the text-interpellator as the originator of understanding. Irony glues meaning to understanding. They can correspond, be different, and even be opposites. The irony is that scholars can better control the correlation between the meaning of the text and its understanding by opening the text and make it aware of the moment of contingency, the surrounding theoretical and social reality, and by acknowledging their own limitations, such as ideology. If we were to use the theory of connectedness, irony is embedded into understanding and is connected to the gaze of the audience, deciphering the meaning of the text. Irony produces understanding from extra-textual information, which also comes from the scholar's omissions.

For instance, in his critique of twentieth-century Western intellectuals supportive of Soviet Russia, Tony Judt (2012) persuasively explained how faith and shared allegiance kept them from exposing the truth at bay, with the lone example of Andre Gide, who made public his findings upon a visit to what was then U.S.S.R. If we imagine T_1 to represent all scholarship about the U.S.S.R., according to Judt, S_2, all Soviet scholars (S_1) deliberately chose to ignore a particular aspect so the Soviet scholarship, S_1, conspired to only reveal half of the truth about the Soviet reality. Ironically, despite all the omissions and fabricated truth that characterized T_1 according to Judt (S_2), he was nevertheless able to find the opposite of what T_1 literally contained. Ideological irony prevailed in the meaning-making negotiation: Judt's ideology (anti-Soviet American postmodern liberalism) prevailed in the meaning-making process over the overtly Soviet ideology of the scores of S_1 he alluded to, shaping our understanding to T_1.

Staying with Judt's criticism on the theory of meaning-making then replacing Soviet Russia with any jurisprudential topic of the day, it seems Judt's remarks remain persuasive among current "progressive" establishment intellectuals – i.e., political human rights are more essential than socio-economic human rights. The reluctance by establishment intellectuals to break ranks and speak against the Regime of Truth of their era – the intellectual position on which they have built their carrier – is not remarkable; it is only human. That sense of allegiance defines not only the "progressive" intellectuals of the 1950s and 1960s and those of the previous two decades (Latham 1966; Warren III 1966), but establishment intellectuals throughout time. A cursory reading of the American social scholarship of the last half-a-century – easily ascertainable from perusing the book reviews published in *The New York Review of Books* – would show that what we perceive today to be the work of the radical right, or the so-called "Red Scare," was in fact a national obsession with anti-Communism. By extension, for scholars, it was an anti-Marxian and anti-Marxist obsession:

> The larger truth [...] will have to wait for a historian who is prepared to see American anti-Communism not as an issue foisted on the rest of us by the "radical Right" but as a continuing obsession, national in scope; and who is prepared to admit, moreover, that not only McCarthyism but our "liberal" bipartisan foreign policy since 1945 can be understood only partially as a response to the real threat of Communism abroad. The obsession with Communism has to be explained principally as a manifestation of certain developments within American society itself. One of these is the failure of liberalism, particularly in the Forties and Fifties, to offer an alternative to the cold war.
> LASCH 1966

In the same vein, the brief property example suggests the same faith-based obsession with the virtue of our current property rules. Without understanding its irony, we derail any possibility of change. That we accept the current corporate monopolies and preach corporate governance, is based on pure faith. Like the hope of the poor to win the lottery one day, that hope incentivizes people to oppose a more progressive taxation on the wealthy and even curtail dangerous encroaches on public services. While at best, in the most progressive situations, data show that the lottery redistributes revenue from poor gamblers to high-achieving middle and upper-class students. Where the lottery is tied to education (California) and individual scholarship (Georgia), the poor still spend money on the lottery dreaming of the life of the rich, because of magic (Cohen 2017), or what I call, corporate propaganda. In other words, unquestioned repeated statements coming from centers of perceived authority and mass-appeal. The lottery is another instance of promoting the virtues of the current private property rules as undisputable truths based on faith. In turn, scholarship in favor and against the strategic role of gambling, whether presenting it as a source of public revenue for community services or as a consumer commodity (property) (Perez and Humphreys 2013), is full of ideological irony. That irony easily extrapolates to any property-based scholarship, but few expose it.

CHAPTER 8

The Bearable Lightness of Jurisprudential Irony

This book's working thesis is that all social theories, including jurisprudence, are part philosophy, part ideology, and part irony, and that this is where their scholastic charm lies. While jurisprudence aspires to be objectified, reasoned narrative or philosophy, most of the time it is only a quixotic quest to objectify ideological subjectivity. Law cannot ever be the Kantian "thing in itself," because law, more than an abstract construct, is an actuated (ironic) human construct (Kant 1890; Blumenau 2017).

Clifford Geertz's ideological explanation applies well to my view of jurisprudence, which is both a diagnostic and an apology, or a justification:

> Where science is the diagnostic, the critical, dimension of culture, ideology is the justificatory, the apologetic one – it refers to that part of culture which is actively concerned with the establishment and defense of patterns of belief and value.
> GEERTZ 1973: 231

Ontologically, jurisprudence can be seen as the result of theory production, communication and meaning negotiation. As in any process involving negotiation, the outcome is rarely clear at the outset. In scholarly communication, despite the fact that both the instigator and the interpellator are scholars, the lack of semantic control remains inevitable. The meaning ascribed to a text might be unintended, or downright the opposite of what its author communicated. This unaccountable difference is the "wild card" of meaning. This situation is due to the difference in cultural baggage between the text-instigator and the text-interpellator, as well as their attitude (ideology) toward it and the power structure enabling it.

For example, the United States Constitution, the fundamental law in the United States, is as abstract as any religious text, but it can also be regarded as an actuated, ironic construct. It is the product of an antiquated form of patriarchy – the Founding Fathers – whose legal and political work is hard to separate from their personal lives. Furthermore, while it has been around for more than two centuries, during this time it has meant many things. Its ideological irony is inescapable, especially in hindsight, due to the clash of subjectivity – ours attempting to make sense of that of its writers, the Founding Fathers.

Building on this example, constitutional jurisprudence is a type of intellectual bridge which connects the social practice of law with the aspiration or ideal of the Rule of Law (Lear 2011: 11). Bridging this gap goes beyond constitutional jurisprudence, it is the animus beyond all legal theory production. If that gap is ignored theoretically, it arguably marks all inner dogmatism with an "expiration date" due faster than otherwise. In turn, a future gap that will arise will subsequently need to be addressed. Ironically, another scholar will take advantage of the predecessor's dogmatism and try to address the new scholastic moment of crisis.

Theoretical misunderstandings are easily solved once the ironic nature of scholarship in general and legal scholarship in particular, has been laid out. Irony is a beginning, the forerunner to the skeptical, "I don't know," which only touches the scholar's subjectivity with discomfort and doubt about her own work. Irony represents the moment when all discomfort with the existing theoretical explanation is actuated into a moment of crisis, or when the scholar detects a discrepancy between an incipient developing change and the existing theory. At that moment, she will most likely experience the "I don't know" epiphany and embark on a process of replacing it.

Irony is inescapable; it exists as actuated subjectivity. It corresponds to a metaphysical need to understand the world. Also, it marks the recognition that such an undertaking is futile because it is temporary. Using Rorty's vocabulary, irony becomes the moment when the theorist seeks a recalibration of the "Plato-Kant canon," whose power over her scholarship dissipates by that very realization (Rorty 1989: 97; Inkpin 2013). While irony might be limited to the tension between scholarship and a specific slice of reality, there is no requirement for that to always be the case. In this light, the scholar may as well be attuned to the larger picture which makes her scholarship ontologically dissonant within a particular discipline.

Marx's work – deeply subjective in its assumption of its politics and ideology, as well as dialectical in that it is the result of a comprehensive interpellation of reality at a very specific historical moment – is ideally suited to unveiling the irony it contains and directing the reader's gaze to all scholastic irony. History is a moment of suspense within dynamic surroundings. To notice historicity is to notice and to acknowledge temporality as a value embedded in any theoretical explanation.

Irony has been noted culturally by legal scholars. For instance, Jedediah Purdy calls irony the marker of our time, of our cultural maturity (Purdy 1999: xi). For him, irony is a manner of living "powered by a suspicion that everything is derivative" (id.: 14).

> The ironic attitude is most pervasive in popular culture, when Karl Marx's dictum that historic events occur twice – "the first time as tragedy, the second as farce" – which had never before been much use except as an insult to alleged second-timers, has found a new vitality. (Id.: 11)

Purdy goes on describing his experience of the 1990s in a book decrying what he perceives to be irony but looks more like social impotence. I cannot talk to that view of irony because it is so limited to the 1990s American urbanism. Like the much-quoted American sitcom of that era, *Seinfeld* (1989–1998), it is too vacuous to matter. It is a mere detachment from engaging in spectatorship, something very well explained in Guy Debord's *La société du spectacle* (1967). Like Debord before him, Purdy noted that action had been replaced by passive enjoyment. From a meaning-making perspective, ideologically, Purdy's irony is Emersonian. His call for common things is a call for reflection against "foolish optimism and idle pessimism" (Purdy 1999: 206), both reasonable and admirable.

Here, irony comes to the forefront from a different perspective. It lies within the sphere of textual understanding, which comes from S_2's engagement with the text (T_1), noting incongruences S_1 left within.

1   Jurisprudential Irony as an Inescapable Trade-Off between Scholastic Ambition and Reality

In "Working Themselves Impure: A Life Cycle Theory of Legal Theories" (2016), Jeremy Kessler and David Pozen noted the cannibalistic nature of scholarship. For them, the core of the meaning-making process, unlike here, is the private process of understanding. How S_2 understands T_1 determines how T_2 cannibalizes or incorporates T_1.

Both they and this project seemingly agree with Stuart Hall's theory that meaning comes from difference. For Kessler and Pozen, the absence of meaning (difference) produces theory feeder. They do not seem to view meaning as a result of a negotiating meaning-making process between S_1 and S_2. Nor is it seen as the result of a symbiotic process. That is perhaps because, for Kessler and Pozen, S_1 is a mythological author who is able to singularly give meaning to T_1. For me, S_1 is a mere text-instigator, whose views are given meaning once S_2 interpellates T_1 and engages S_1's subjectivity in the meaning-making process.

This difference of views may be responsible for Kessler and Pozen's theory of "meaning adulteration." By talking about meaning adulteration they ignore the role of communication. They disregard that S_2 is first a text-interpellator before becoming a text-instigator. To cannibalize T_1 and produce T_2, S_2 needs to engage T_1. This engagement can happen only if T_1 is communicated. It is possible that Kessler and Pozen assumed communication because it is so natural, or using Seana Shiffrin's explanation:

> In human social life, the principal object is to communicate our attitudes, and hence it is of the first importance that everyone be truthful in respect of this thoughts.
> SHIFFRIN 2014: 5

Irrespective the reason for skipping communication, skipping it makes the meaning-making negotiation invisible. All scholarship is produced to become public knowledge (K). That is why it is communicated, and that is why I talk about the negotiating meaning-making process.

Understanding T_1 is a segment of the meaning-making negotiation between S_1 and S_2. Meaning-making is contingent on the public level of understanding at a particular moment and on the Regime of Truth and its imbedded ideology. Actuating meaning is a process which S_1 can only partly control, especially through a very transparent theory-production process. Kessler and Pozen have too much confidence in S_1, and as such in T_1 to speak for itself and to actuate understanding, which subsequently may be adulterated. The irony is that meaning-making is a process where individual and public understanding melts into some representational information, and sometimes, when lucky, public knowledge (K). What they call adulteration is an essential part of meaning-making and subsequent understanding.

Presenting meaning as a process makes irony possible while denying scholarship its neutral singularity. Kessler and Pozen themselves noted that no text works in its pure literal meaning. Statements come with a penumbra, or a residual meaning, which goes beyond linguistic ambiguity, and whose meaning is actuated in the process of understanding. This is ironic meaning impregnated with ideology, that of the text-instigator, S_1 and that of the scholar, T_1, interpellates, S_2.

While Kessler and Pozen noted that irony springs from what is expressed and what is achievable, they mislabeled it as an "adulterating" factor. For Kessler and Pozen, meaning preexists, rather than embeds, irony. Irony adulterates it.

> The belief that law can "work itself pure" ironically underwrites the contradictions and compromises of prescriptive legal theories. Those

> theories that suggest that a divisive legal practice can be redeemed, and political debate quieted, through the adoption of proper decision-making techniques always already contain the seeds of their own decay. There may be an inescapable trade-off between a legal theory's ambition to transcend social conflict and its susceptibility to impurification.
> KESSLER and POZEN 2016: 1824

Certainly, sugar is an additive to tea, and we know that because tea can be, and is, consumed without sugar. Jurisprudence is ironic, and thus it cannot be understood without its irony. T_1 creates meaning and in the process of socializing T_1, it is understood.

Understanding is a consequence of engaging, or interpellating the text. At this level, the scholar becomes a text-instigator, whose work is understood within the context of engaging T_1. It is at this moment that irony is actuated, during the engagement with the text, which does not happen in some vacuum but in the context of existing scholarship and the contingency of the engagement. "The belief that law can 'work itself pure' ironically underwrites the contradictions and compromises of prescriptive legal theories" (id.), and in the process, it marks the historicity of its textual interpellation.

2   Jurisprudential Irony and the Socratic Method of Teaching Law

As explained here, statements come with a penumbra, or a residual meaning, which goes beyond linguistic ambiguity, and whose meaning is actuated in the process of understanding. This is the ironic meaning impregnated with ideology.

Irony is connected to textual production and communication. Within the realm of jurisprudence, it comes as direct criticism, often employed in law school teaching.

For example, the law student is acutely aware of the imbalance of the Socratic method of teaching. The irony in the Socratic Method of teaching – the lectures from an ivory tower of knowledge presented as ignorant questioning – while present, is not particularly engaging (Davis and Neacşu 2014: 481). The Socratic Method uses irony to establish and maintain the teacher/student power structure. Perhaps because this power relation is asymmetrical while preserving the appearance of polite criticism, this use of irony is mostly circumscribed into today's law school culture. "An instance of irony provides also an instance of criticism" (Barbe 1995: 89). This is an instance where the Irony Principle, "speakers can be impolite while appearing polite," (id.) seems to fit perfectly. Irony keeps conflict at bay because, while emotionally painful, it is not an open insult, as this fictional exchange from the movie *Paper Chase* (1973) accomplishes very well.

> PROFESSOR KINGSFIELD: Mr. Hart...will you recite the facts of Hawkins vs. McGee? I do have your name right? You are Mr. Hart?
> HART: Yes, my name is Hart.
> PROFESSOR KINGSFIELD: You're not speaking loud enough, Mr. Hart. Will you speak up?
> HART: Yes, my name is Hart.
> PROFESSOR KINGSFIELD: Mr. Hart, you're still not speaking loud enough. Will you stand? Now that you're on your feet, Mr. Hart ... maybe the class will be able to understand you. You are on your feet?
> HART: Yes, I'm on my feet.
> PROFESSOR KINGSFIELD: Loudly, Mr. Hart. Fill this room with your intelligence. Now, will you give us the facts of the case?
> HART: I haven't read the case.
> PROFESSOR KINGSFIELD: Class assignments for the first day ... are posted on the bulletin boards ... in Langdell and Austin Halls. You must have known that.
> HART: No.
> PROFESSOR KINGSFIELD: You assumed this first class would be a lecture...a n introduction to the course.
> HART: Yes, sir.
> PROFESSOR KINGSFIELD: Never assume anything in my classroom. Mr. Hart, I will myself give you the facts of the case. Hawkins vs. McGee.
> BRIDGES 1973

The irony is not expressly signaled in this exchange, but it is rather obvious in Kingsfield's words: "Fill this room with your intelligence." One might say it is a lowbrow use of irony.

It begs to reason that such ingrained exposure to irony is doomed to become conceptualized into the jurisprudential writings of the best law school students. Furthermore, the jurisprudential attraction for irony may lie also in the type of argument it enables. For instance, when Socrates engages in the strictness of argument, he leaves a lot unsaid, thus enticing his pupils to understand what is not said. This is the other type of irony Plato ascribes to his teacher. In his ten books of the *Republic*, Plato alters his method of introducing us to Socrates' irony. Socrates no longer comes forward with questions in the character of an ignorant man only seeking greater ignorance in the service of a larger meaning, but rather as one who has already followed what he seeks. There is no dialogic embellishment, but instead an enticing irony, which contains the strictness of argument. In the *Republic,* as Kierkegaard points out, irony has a theoretical or contemplative aspect.

3 Jurisprudential Irony – Byproduct of Legal Hegemony

Extrapolating Antonio Gramsci's view of hegemony (1971), legal hegemony is a modern way of control and domination which ensures willing obedience to our Rule of Law. An imperfect visualization of how legal hegemony works rests with hard-as-nails Lily Dillon in *The Grifters* (1990). Dillon, played by Anjelica Huston, works as a swindler for dangerous bookie Bobo, played by Pat Hingle. In order to exert control, Bobo beats her with a luscious hotel towel filled with high-quality oranges. However, he only hits her over her body and leaves her face untouched. The beating stops with Bobo breathless by the amount of force used in the assault. Though terrified, Lily's body showed no sign of abuse. The irony rests in the result which is not apparent at first blush, or even opposite to what is apparent.

Likewise, legal institutions have been propped up to promote ideals that they cannot ensure. Jurisprudence assigned itself the chore of making that job salient.

In the nineteenth century, property developed into the curricular object of *Real Property, Contracts*, and arguably, *Torts*. Within this ever more refined institutional hierarchy, the teaching of property became more and more ideological as it needed to legitimize the inevitable material of social inequality. In a liberal democracy, whose overarching Rule of Law is attached to social stability, the property rules needed to be present a nature-inspired technicality, so both the haves and the have-nots would voluntarily obey them. Thus, property became described as individual rights to things, rather than the individual's rights with respect to others regarding various aspects of the use of things. The regime of property was determined by things owned as if outside of human intervention.

Ownership imbalance had existed long before jurisprudence came around and felt the pressure of hegemony to propose an enriched vocabulary for legitimizing inequality, all the while preserving it and making it a necessary part of the fabric of our society. The realm of all rights to things (including real property, the most valuable at the time) became taught as being separate, but equal to the realm of other individual rights, freedoms, and entitlements. The tilted balance was settled with abstract vocabulary, avoiding any discussion about the morality of having very few individuals with rights to most "things." Blackstone's heavily ideological *Commentaries on the Laws of England* (1765) was published during the time England was going through its industrial revolution. Blackstone's work legitimized inequality in many ways, starting with its table of contents *Das Recht Des Besitzes: Eine Civilistische Abhandlung, 1803*: the title of Book I is, "The Rights of Persons" and Book II, "Things."

In continental civil law countries, Friedrich Karl von Savigny (1848) was working in the same vein. His *Das Recht Des Besitzes (The Law of Possession)*, legitimized the same process by reclaiming its Roman roots in dealing with the new post-feudal, capitalist reality. Savigny presented law as having no existence of its own. For Savigny (1848) law's nature was human life looked at from a particular angle and he relied on the customary nature of Roman law for support.

In time, private property became the cornerstone of liberal democracy, a matter of rational happenstance, as well as, a political gambit for its proponents, such as Hobbes and John Stuart Mill. The regime of rights developed and so did the object of property. For instance, the rules of property multiplied, thus, eroding the absolute nature of property and creating new, additional rights, such as servitudes. If continental Europe started with only one male member per household holding property, America abolished the primogeniture rule, and Tocqueville credited this institution with the basis for our successful democracy (1992: 55).

With the change from feudal to what Marx called *bourgeois* property, everybody could dream about owning property. For the working masses, ownership represented possession over some tangible household objects and the *pater familias*'s salary. The industrial revolution gave birth to more and more technology, and technology soon made it easy for people to reach a state of faith in some future where there was the possibility of more ownership. Fearing that such faith might disappear especially with the advent of wide-spread education, liberalism expanded the meaning of property. Private property became connected to individual freedoms and evolved into the staple of liberal legal theory. Freedoms to speak then to vote, for instance, morphed into separate individual rights. In times, more and more citizens basked in this republican abundance. Over the years, civil and political freedoms grew as the rights to the sources of wealth, to "things" stagnated in the hands of the few. As such, the capitalist structure was by then solidified for the ages. All it needed were rules that were elastic enough to mask its rigidity.

The expansion of the realm of property has continued both with outer space and new human creations such as digital commons. The diversity of rights and freedoms seems to accompany the concentration of wealth, as if to distract attention from and even mask the disparity. Interestingly, the redistribution of digital space parallels the colonization of the world with big corporations playing the role of super-powers. As that process is underway, people are not forgotten. They are invited to participate in "shadow work," to borrow Ivan Illich's terminology for unpaid, gendered, household work, which was the necessary condition for the existence of wage labor (1980).

Presented in another light, the mobile-device industry subsists on the information it accumulates from its users to improve the products it sells back to its users. Through myriad applications, users volunteer information that is, in turn, used in the creation of other, new products, which are better equipped to grasp and create new wants seemingly satiable only at higher prices. The Cartesian saying, "I think, therefore I am" (*cogito ergo sum*) (Decartes 1637) has morphed into "I play, therefore I gift surplus value to someone I don't know." Much in the way Wikipedia editors create value to the owner of the Wikipedia Foundation and its employees, the workers provide an unpaid surplus of labor and value to corporations. While all this social hierarchy expands, jurisprudentially we are flooded by a multitude of rights and freedoms that every claim we make for some reimbursement has the ring of an entitlement tantamount to that of a billionaire over his wealth.

This brief review of property jurisprudence is aimed at ensuring that irony's presence is acknowledged. While politics is the pervasive common thread among all legal institutions, few are so often used for political gains, resulting in an opening of the field of jurisprudence to so many views and interpretations.

Ideological irony is an intrinsic part of property jurisprudence. For instance, in a 1998 law review article, Michael Heller worked on an implied criticism to Marx's bourgeois property when he promoted institutions to help the Russian transition from state capitalism to a more orthodox form of capitalism. Heller was arguing in favor of a new regime of property called the anticommons, whose strength resided in its beneficiaries' exclusion of others access to resources (Heller 1998: 662–665). According to Heller, during the twentieth century, property had been re-imagined past its classic "fee simple" to be viewed as a bundle of rights, claims, privileges, powers, and immunities. This included the more classic rights to exclusive possession, personal use, and alienation. The most important element of property for Heller was that it could not have been decomposed to a level of non-use. "Property has to be kept available for productive use" (id.).

Heller's pontifical of private property came in response to his empirical studies in former Soviet Russia, and its Warsaw Pact allies. He identified anticommons property on the sidewalk kiosks located in front of empty Muscovite storefronts in late 1990. Because multiple owners had the same rights of use in the space, as well as exclusion privileges keeping others from setting up their own kiosk, Heller deplored the situation as *the tragedy of the anticommons*. Never did Heller favor the commons as an alternate use to both private property and anticommons. His conclusion was that opting for anticommons, as opposed to a fee simple private property, was detrimental.

On the tragedy of the Moscow "storefront anticommons," Heller said:

> Empty stores result in forgone economic opportunity and lost jobs. As of 1995, about 95% of commercial real estate in Russia remained in some form of divided local government ownership. Of this commercial real estate, a significant portion was unused.
> HELLER 1998: 639–640

The irony is in Heller's distraction. He was so sure of the end result (fee simple private property) that he deplored the experiment, regarded as fruitless by the standards employed. And we continue to persist to talk about transition and corporate governance as the only solution. But is it? Or, is this the same ideological irony I can see in Marx's own views on bourgeois property altogether? Although, Marx put out the idea of social and institutional change when "the productive forces at the disposal of society no longer tend to further the development of the conditions of bourgeois property," his scholarship is ignored because his ideology proved a bigger deterrent than anyone expected. No property theorist seems to consider anything else for today's society but the private property.

However, paraphrasing Richard Rorty, "Like it or not, gentlemen, the future of your property depends on your ability to accept limits to your own today" (Rorty 1990: 1817), acknowledging our ideological limits would only open scholarship to its fullest meaning. S_1's acknowledged ideological bias would be taken into consideration by S_2, who, acknowledging their biases, would formulate criticisms which would be forced to reckon with the existing biases, and if unable to adjust or overcome them, would be discarded as epigones. Rather than congratulate each other on our small thoughts, we could become ironic because we want to see more.

The Rule of Law of our democracy has been often amended and improved. Justice Holmes' dissent in *Lochner v. New York,* 198 U.S. 45 (1905) is such an example. *Lochner* is a particular property controversy over what constitutes a sufficient number of hours spent continuously laboring so one earns a living wage. Two renowned scholars incorporated it in their work: Richard Rorty and Richard Posner. Referring to it, Rorty lacks Posner's enthusiasm.

Richard Posner seems unaware of the perils of repetition, as Marx put it so well in *The Eighteenth Brumaire of Louis Bonaparte* (1852):

> Hegel remarks somewhere that all facts and personages of great importance in world history occur, as it were, twice. He forgot to add: the first time as tragedy, the second as farce.

Posner's fawning over Holmes was expressed both in *Law and Literature* (1988) and *Overcoming Law* (1995). Twice, Posner exuberantly assured his readers that Holmes' dissent in *Lochner*, 198 U.S. at 74–76 "is the greatest judicial opinion of the last hundred years" (Posner 1988: 285). For those unfamiliar with Holmes' dissent, it is an ideological refusal to accept an ideological view of scholarship.

> The 14th Amendment does not enact Mr. Herbert Spencer's Social Statics.
> *Lochner v. New York*, 198 U.S. at 75 (1905)

Ironically, Posner seems to admire Holmes' subjectivity, his "instinct." Otherwise, why would Posner say in *Overcoming Law* that judges should "accept[] the role of personal values in adjudication [curtailed only by] empirical data" (Posner 1995: 194–195)? Stretching pragmatism to be whatever it need be to support the decision of the day, Posner does what he accuses Wechsler of doing, forgetting to play the neutral game by exhibiting his "inner mental state." Moreover, Posner derides Wechsler as a "self-conscious ... master crafts [person] of the guild of lawyers" who "assumes [his] inner mental state, his doubts or confidences, have a significance independent of the reasoning or evidence he offers in support of his views," (Posner 1995: 70, 71). The ideological identity data submitted by Wechsler is a splinter compared to the plank of such data provided by Posner for his readers.

In *Overcoming Law*, as Jeffrey Rosen noted, Posner becomes a jarring spectacle of inconsistency (1995: 588). Posner glorifies one of the most intellectual judges, Holmes, not for his reason, but for his subjectivity, his instinct. Unaware, Posner supports my position about ironic ideology actuating jurisprudential meaning, despite using different terminology. Being open about one's subjectivity, ergo ideology, judges can overcome "all that is pretentious, uninformed, prejudiced, and spurious in the legal tradition" (id.: 21). Too bad Posner does not understand the irony of his own criticism.

Rorty's fascination with Holmes' dissent comes across different than Posner's. What is so great about that dissent Rorty asks *his* readers? What exactly does it say?

At first blush, Holmes sidestepped any moral judgment over a living salary in exchange for sixty hours of weekly labor or ten daily hours as limited by the New York statute. In this respect, irony in Holmes' dissent appears from what is omitted, and which Rorty partially noticed. Despite the appearance to the contrary, Holmes' rejection of "Mr. Herbert Spencer's Social Statics" is not necessarily because he thinks judges should be neutral. It could easily be a dislike. Either way, he opens the door to other philosophical schools of thought than Mr. Spencer's to influence the 14th Amendment jurisprudence:

> The liberty of the citizen to do as he likes so long as he does not interfere with the liberty of others to do the same, which has been a shibboleth for some well-known writers, is interfered with by school laws, by the Post office, by every state or municipal institution which takes his money for purposes thought desirable, whether he likes it or not. The 14th Amendment does not enact Mr. Herbert Spencer's Social Statics.
> dissenting opinion in *Lockner*; HOLMES 1905: 75

Second, Holmes' irony expands the meaning of his dissent in a direction that Rorty noticed. For instance, we can read his dissent as an invitation to his esteemed colleagues to recognize the expansion of the political power players, and include among the "people of New York" those who pressured the New York legislative vote to be mindful of the job seekers' health: trade associations. "Like it or not, gentlemen, trade unions are part of our country too," Rorty reads Holmes' dissent. Here, I can see Holmes' pragmatism in it (1990: 1817). Sadly, there is no single U.S. Supreme Court Justice left on the bench to make such pragmatically tolerant arguments nowadays, even by omission.

In *The Banality of Pragmatism and the Poetry of Justice,* Richard Rorty distills the irony in our most treasured, iconic U.S. Supreme Court landmark cases. Rorty does so in ways that if pointed out when they were passed, their implementation would have been perhaps less culturally traumatic for both their proponents, but also for those opposing them, ideologically. With regard to one U.S. Supreme Court decision, *Bowers v. Hardwick*, 478 U.S. 186 (1986), Rorty presciently gave the justices the template for its subsequent reversal in *Lawrence v. Texas*, 539 U.S. 558 (2003) – make the issue banal:

> I think of Brown as saying that, like it or not, black children are children too. I think of Roe as saying that, like it or not, women get to make hard decisions too, and of some hypothetical future reversal of Bowers v. Hardwick as saying that, like it or not, gays are grown-ups too.
> RORTY 1990: 1818

Irony is part and parcel of our jurisprudence. Using this perspective when we teach law to our future guardians of the law, the entire meaning of jurisprudence would become open to experimentation. In the instance of the three

Supreme Court decisions Rorty refers to, *Brown v. Bd. of Ed. of Topeka, Shawnee County, Kan.,* 347 U.S. 483 (1954), *Roe v. Wade,* 410 U.S. 113 (1973), and *Bowers v. Hardwick,* 478 U.S. 186 (1986), law students would learn that less is more. Instead of holding them on some sacrosanct pedestal, cultural trendsetting decisions could have faster and far-reaching positive effects if jurists were encouraged to point to what is not expressly said, but culturally more acceptable in the moment. What is inferred might very well assuage the bigotry of those opposing their implementation because it elevates their non-threatening human element. Rather than letting those decisions stand on their explicit politics, and create a privileged "other" status for black children, women, and gays, Rorty suggests, and I support his position, members of subordinate classes would enjoy more rights faster if they were perceived in a more banal way, as part of the anonymous everybody. Their status would lose some court-based privileged aura, but also their marginalization.

If that is true using a liberal philosopher's position, Rorty's, what is the point in resuscitating Marx? Haven't we spent enough time dismantling Big Theory and all "systemic" or "structural" approaches to knowledge production? We certainly have, but while we have attacked Big Theory, ironically, we have continued to envision and celebrate the author's high degree of mastery and ambition. I would dare say that no minimalist theoretician sees herself as a tinkerer or technician. So here we are with Small Theory and Big Ego Authors, in the realm of post-modern irony.

Irony is a product of small and big theories. There is plenty of irony in Marx: as much as in any of his epigones or detractors. I suggest resuscitating Marx because he remains an outlier in American scholarship, while his scholarship persists to be as relevant today as ever; despite adopting an ideology foreign to the one embraced by the American establishment intellectual. This is not a call for Big Theory and especially not for structuralism, in light of my emphasis on irony because they are somehow complementary synergistic. Irony is actuated by all ideologies, even by differences within the liberal tent of American jurisprudence, as shown below. I believe that studying Marxian irony becomes more easily detectable. Once we can recognize the irony in jurisprudence, cultural bridges between opposite ideologies could be brokered more easily, and scholarship would become enriched by our opposite views.

4   Encoded Jurisprudential Irony

Jurisprudence is filled with irony residing in the text. Jurisprudential concepts contain encoded irony. The reasoned narrative is filled with ironic meaning. The heavily footnoted style is ironic. Here are some examples.

One of the most revered concepts in American jurisprudence is "justice," and its counterpart, "just." *The Preamble to the United States Constitution* (1787) mentions *justice* as a goal attainable by following and obeying the rules that the Founding Fathers established for our nation.

> We the people of the United States, in order to form a more perfect union, establish justice, insure domestic tranquility, provide for the common defense, promote the general welfare, and secure the blessings of liberty to ourselves and our posterity, do ordain and establish this Constitution for the United States of America.

Kierkegaard (1965) would have noted its irony, in the vein of the happiness promised to Christians who followed the Ten Commandments (280). Similarly, "just" is mentioned in the *Preamble* to the *Declaration of Independence*, in the context of the "just powers" of the government being derived from the consent of the governed when only some of those governed could actually give their consent: white, propertied adult men.

In *Republic*, Plato introduces justice through irony with a story about Socrates and Glaucon traveling to a festival. While on their way, they accept the invitation to spend the night at the house of the elder Cephalus. While there, a conversation develops. The circumstance that Cephalus has partly inherited and partly acquired his rather noticeable fortune is the starting point for Socrates to begin inquiring about what constitutes justice, and what can be considered just. Eventually, Plato will settle for justice as the outcome of following the rules, because the only existing rules would be justly approved and following them would thus produce a just result and justice for all.

In Plato's *Republic*, the justice debate was about speaking the truth and paying one's debts, whether there are instances when it would be unjust to repay the debt. For example, if one were to return a gun to a friend at a moment the friend is unhinged, a gun which the friend himself had handed over when he was in his right mind, would that be just? Plato leaves just such a query with the reader. He moves the discussion about justice to Cephalus' son, whose ideal of justice is to repay the debt, "to render each his due." But how does one know what is due? Socrates is quizzical, as knowledge severely restricts the sphere of justice, which then is in danger of becoming another way of satisfying the interest of the stronger. "I proclaim that justice is nothing else but the interest of the stronger" (Kierkegaard 1965: 145).

In addition to the ironic discrepancy between text and expectation, jurisprudential irony comes from poor textual execution. For instance, in "Morton Horwitz Wrestles with the Rule of Law" (2010), Levinson and Balkin (2010) observe that jurisprudence seems to be prone to irony because it cannot offer a balanced reading of the law, which is a political, deeply ideological artifact. All schools of jurisprudence have emphasized its political bias, inadequately though: Marxists were too reductionist, while the *Crits* too timid. Given this error in execution, Levinson and Balkin admire in Horwitz stance. His jurisprudence can cure the ills attributed to the Rule of Law within the limits Horwitz has established:

> Law might "create formal equality" – a not inconsiderable virtue – but it promotes substantive inequality by creating a consciousness that radically separates law from politics, means from ends, processes from outcomes.
> LEVINSON and BALKIN 2010: 498

Interestingly, the ideological ironic approach to jurisprudence is Horwitz's italicized reference in the last paragraph of the work Levinson & Balkin analyze, which they ignored:

> So can we say that the rule of law is an "unqualified human good"? Only if [we] accept the Hobbesian vision of the state and human nature on which our present conceptions of the rule of law ultimately rest. It *is* a conservative doctrine.
> HORWITZ 1977: 566

Given the political nature of law and jurisprudence, is it possible to imagine and implement progressive standards and achieve greatness? Horwitz believes that law could not implement progressiveness. For Horwitz, there is just the opposite. Such a trenchant attitude opens Levinson and Balkin to irony. Inasmuch, I ask, how can they as S_2 negotiate a meaning of Horwitz's work (T_1) that Horwitz (S_1) denied? Law is conservative. Law is the human good which in its most progressive iteration promotes status quo. Naturally, irony resides in the scholarly execution of the reasoned narrative, if they promote progressive standards that cannot be supported by law itself.

In addition to this type of textual irony, jurisprudence is prone to irony because of its chosen style. Think only about the jurisprudential devotion to lengthy and copious footnotes. The irony of so much formal rigor raises questions (or it should) about pedantry for the sake of pedantry. How many of us ponder over the signals of rigor, and think whether footnoting is a sign of vacuity and derision? Isn't that ironic because it denotes the opposite of rigor? None other than Judge Posner wrote along these lines:

> the superficial dominates the substantive. The vacuity and tendentiousness of so much legal reasoning are concealed by the awesome scrupulousness with which a set of intricate rules governing the form of citations is observed.
>
> POSNER 1986: 1344

As noted earlier, Posner enjoys quoting himself (and he's not alone!). In his 2011 diatribe against *The Bluebook: A Uniform System of Citation* (2010), the manual of style employed to publish jurisprudence, Posner suggests that the function of the law reviews' hyper-meticulous footnoting practices is to conceal with apparent rigor, an intellectual sloppiness that lurks beneath – to make legal scholarship look scientific when it is not. But what if the function of the footnotes (as well as of the philosophical pretensions of jurisprudence more generally) is not to ensure rigor but to conceal intellectual sloppiness?

A brief survey of the use of footnotes in the fifty-two law review articles published within the first 21 days of this year (2019) should be as illuminating as any random sample would be. Out of the 52 articles, 21 are peer-edited; 21 are refereed, and only 10 are student-edited. The peer edited articles come from *Preview of United States Supreme Court Cases* (12) and *Criminal Justice and Behavior* (9). The refereed articles come from *Innovation Policy and the Economy* (6) and *Trusts and Estates* (15). The student-edited articles and comments come from UMKC *Law Review* (5 + 3), and *Widener Commonwealth Law Review* (5 + 2). The five articles in *Widener* had 738 footnotes, with a median of 105 per article or 4.3 footnotes per page. In summary, the student-authored comments had more footnotes than the other articles. My simple empirical anecdote can be further amended by showing that first-tier law journals publish articles with even more numerous and larger-in-content footnotes. Let it be.

My guess is that footnotes have become proof of intellectual pedigree. Quantitatively, they tell little about the quality of the article because they are so easy to beef up with unlimited "id.," "see supra," etc. But also, when they are substantive, I wonder why the content has to be in a footnote. Is it necessary for the argument? If so, then put it in the body of the article. If not, then erase it. Otherwise, footnotes offer little else than a façade behind which to hide. Perhaps more telling about the intellectual impact of an article is the number of times the article's author was cited. But footnoting in itself creates only one certainty, it imposes on law library collection's unnecessary development of "Bluebooking rules" – or asking *American Bar Association (ABA)*-required institutions to purchase in-print primary sources where there should be no need.

Jurisprudential irony resides also in its prescriptivism – on supplying practical solutions that can be implemented by government actors – when the current form of liberalism hails private enterprise and assails the very legitimacy of state actors. That irony is rich. Heavily ideological, such practical solutions would need a disclaimer. They build on the current status quo, so those solutions are limited in scope, leaving the reader, the textual interpellator hungry for more, at the very least. At most, the textual interpellator craves an alternative proposal which would need to be imagined. For instance, even when producing an article about how the jury system is implemented (T_1), S_1 may write an implied, or overt criticism, or just pure approval. S_1 can do it in a discreet disingenuous manner, or encourage the reader S_2 to see the ideological limits of the writing, bridging a cultural gap, if any between S_1 and S_2 over the meaning of T_1.

Irony is equally evident in jurisprudence on depoliticized, process-oriented arguments that purport to transcend traditional ideological and political divides. For instance, when David Pozen wrote about elective versus non-elective judiciaries, he discovered three ironic – unexpected, even opposite – effects of the normalization of judicial elections (2008). One of his examples is perhaps the clearest instance of scholastic irony: a law review article exploring the ability to talk about judicial elections as having equally reached both radicalization and normalization because of their campaign spending, partisan rancor, and political speech:

> all [these] new features [...] we have come to expect, if not entirely to embrace, in our legislative and executive races. In the broader scheme of electoral law and politics in the United States, judicial elections have not gone wild; they have gone normal. The double nature of these developments–the way they represent both a mainstreaming and a radicalizing phenomenon–helps explain why they pose such a difficult challenge for critics of judicial elections and why many participants in the conversation can appear to be talking past each other.
> POZEN 2008: 307–308

Pozen's noted irony, supplemented by two additional ironic situations in his intriguing work, might even be described as procedural. The end results, the elected judges are not much different than the appointed judges. They have the same background, the same education, and probably the same ideological baggage. The only difference might be their private subjectivity, their alienation, their individual way of incorporating the public power structure, or how they view themselves within the system, not how the system views them (all are vetted if reach judgeship). So, the irony I see in Pozen's work is that Pozen does not see the normalcy of the elective judiciary in the very results it produces. In my opinion, Pozen's work supports the status quo. Empirically speaking, elective judges might protect the status quo even more zealously because they are elected along the existing two-party system. Had those judges been elected otherwise, then, that would be a different situation, wouldn't it?

Finally, jurisprudential irony is also substantive. The issue is too vast to be addressed here, but I will accept the challenge posed by David Pozen about the irony behind the widely felt imperative to be "faithful" to our (im)perfect Constitution (Pozen 2016).

> Americans want to believe they are being faithful to the Constitution, Balkin observes; "they need it to be so." (Id.: 946)

This imperative is felt by judges as well as by the academe. In a monumental law review article, *Our Perfect Constitution*, Henry Paul Monaghan (1981) engaged in the most articulate and intellectually honest legal scholarship conceivable on the issue of constitutional meaning. Monaghan is a proponent of originalism that is moderated by *stare decisis*. As a scholar, S_1, Monaghan made his biases explicit in footnote 53, rather than in the body of the text, which may raise the issue of the chosen location of this announcement:

> I reject any thesis that treats constitutional doctrine as simply an epiphenomenal manifestation of some deeper determinant, such as the economic organization of society.
> MONAGHAN 1981: 360

More explicitly, Monaghan is neither a Marxian nor a Marxist. For Monaghan, law is not part of the superstructure, determined by the economic organization of society, but while he seems to subscribe to the theory that law is a human product that escapes many of the rules affecting human products, we cannot tell whether law has a limited lifespan or whether it can be preserved for eternity (like religion). That, Monaghan does not say. This is vastly different from Justice Stephen Breyer's position, for instance, who subscribes to a view of law and constitutional jurisprudence which weighs consequences, "in terms of basic constitutional purposes," much more than legalese, be them: "language, history, tradition, and precedent alone" (Monaghan 2004: 32). While Breyer is no Marxian either, Breyer seems to add real limits to jurisprudence: contingent consequences. Monaghan decries such jurisprudential conception devoid of the abstract constraint of the original content of the law (id.).

A quarter of a century later (2004), when writing about Justice Ginsburg's constitutional theory, Monaghan adds historicism to his originalism. He seems to align his views with those of Justice Ginsburg, whose theory he calls the correct version of originalism because it considers "historically constrained evolution" (36–38). This original understanding relies on evolution that is not "too much change" (id.: 38).

I am not here to promote or demote any particular views: inherently all scholastic relevance is temporary. I just question whether there is a strong connection between a scholar's ideology and the "reasoned narrative" it chooses. Furthermore, because, Monaghan makes his ideology clear, his writing has little ambiguity and irony.

The irony I detect comes from the (lack of) difference between his 1981 and the 2004 version of his theory. In other words, how much influence does one's ideology have over one's legal argument? And that is the main jurisprudential irony: we can only write what we can imagine, and we imagine what is ideologically accessible. Would Monaghan (1981) write, "In short perhaps the constitution guarantees only representative democracy, not perfect government," (396) had he let himself imagine writing an argument from a different ideological perspective? I don't know. But I do know that he thinks his views similar to those of the late Justice Scalia due to their similar private subjectivity – education and upbringing. Both were brought up in pre-Vatican II Roman Catholicism. I can only admire the scholar for his thought processing transparency. And I engage their works with a similar meaning-making outcome.

Monaghan's ideological transparency makes it easier for subsequent scholars to understand his theory without substituting, or meaning-guessing, because of ideological omissions. Rather than guessing, criticism would be built on a strong foundation devoid of lacunae. The irony, as actuated by S_2's ideology, would add to T_1 and would only interject meaning rather than supplant it. For instance, to Monaghan's conclusion that constitutional jurisprudence cannot ever promote a perfect government, but only a representative democracy, S_2's ideological irony could add that a perfect government is a representative democracy. However, that representative democracy cannot rest on some July Fourth 1776 formula. If we are still unsure why that is undesirable today, I believe reading Marx, and American Marxists such as Claudia Jones, would make those reasons easily apparent.

5 Jurisprudential Irony and the Supreme Court: The Case of Justice Antonin Scalia and Justice Neil Gorsuch

Meaning-making is heavily influenced by the textual instigator's (S_1) and the textual interpellator's (S_2) subjectivity. Case in point is the fluctuating meaning of Thomas Paine's work *Common Sense* (T_1), which reclaims different meaning within different historical contingencies. The difference of meaning is ironical.

The only difference is the textual instigator's ideology (S_2) and the historical contingency. Here are Paine's words:

> But where, say some, is the King of America? I'll tell you, friend, he reigns above, and doth not make havoc of mankind like the Royal Brute of Great Britain. Yet that we may not appear to be defective even in earthly honors, let a day be solemnly set apart for proclaiming the charter; let it be brought forth placed on the divine law, the word of God; let a crown be placed thereon, by which the world may know, that so far as we approve of monarchy, that in America *the law is king*. For as in absolute governments the king is law, so in free countries the law ought to be king; and there ought to be no other.
>
> 1922: 35–36; emphasis in the original

There are instances showing that *Common Sense* (T_1) had different interpellated effects at the time of its writing and centuries later. The ironical difference of meaning can be explained by the ideology of the interpellator (S_2). At the time of its writing, American revolutionaries (S_2) actuated its Republicanism, and the ideological identity between the text-instigator and the text-interpellator gave meaning to the textual embedded irony. At the end of the twentieth century, the late Justice Scalia (S_2) actuated his ideology and supplanted it for Paine's. The ideological difference between the two is so noticeable that the irony of meaning in Scalia's understanding of Paine's work is only increased by its oppositional reading.

When Paine (S_1) penned these ideas, his Republican ideology was matched by that of the American revolutionaries (S_2) for whom it was written. Their ideology negotiated the meaning of Paine's metaphor about "the law is king" (id.). At that historical moment, Paine's uninhibited Republicanism was shared by his audience. His words were given meaning according to the textual irony Paine embedded in his text. Accessed in pubs and other open spaces, *Common Sense* was a scathing critique of Britain.

Paine asked for a government of laws as norms to be passed by duly elected legislative bodies following pre-approved procedures. He rejected the tyrannically whimsical monarchy. From his purview, the Rule of Law would oversee a republican government whose foundation was an institutional system of checks and balances. His writings show that he favored as little individual input as possible, while fully aware that the American legal common law system, unlike the continental civil law system, enabled all judges to create law within the limits of the binding precedent.

Nothing about Paine's *Common Sense* could be explicitly construed either in favor of or against a privileged position for jurists. He did not address the issue of particularly situated judges, though, he thought that he made his intentions clear and in light of how the American Revolution happened. The negotiating meaning seemed to be close to the literal meaning of the text. I call that omission the dormant irony, which conditions the meaning of Paine's metaphor: *law is king.*

Paine's republican ideology has been influential throughout the centuries and has been assumed by subsequent textual interpellators of his work (S_2). His metaphor about the role of the Rule of Law remained popular. Its meaning seemed all settled for eternity, for it dominated Paine's ideology and the contingency of its creation: the time of the American Revolution.

It is thus unexpected to discover a fluctuation in meaning regarding Paine's famous metaphor. Two hundred years later, the only objective difference is the historical contingency and the scholars' subjectivity. However, because the meaning negotiated between Paine and the late Justice Scalia is so wildly and ironically different from the earlier meaning, it means that whatever happened to change the balance is meaningful. While Paine's ideology was indubitably Republicanism, Scalia's evolved into Oligarchism.

In 1989, Scalia (S_2) engaged Paine's work (T_1), in his article, "The Rule of Law as A Law of Rules," published *The Chicago Law Review.* That article, devoted to the American Rule of Law, ironically, started with an ode to a monarch, Saint Louis, who, ten centuries ago, devoid of any formal legal education, dispensed justice under a tree:

> Louis IX of France, Saint Louis, was renowned for the fair and even-handed manner in which he dispensed justice. We have the following account from The Life of Saint Louis written by John of Joinville, a nobleman from Champagne and a close friend of the king:

> In summer, after hearing mass, the king often went to the wood of Vincennes, where he would sit down with his back against an oak, and make us all sit round him. Those who had any suit to present could come to speak to him without hindrance from an usher or any other person. The king would address them directly, and ask: "Is there anyone here who has a case to be settled?" Those who had one would stand up. Then he would say: "Keep silent all of you, and you shall be heard in turn, one after the other."

> SCALIA 1989: 1175

Employing a remnant of Socratic Method, Scalia wonders how Paine would have felt about this particular monarch. He then goes on and cites the famous words of Paine:

> [L]et a day be solemnly set apart for proclaiming the charter; let it be brought forth ... [so] the world may know, that so far we approve of monarchy, that in America *the law is king*. For as in absolute governments the king is law, so in free countries the law *ought* to be king; and there ought to be no other.
>> Id.: 1188; emphasis in the original

In his writings, Scalia wants to talk about the virtues of the American Rule of Law as a Law of Rules, presumably opposed to the Civil Law Rule of Law, which it is not.

> It is this dichotomy between "general rule of law" and "personal discretion to do justice" that I wish to explore.

Paine's view on the Rule of Law has been so easily accepted that it has become like Nietzsche's metaphorical knowledge, which, through frequent usage, fills in as an approximation of hegemonic acceptance (Nietzsche 1999: 400). Given the mythical status of Paine's Republicanism, Scalia's interpretation of Paine's opinion on the Rule of Law is noticeably different:

> In a democratic system, of course, the general rule of law has special claim to preference, since it is the normal product of that branch of government most responsive to the people. Executives and judges handle individual cases; the legislature generalizes. *Statutes that are seen as establishing rules of inadequate clarity or precision are criticized, on that account, as undemocratic – and, in the extreme, unconstitutional – because they leave too much to be decided by persons other than the people's representatives.*
>> Id.: at 1176; emphasis added

However, the unconstitutional and undemocratic nature of statutes is too much to swallow in a thirteen-page article. So, Scalia limits his discussion to instances where a common law judge, who follows well-established rules, is free to "make law" in the absence of precedent.

> For I want to explore the dichotomy between general rules and personal discretion within the narrow context of law that is made by the courts.
>> Id.: 1989

Before he explores that dichotomy, from a comparative perspective, Scalia presents his view of common law system. Scalia explains, admiringly, because it does not rely upon overarching generalizations. Moreover, it leaves "considerable room for future judges" (id.: 1177), and that is "the genius of the common law system" (id.). He continues, by stating that the Continental civil law system does not offer judges such roles. He contends that they are supposed to follow the letter of the codified statutes, published in "codes." Although Jean Guillaume Locré (1827), as Peter Strauss (2014) points out, clearly explains that this textual slavishness is mostly imagined by the non-civil law academe.

A product of American Ivy League Schools, Scalia continues with what starts to seem like false admiration, as if planting the seeds of irony.

> When I was in law school, I was a great enthusiast for this approach – an advocate of both writing and reading the "holding" of a decision narrowly, thereby *leaving greater discretion to future courts.*
> 1989: 1178; emphasis added

By now, Scalia's use of Paine's work is almost confusing. On one hand he admires Louis IX's acting as the supreme law and he calls statutes undemocratic, and on the other hand he refers to the genius of the Common Law. However, there are clues. At one point, Scalia almost references the United States Supreme Court monarchically when he says, "*my* Court" (id.). In itself, this appellation may mean nothing more than a mere identification with the locus of the Court as the supreme court of the land in his heart. Or, it may mean a megalomaniacal appropriation of the institution, like a monarch discussing his court.

From that hierarchical position of power, Scalia goes on to declare that the genius of the common law, that very freedom of all judges – both present and future – to be antiquated. And if it needed more clarification, he adds, the common law "discretion-conferring approach is ill-suited" (id.: 1178). The solution seems to be that future judges should follow Scalia's precedent as if he were Saint Louis.

The pretense of admiration apparently ended perhaps when Scalia discovered the rift between practicing judicial ascendancy, using Peter Strauss' vocabulary. Preaching judicial subordination, Scalia started to admire certain judges within the common law system who could act as if they were the law codified in the civil law system. Those were the individual judges whose decisions could replace the codified law because of the power of their judgment.

As well, Justice Scalia's judiciary admiration endorses unfettered powers for particular members of the judiciary. He seems to be amending John Adams' words in Art. XXX of Part First, Massachusetts Constitution of 1780. Additionally,

Scalia endorses the end of the government of laws replacing it with a government of (nine) men.

> In the government of this commonwealth, the legislative department shall never exercise the executive and judicial powers, or either of them; the executive shall never exercise the legislative and judicial powers, or either of them; the judicial shall never exercise the legislative and executive powers, or either of them; to the end it may be a government of laws, and not of men.
>
> SWINDLER 1979: 96

This roundabout presentation of the contextual reading of Paine's metaphor in Scalia's textualism indicates a development of the metaphor's connotation to mean its opposite: the American Rule of Law is a Law of Nine Justices. There is irony of meaning between Paine's work centuries ago, and that which is negotiated by Scalia, the text-interpellator. Scalia seems to use Paine's metaphor devoid of meaning, as mere procedure. Or worse, to endorse not the Rule of Law, but its guardians. Or better said, its Highest Priests, the Justices of the United States Supreme Court, "ought to be king."

This difference of meaning is possible because all scholarship based on linguistic theoretical explanations, reflects the textual instigator's, S_1, and interpellator's, S_2, subjectivity – their alienation and ideology. Irony actuates the tension between the existing state of scholarship as viewed by S_1, and its potentiality, as viewed by S_2. Often dormant until S_2 engages the text, T_1, irony actuates how the world views the particular scholarship in the process of understanding the text, by interpellating it.

To be able to judge irony, thus, actuating T_1's subjectivity, let's focus for a moment on some philosophical roots that American jurisprudence shares with Marx's works.

Talking about appointed judges and justices, I find it ironic that the man whose own relatively recent rise to judicial prominence as a member of the highest court in the nation, a man whose role it is to make sure that the Rule of Law is respected, is himself a symbol of the illegitimacy of his own appointment. While President Barack Obama nominated a different candidate for that same job (Eilperin and DeBonis 2016), the Senate refused to act (Boyer 2016). Then Obama's successor appointed Neil Gorsuch, and the Senate got the job done. In the process, the Republican Senators destroyed filibuster rules (Davis and Landlerjan 2017).

Another irony comes a couple of years earlier when Gorsuch, then a federal circuit judge, wrote a piece entitled "Law's Irony," published by *Harvard Journal of Law and Policy* (2014). Like Dickens in *Bleak House* (1853), or even like Johann Wolfgang von Goethe (1882), who apparently abandoned the practice of law after witnessing thousands of aging cases waiting vainly for resolution in the courts of his time (119), Gorsuch views the delay in the administration of justice with an ironic eye. He points out that the adoption of the "modern" rules of civil procedure in 1938 marked the start of a self-proclaimed "experiment" with expansive pre-trial discovery – something previously unknown to the federal courts. Gorsuch jokes about the appellative "new" and "modern" for the rules of civil procedure, more than 70 years later,

> [n]ow, that's a pretty odd thing, when you think about it. Maybe the only thing that really sounds new or modern after seventy years is Keith Richards of the Rolling Stones. Some might say he looks like he's done some experimenting, too.
> GORSUCH 2014: 745

The banter continues, without much explanation as to why this is possible in law. Gorsuch points out that the 1938 assumption about the importance of readily available access to an opponent's information in civil disputes, which would apparently achieve fairer and cheaper merit-based resolutions, actually proved inaccurate (Sunderland 1939). In fact, Gorsuch cited the Interim Report on the Joint Project of the American College of Trial Lawyers. While that may be true for parties with monies to start the process,

> eighty percent of the American College of Trial Lawyers say that discovery costs and delays keep injured parties from bringing valid claims to court.
> ACTL and IAALS 2008: A6

Using irony, Gorsuch is able to mediate between idea and actuality. By pointing out the contradictions, he shows how the rules of civil discovery are not doing what they are meant to do. Gorsuch is critical of the situation he is discussing, and how the 1938 rules of discovery are applied in the twenty-first century.

Irony is particularly suited for legal theory because legal theories challenge actuality and posit a replacement. They have a standpoint, and more importantly, their polemic is an introduction that is simultaneously a conclusion. The oppositional new principle is introduced as a possibility, as Kierkegaard (1965) would have said (237).

As Gorsuch illustrated, law is full of incongruous tensions. On one hand, the law must regulate the authenticity of its own instruments (contracts, wills, statutes, recommendations, etc.), and in this self-regulation, the aspects of the central cases are in tension. A civil lawsuit centered on a contract focuses on two aspects: the content of the agreement of the parties and the legitimacy of the parties. In other words, the contract needs to be legal (a good agreement).

Not everything that represents the freedom of the parties can be negotiated into an agreement which would be recognized in court as a contract. Ironically, the definition of contract rests on precisely that. To put it in another way, think only about the studio session of R&B star R. Kelly filled with 14-year-old-girls, to understand that not every freely negotiated freedom becomes an enforceable contract. This type of irony, which is embedded in law, is perhaps made clearer by this statement from Cicero (1895), in defense of Cluentius: law makes servants of us all for the very purpose "to set us free." (LII).

The irony surrounding Gorsuch continues. In his new capacity as a U.S. Supreme Court Justice, he joins Justices Clarence Thomas and Samuel Alito in chipping away at our Rule of Law. In recent Court decisions, such the *per curiam* decision in *Trump v. International Refugee Assistance Project*, 582 U.S., 137 S.Ct. 2080 (2017), Gorsuch agreed to hear arguments on President Donald Trump's travel ban, *Executive Order No. 13769, Protecting the Nation from Foreign Terrorist Entry Into the United States (EO-1)*, 82 Fed.Reg. 8977. In the ruling, its highest priests and guardians, the justices, gave it a disastrous blow. Hopefully, this is all temporary, especially if we persist in exposing the irony behind all procedural stuffiness.

CHAPTER 9

Philosophical Camaraderie, Ideological Difference, and Irony

Marxian theory is abstract and often its language is filled with references to German philosophy so hard to decipher that it might come across as intellectual snobbism. Ironically, his highbrow cultural background did not endear him to the elite echelons of our jurisprudential representatives, whose legal theories abound in interdisciplinary references, many found in Marx's work as well.

Long ago, Justice Holmes (1881) pointed out the intellectual mélange of jurisprudence. He did not say that jurisprudence melts all of its components into thin air, and neither did he compare them to *Gallerte*. For Justice Holmes, the prevalent moral and political theories – past and present – and even the "prejudices which judges share with their fellow-men" (Holmes 1881: 1), represented the substance of our law and jurisprudence.

Wolfgang Friedmann argued last century that jurisprudence reflected the existing conceptions of man both as thinking individual and political being. Friedmann was playing with the idea of jurisprudence as an intellectual potpourri, a mixture of many things. More interestingly, he differentiated between the "thinking individual" and the "political being." This tension perhaps explains the particular ironic nature of jurisprudence. By pretending to be something it is not, it opens itself to meaning, which denotes the different, the opposite, or even the travesty of what the text *purportedly* – in legal jargon – says. Perhaps, that is why he then continued,

> all legal theory must contain elements of philosophy – man's reflections on his position in the universe – and gain its color and specific content from political theory – the ideas entertained on the best form of society.
> FRIEDMANN 1967: 3

Friedmann referred to jurisprudential scholarship from a textual perspective, ignoring irony as a secondary construct of meaning actuated in the process of communicating the text, and understanding it, during the meaning-making process. Most jurists ignore the communication element in their writings, perhaps, because all jurists believe that there is a method of legal writing that makes all ideas clear and unambiguous.

Or, maybe Friedmann, like many theoreticians, limited irony to the work of the ironist, or more specifically, "the explicitly intentionalist" (Hutcheon 1995: 111). These are the "intentional" ironies, or the "stable" ironies, which are intended, and overt as Linda Hutcheon (1995) explains, were meant to be "reconstructed" (id.) by the textual interpellator. While interesting, this aspect of irony is only a facet of the process discussed here, which covers both the encoded irony – sometimes open and obvious – but especially the decoded irony – whose growth comes from the encoded and decoded irony. Or, the irony which exists in the eye of the beholder.

Jurisprudence is one of those clear concepts that does not hold the same theoretical position for all. For some, jurisprudence represents the hallmark of American legal thought. For others, it comes close to Althusser's view of chauvinism, which can take the "form of the simplest kind of stupidity: ignorance" (Althusser 1959/1972: 163).

For those detractors, legal theory or "jurisprudence"

> is of importance only if it contributes to problem-solving for our profession and society, and if it does not, then, there is no reason why it should be incorporated in the law school curriculum and distract the attention of those preparing to serve their communities and fellow citizens from matters of real importance.
> REISMAN and SCHREIBER 1987: 11

Jurisprudence in this instance is viewed in opposition to the life that the average legal practitioner leads: a life closer to the job of a plumber than the office of a priest (id.). Legal theories, like history or literary criticism, have a limited value: they "advance one's understanding of the intellectual discipline which is its subject" (Mirfield 1989: 986). Still, there is significant value in that role, and there is meaning derived from the ways in which that role is achieved. For instance, legal theories advance legal understanding while creating an epistemological hierarchy of importance. Issues which are not presented at the top will not be perceived as primordial. Employing different standards, legal theories clear their normative path of reality using or dispensing with descriptive narratives.

American legal jurisprudence, to the extent it promotes and protects a business-like individualism, has always been deeply pragmatic within the Jamesian "whatever works is right" (James 1912: 1009) mentality. As earlier, Marxian thought is very pragmatic in its search of action and practical implementation of theoretical narratives. American jurisprudence is also much indebted to Western European thinkers formed during the scholastic tradition of Antiquity, the Entitlement, and various subsequent social and political revolutions.

This chapter contains a brief history of the philosophical roots of American jurisprudence, pointing out their remarkable essentialism, binary terminology, along with labels identifying fluid concepts, utopian arguments, and a thorough construction of legal apologies for political decisions. The shared philosophical roots between American jurisprudence and Marxian thought will point to yet another aspect of the North American Marxian paradox – rejection in the absence of knowledge. Or, to continue paraphrasing Jeremy Bentham and his concept of contextual definition, one might refer to the Marxian rejection by American jurisprudence as contextual rejection.

Marxian thought may become inspirational because of its devotion to history and reality viewed in all its beautiful cacophony. Law embodies the story of a nation's development through many centuries, and it cannot be dealt with as if it were a book of mathematical axioms or, perhaps worse, facts that were rounded to fit particular experiential theories.

On the other hand, dialectics, a method of inquiry that has influenced our highly regarded Founding Fathers and those emulating them, still suffers because of its contextual connection with Marx. But dialectics itself is a concept widely misinterpreted. A dialectical approach might involve raising questions, as in Plato's *Dialogues*, to expose contradictions within an opponent's position. For Plato, it was supposed to make the coherent and defensible answer irresistible. In that representation, ironically, dialectics still remains the dominant method of teaching in American law schools even today. It is known as the Socratic Method, and it is far removed from how Marx used it.

Like any other theoretical systems, American jurisprudence is much indebted to that which preceded it, as many scholars have pointed out. However, others, including Richard Posner or Bruce Ackerman, believe the reverse. Ackerman wrote:

> To discover the Constitution, we must approach it without the assistance of guides imported from another time and place. Neither Aristotle nor Cicero, Montesquieu nor Locke, Harrington nor Hume, Kant nor Weber will provide the key.
> ACKERMAN 1991: 3

Certainly, law by its very government of human relations is dynamic and heavily contextualized. To the extent that law is taught and administered by people, their cultural matrix (including, of course, its philosophical traditions) will affect that particular legal regime, irrespective of any desires to the contrary that one may have. It is this cultural matrix in action that I am trying to understand, while briefly exposing the pedigree of American jurisprudence.

Like the country's political agenda nowadays, the academic intellectual agenda seems to be driven by conservatives. Consequently, the Left has been derisively limited to the linguistic position of political correctness, which is further derided as the vocabulary of the existing Regime of Truth, "code" for aloof entitlement.

> It is well documented that American universities today are dominated, more than ever before, by academics on the left end of the political spectrum. How should these academics handle opinions that depart, even quite sharply from their "politically correct" views?
> WAX 2018

Given that jurisprudential meaning-making has a disproportionate role in the existing Regime of Truth, and that the vocabulary in use is that of political correctness, meaning-making is heavily under attack by the conservatives and with relatively little import for promoting communitarian well-being. As a result, we are faced with a crisis of values to the extent that values are scholarly-promoted. Understanding the cloak of subjectivity of all scholarship, be it alienation or ideology, this would add to the process of exposing knowledge production, as well as the prevalence of a particular Regime of Truth imbedded with a particular ideology.

1   Plato's Concepts of Just and Justice

While some scholars believe that Plato has been neglected in American jurisprudence (Hall 1949: 566), others' work (Brennan 2002; Yoshino 2005) urges the opposite. For me, Plato resonates with Thomas Paine's guardians of law, which makes his teachings so relevant. I shall explain.

In Plato's better-known dialogue, *The Republic*, the political rulers and guardians of Utopia were the thinkers and the philosophers. Plato has a complex view of philosophers, similar to Arendt's "public intellectual," I would argue. In *Republic, Book* IV.*421a*, Plato views them as "guardians of the laws and the city," (Plato: 98). When he decides that philosophers also "must rule," Plato goes a step further. Philosophers stopped being theoretical: in *Republic, Book* VI, *500a*, they become "orderly and divine, to the extent possible for a human being" (id.: 180). In becoming guardians, philosophers are ready to act as warriors too, able to complete their assigned duty. Thus, they are and behave in a *just* manner: like all others, they do "what's appropriate," to their status, "minding their own business" (id.). In the process, they made the city *just*.

Plato might not have invented powerful descriptors, or what we perceive today as easily-dispensable labels. Nor, might he have been the first to introduce binary terminology, which continues to be widely used. But, surely, he exploited it. Since his time, *just* and *unjust*, for instance, have been commonly applied in legal philosophy. For Plato, a ruler can be just and is *just*, despite his quasi-absolute exercise of power over his subjects:

> And you are so far off about the *just* and *justice*, and the *unjust* and *injustice*, that you are unaware that *justice* and the *just* are really someone else's good, the advantage of the man who is stronger and rules, and a personal harm to the man who obeys and serves. *Injustice* is the opposite, and it rules the truly simple and *just*; and those who are ruled do what is advantageous for him who is stronger, and they make him whom they serve happy but themselves not at all. And this must be considered, most simple Socrates: the *just* man everywhere has less than the *unjust* man. First, in contracts, when the *just* man is a partner of the *unjust* man, you will always find that at the dissolution of the partnership the *just* man does not have more than the *unjust* man, but less. Second, in matters pertaining to the city, when there are taxes, the *just* man pays more on the basis of equal property, the *unjust* man less; and when there are distributions, the one makes no profit, the other much.
>
> PLATO, *Book* I, ⁋ 21: 343

Plato, the legal theorist, never leaves philosophical abstractions aside when he talks about law and the city-state as a legal entity. Thus, he is never innocent of using labels as misnomers: In *Republic, Book* V, *479d9–480a11*, Socrates asks Glaucon, "Must we call [the rulers] philosophers, rather than lovers of opinion those who delight in each thing that is itself [and why]?" Indeed, when you have the power to define your work and your title, does it make any difference whether you are called a philosopher or a guardian of the law and the city? It does if peace is valued more than chaos and anarchy. Thus, Plato engages in legitimization. Since then, all legal theorists have done the same.

Plato's "Utopia" does not profess equal justice. Utopia is merely *just* with its people because its rulers do what is legal and what is allowed. Plato's circular argument seems to be formal: what is legal is *just* and vice-versa. In *Nichomachean Ethics, Book 5, 2.* Aristotle uses the same formalism in his discussion of justice. In Plato's Utopia, the guardians' privilege were *just*, because they were legal. Now, if it were to stop there, Plato's argument would have been forgettable. But he continued, stating that power inequality was *just* because of the people who exercised it: the philosophizing-guardians were wise and educated, thus expected to act for the good of the community and of the commoners, as well as of the soldiers.

Plato's intellectual exercise is worth mentioning because he legitimizes moderation (for haves and have-nots) as a way to ensure a *just* state. For Plato, a *just* state takes care of its less privileged population, the commoners and soldiers, while bestowing the most benefits, education, and social honor on the guardians (philosophers). He never opens the discussion questioning whether such a way of taking care of people is *just*. Perhaps, because he preempts that question by extolling the benefits of cooperation, people cooperate and do their assigned jobs. The *just* state assigns soldiers the job of soldiers, commoners that of farmers, and the guardians receive the task of watching over everybody doing their job.

Plato's *just* label relies on the perception that "doing one's assigned job" is what society values most and Utopia's guardians ensure this *de minimis* welfare state. Utopia could ensure that its citizens are safe from military occupation and are able to avoid famine. If we think about Plato's own experience, having lived through famine and defeat in Athens, perhaps that was the most justice he could have expected from a just state.

I view Plato's *Republic* as the debut of legal theorists as thinkers about the law and its legitimacy. He introduced concepts to both explain and legitimize law-making and adjudication at a particular moment in society – all of which were according to his own set of values and ideology. Though apparently historically limited, Plato's concepts have become, perhaps ironically, a perennial benchmark in legal and political theory. By now, this binary terminology is the epitome of human and state action – *just/unjust* and *justice/injustice*.

At the same time, material wealth (what we have called capital since Marx) was viewed by Plato as a political issue, and he focused on its societal impact in a way that resonates with Marx. Plato presented wealth as destructive as, if not more so, than poverty:

> "So, as it seems, we've found other things for the guardians to guard against in every way so that these things never slip into the city without their awareness."
>
> "What are they?"
>
> "Wealth and poverty," I said, "since the one produces luxury, idleness, and innovation, while the other produces illiberality and wrongdoing as well as innovation."
>
> "Most certainly," he said. "However, Socrates, consider this: how will our city be able to make war when it possesses no money, especially if it's compelled to make war against a wealthy one?"

> "It's plain," I said, "that against one it would be harder, but against two of that sort it would be easier."
> "How do you mean?" he said.
> "Well," I said, "in the first place, if the guardians should have to fight, won't it be as champions in war fighting with rich men?"
> "Yes," he said, "that's so." "Now, then, Adeimantus," I said, in your opinion, wouldn't one boxer with the finest possible training in the art easily fight with two rich, fat nonboxers?"
> PLATO, *Book* IV *421e–422a, b,* ₽ 99

Perhaps Bertrand Russell took his cue from Plato when Russell (1945) observes that every *society* has known its guardians, "the Jesuits in old Paraguay, the ecclesiastics in the States of the Church until 1870, and the Communist Party in the U.S.S.R." (109). But, Russell neglects to include the guardians of liberal democracies such as ours. Could it be that, ironically, the beneficiaries of privilege in our more democratic societies, unlike the guardians of Utopia, find the simple life devoid of ostentatiousness repugnant? I dare say, yes.

> [T]o the extent that the work of the guardians is more important, it would require more leisure time than the other tasks as well as greater art and diligence.
> PLATO, *Book* II: 51

2 Aristotle's Dialectical Universals

Both John Adams and Thomas Jefferson regarded Aristotle "as one of the first formulators of the principles of the American founding" (Johnson 2002: 29). The influence of Aristotelian philosophy on legal theory is evident, and Jerome Frank discussed at length the transmission of Aristotle's Rule of Law into American jurisprudence (Frank 1942: 190–211). Aristotle's ideas have had an enormously beneficial effect on modern theories of justice and equality. His treatises on logic are inextricably linked to the tradition of legal reasoning underlying modern and historical American jurisprudence

Focusing on the binary vocabulary, Bertrand Russell tells us, Aristotle espoused his theory as a professor who was extremely fond of universals, whose content defines terminology, and labels, not vice-versa (Russell 1945: 161). *On Interpretation*, Aristotle (350 B.C.) wrote:

> Some things are universal, others individual. By the term "universal" I mean that which is of such a nature as to be predicated of many subjects,

by "individual" that which is not thus predicated. Thus "man" is a universal "Callias" and individual.

ARISTOTLE 2000: 3–5

While it may seem a bit convoluted, still, it is reasonable to say that for Aristotle, the "universal" label defined something that could not exist by itself, but only in particular things. Man could exist only as Callias in his example.

Aristotle also labeled behavior in virtues and vices, where virtues were taught and acquired. Among the latter was *justice*. However, the meaning of *justice* was not clear from its name. In *The Art of Rhetoric*, Aristotle further qualified *just* and *justice* as "beautiful" because of the effect they produced on those who did not possess them, and then declared *justice* to be a legal label connected to ownership:

> *justice*, indeed, is a virtue through which everyone legally possesses what is his own; and *injustice* is that through which a man possesses the property of others, contrary to law.
>
> ARISTOTLE 1818: 51; emphasis added

Additionally, *justice* also resulted from the mere act of judging in a "court of justice." As a result, in the fifth book of the *Nichomachean Ethics*, Aristotle opposed *justice* and *injustice* formally, while he bequeathed several meanings on both terms.

Aristotle further explained that there were instances in which meaning could not be conveyed clearly by individual examples, labels or definitions. Labels were insufficiently clear and their conveyed meaning ambiguous, "as the different things covered by the common name are very closely related, the fact that they are different escapes notice" (id.). For those instances, Aristotle found a more reliable way to express meaning: metaphorically. Two opposite labels would provide meaning to each other. In this way, Aristotle escaped the need to define concepts. Even when he talks about "justice" and "injustice," concepts which seem clear because of each other but which are not so clear when the ambiguity is simply not noticed. Not that it does not exist, but the correlation is sufficient to make the terms workable.

In Aristotle's *Book 5.1* and *Book 5.3*, "justice" and "injustice" seem to be ambiguous. But, because their different meanings approach near to one another, the ambiguity escapes notice and is not obvious as it is, comparatively, when the meanings are far apart. This way of creating meaning through contextualization rather than mere literal definitions has been embraced by all scholarship, especially when concepts are too complex to explain. Contextualization seems to contain the seeds of deflating misperceptions. Perhaps, if the scholar's attempts would be prefaced with an acknowledgment of the subjective bias it includes, this would not happen.

Ironically, the Aristotelian conflicting views on justice have had the most traction in American jurisprudence from its formal to its more substantive meaning. What is often forgotten though, is the method Aristotle used to give meaning to this ambiguous virtue. Aristotelian dialectics incorporated Plato's formal thinking (justice is that what is legal) then built on it to the extent that it negated its perceived shallowness. In the end, justice became a universal label with a rectifying effect, and in the process, justice also took on a facet of equality.

From Aristotle onward, we can talk about *unjust* as unequal and by default of *just* as equal: "If then, the unjust is unequal, just is equal, as all men suppose it to be." But, what their meaning exactly covers is anybody's guess, until all is put in the historical perspective of that moment.

Marx, too, was fond of creating meaning outside of the strict confinements of definitions. As shown earlier, in *Capital*, for instance, talking about commodities, Marx explains the concept of exchange value as a metaphor for *Gallerte* (gelatin) (Sutherland 2011: 37), "a mere congelation of homogeneous human labor" (Marx 1887: 5). At first blush, it looks like a quantitative relation, as the proportion in which values in use of one sort are exchanged for those of another sort (id.). But for two items to be exchangeable their value has to be equal to a "third which in itself is neither the one nor the other" (id.: 4). Step by step, Marx brings the reader to the realization that the commonality among all the items exchanged on the market is their use-value which comes from their property of being "products of labor" (id.). Their existence as "material things" disappears and what is left is their embodiment of "human labor in the abstract" (id.).

Marx does not let ambiguity take over understanding. As Parekh (1982) shows, Marx went for the socio-economic historical context of his analysis. And where definitions were missing, Marx searched for metaphorical visualization. The human labor in the abstract he describes as gelatin, in German, "*Gallerte*." Sutherland (2011) believes that the image of a somewhat disgusting semisolid, tremulous, comestible mass, which cannot be converted back to meat and bones, expresses best how the laborer's efforts are viewed by the capitalist (37–42). The capitalist, who is the beneficiary of the use-value incorporated into each commodity, and who lives off the laborer's efforts, nevertheless is disgusted by the source of his living. This attitude, perhaps, explains Marx's embrace of the exploited masses' ideology, because I know it explains mine.

3 Thomas Hobbes and John Locke's Ideological Differences Lead to Diverse Epistemological Conclusions

Thomas Hobbes, with John Locke, Jean-Jacques Rousseau and Jeremy Bentham, provide American jurisprudence with its most well-known pedigree. The famous debate between H.L.A. Hart (1958) and Lon Fuller (1958) over positivism never reached that level of philosophical respect.

It is widely accepted that Thomas Hobbes, John Locke, and Jean-Jacques Rousseau had influenced most our Founding Fathers due to their work on the social contract theory that articulates the dichotomy between government power and individual liberty. Generally, Hobbes is credited with first articulating the social contract theory of government formation in response to an unappealing picture of life in the state of nature (Watts 2014). To begin with, Hobbes and Locke were both similar, and yet, conspicuously different. How can two outstanding scholars with similar cultural background produce such dissimilar work? One, Hobbes,' is subservient and thus perceived as steeped in fear, while Locke's is remarkably programmatic.

Hobbes' *Leviathan* was written in response to Cromwell's politics. Because of this direct connection to the politics of his time, some believe that Hobbes placed his scholarship in the service of unquestioned subservience. Perhaps. But what is notable are Hobbes' research methods. He employed empirical observation to legitimize monarchal legal authority and unlimited state powers. Hobbes rationalized his position by stating that people could not be trusted to govern themselves because they were not run by reason, but by unlimited love for freedom, which came at the expense of others' freedom. Briefly, the result would have been unending war unless they agreed to submit to a state, called Commonwealth, or *Leviathan*.

Hobbes' state was supposed to take care of its subjects, much within the limits of Plato's *Utopia*. While in the state of nature all humans were equal in pursuing their destructive freedom, within the *Leviathan* they submitted to the authority of one person, the Sovereign, preserving only one freedom, that of self-defense. Ironically, Hobbes did not see any instance when the freedom of self-defense would amount to civil disobedience. That was perhaps because Hobbes did not see any discrepancy or conflict between the absolute social obedience of the subjects and the absolute – undivided and unlimited – sovereign power. Contractually speaking, which is the lens with which Hobbes viewed and analyzed the relationship between sovereign and subject, both the absolute obedience and the absolute power were the two facets of the consideration for entering the "social contract" between the sovereign and his subjects.

Rather than that of a fearful scholar, Hobbes' work is usually, described as lacking optimism. By contrast to Locke's (Seidman 2014), I view Hobbes as an ideologue working to defend absolute monarchy. In the process, Hobbes nevertheless brings law, and all its legal institutions, including property rights, back down to earth: all rights are derived from the state, which is "the commonwealth." In turn, property becomes a right created by the Sovereign, rather than a natural right.

As Russell explains,

> The laws of property are to be entirely subject to the sovereign; for in a state of nature there is no property, and therefore property is created by government, which may control its creation as it pleases.
> RUSSELL 1945: 551–552

Hobbes seems able to easily legitimize or delegitimize an institution, though they are brief conceptual explanations. A monarchy, a government by one person, can easily become a "tyranny"; and an aristocracy, a government by a sector of the population, can develop into an "oligarchy." Hobbes noted:

> For they that are discontented under monarchy, call it tyranny.
> HOBBES: 89–90

Ironically, in his quest for legitimizing absolute monarchy with what I call expedient terminology, Hobbes achieves the opposite. Inadvertently, perhaps, Hobbes enables his opponents to understand their lack of rights. He disregards their position in unflattering terms, but gives them much-needed vocabulary and logical explanations to express new political demands:

> [T]hey which find themselves grieved under a democracy, call it anarchy, which signifies want of government. (Id.: 90)

But those who did not find themselves, grieve under a democracy, they call "popular commonwealth" (id.: 89). With this, Hobbes' writing contains the much-needed vocabulary to express new political demands.

Within this political realm, Hobbes defines "justice" as a human characteristic, or a "law" inherent to human nature. It both pre-and-co-exists with the legal norms of the commonwealth, but only to a limited extent. From a jurisprudential point of view, Hobbs defines legal norms as "civil law," from the Latin *civitas* or state (id.: 123), or, what we call today the sovereign domestic legal system. A natural law promoter, Hobbes defines it as to each human his own. When *juris prudentia* cannot work (the obedience of subordinate judges), Hobbes defers to the sovereign's judgment in all areas. Hobbes calls *juris prudentia*, "the wisdom of subordinate judges" (id.: 125).

At about the same time when Hobbes was writing, John Locke was becoming the "apostle of the Revolution of 1688, the most moderate and the most successful of all revolutions" (Russell 1945: 604). Both his *Essay Concerning Human Understanding* (1690) and his two *Treatises on Government* (1689) were completed by the time of the Glorious Revolution and published in its immediate aftermath. If the Revolution met its aims so perfectly that no subsequent revolution would be necessary in England, as Russell explains, perhaps Locke deserves some of the credit.

Unlike Hobbes' *Leviathan*, whose sovereign controlled his subjects and provided security and peace, Locke refused to substitute an all-powerful tyrant for the many petty tyrants of the state of nature. Locke was also an ideologue. Only, unlike Hobbes, he incorporated revolutionary ideology: his writing represents *the* theoretical tool to promote and legitimize the new type of government. To that extent, Locke's views also shaped American as well as French constitutionalism.

Locke's more theoretical work, his *Essay*, can be seen as a treatise on the usefulness of labels (and their shortcomings). Theoretically, all labels are useful if they make knowledge manageable, but their organizing quality tends to discourage inquiry into the concepts behind them and most probably makes it seem more efficient to prefer labels over analysis. Locke addresses the established opinion that there are primary qualities, notions, truths, or "labels" that help us organize our experiences. In a dialectical manner, Locke argues against the dichotomy of primary and secondary qualities, which he views as dogmatic. His work has little rigidity of thought, as he makes a superhuman effort to consider opposing values, such as the existence of God and scientific truth (mathematics). Furthermore, Locke is able to anticipate Bentham's relativism, so much touted but so different under current liberal theories, in his chapter on "Modes of Pleasure and Pain" (Locke 1884: 128 et seq.).

Things then are good or evil, only in reference to pleasure or pain. That we call good, which is apt to cause or increase pleasure, or diminish pain, in us; or else to procure or preserve us the possession of any other good, or absence of any evil (id.).

He used this relativism in jurisprudence as well.

> [O]ur actions are considered as good, bad, or indifferent; and in this respect, they are relative, it being their *conformity to, or disagreement with some rule that makes them to be regular or irregular*, good or bad: and so,

as far as they are compared with a rule, and thereupon denominated, they come under relation. *Thus the challenging and fighting with a man, as it is a certain positive mode, or particular sort of action, by particular ideas, distinguished from all others, is called dueling: which, when considered in relation to the law of God, will deserve the name sin; to the law of fashion, in some countries, valor and virtue: and to the municipal laws of some governments, a capital crime.* In this case, when the positive mode has one name, and another name as it stands in relation to the law, the distinction may as easily be observed, as it is in substances, where one name, v. g. man, is used to signify the thing; another, v. g. father, to signify the relation.

Id.: 209; emphasis added

Locke's penchant for weighing opposite thoughts makes him see the origin of the state in human prudence, and then preach its value in government, (1689). Other Lockean binary terminology is the dichotomy of private versus public interests. Over the long run, the interplay between those opposed domains, would bring true freedom, Locke asserts:

Government of our passions was the right improvement of liberty.

1689: § 54, 152

Locke refuses to bring the logic of an argument to its inevitably absurd consequences. He substitutes a sounder judgment for a looming extreme dogmatism. This pragmatism gives him the lens to see contradiction and nevertheless embrace it. What few have realized is that Locke's theory explains the essential unseen dogmatism of the liberal perspective generally. As a religious man for whom revelation was a source of truthful knowledge, Locke nevertheless was willing to accept that knowledge is often built from even thinner air (than reason or revelation):

I mean enthusiasm: which, laying by reason, would set up revelation without it. Whereby in effect it takes away both reason and revelation, and substitutes in the room of it the ungrounded fancies of a man's own brain, and assumes them for a foundation both of opinion and conduct.

Id.: § 3, 429

Locke observes that people may be inclined to embrace beliefs labeled truths, although they are not supported by either proof or revelation. But, he is not willing to conceive the illogic of revelation, perhaps because, like Hobbes,

Locke lacks a sense of irony, too, which can be the reason for Locke's earnest belief in intellectual dualism that supposes knowledge comes from experience (empiricism), but superior knowledge comes from revelation. From here, Locke's principle of the division of powers is only another step, which Montesquieu would take in his *De l'esprit des lois* (1748).

Locke's sense of division, both among the sources of knowledge, as well as those of governmental authority, seems to have traveled into the realm of American jurisprudence. For instance, courts have the last word, unless it is a first level social issue, when only a constitutional amendment will do. But theoretical constructs, whether philosophies or jurisprudences, Russell reminds us, have a dual nature because they are systems of knowledge. As such they need both consistency and credibility, though few manage them equally, Russell forgets to add.

Recognition of the irony that comes with every system of knowledge would force all philosophers, Locke included, to understand that both credibility and consistency can happen only within a given historical frame. This is due to the fact that they are so deeply interconnected. Credibility is a value that comes from using the same lens of interpellating reality consistently: ideology. All theory is credible to those who are inclined to find it credible. Additionally, the method of investigation may add to the credibility of a theory because it brings to the surface the author's knowledge. Extrapolating to Marx's writings, if his ideology is the reason for his lack of credibility, I argue here that his interdisciplinary dialectical method of always taking into consideration the moment of contingency that assures his work's internal consistency and consistent influence (outside the American academe).

4 The Intersection between the Abstract and Concrete Facets of the Law according to Montesquieu, Kant and Rousseau

Montesquieu incorporates the contingency of culture and geography into normative theory. In a manner not entirely unlike the one I adopt here, Montesquieu mixes irony and epistemology to evaluate Catholicism. In *Lettres persanes/Persian Letters* (first published in 1721), the baron makes his assessment under the guise of two Persians traveling through Europe. Thus, his criticism comes across as less poignant because it comes from non-Christians. His poignancy derives, perhaps, from his dialectical method. He ridicules Catholicism, an abstract body of thought, when he describes it in empirical terms of the political regime and geography – two degrees of latitude, and an overly harsh sky – and the manners of practicing merchants.

In *De l'esprit des lois/The Spirit of the Laws* (1748), Montesquieu makes use of dialectics when he uses detailed contingency, an encyclopedic survey of historical and current laws from various countries and political regimes. Montesquieu conducted a comparative study of laws and governments aimed at freeing the law from its theological state. Former Harvard Law School Dean, Roscoe Pound, credits French positivism as highly influential in American jurisprudence, especially Montesquieu's view that "Law in general is human reason," which through positive laws determines "what is commanded or forbidden [relative] to the governors and the governed" (Hall 1949: 549–550).

Montesquieu remains best known for his separation of powers among the three branches of the government, a position eagerly embraced by our Founding Fathers. The doctrine of separation of powers – developed by both John Locke and Montesquieu – was subsequently incorporated into the structure of our Constitution, though the label itself, "separation of powers," does not appear textually in the Constitution. The Constitution builds the branches of the government, so each branch has powers that restrain the other two in a system of checks and balances. Its obvious aim is to prevent the concentration of powers in one branch and thus to avoid any abuse of power.

Kant takes up Montesquieu's doctrine of the three basic state functions, but differently, opposing the baron's quest for moderation in favor of clarity and decisiveness. Perhaps because of this, Russell introduces Kant as a follower of Locke, and his commitment to freedom and equality. Kant, like Hegel, was a university professor, well versed in addressing learned audiences, while Locke, was one of the philosophizing "gentleman of leisure addressing amateurs" (Russell: 704). To the extent that we remember that, unlike many of his followers, if Kant was a liberal, a democrat and a pacifist, then Russell's statement is correct (id.: 642). Kant was admittedly influenced by Rousseau's *Emile*, mostly because of its style. And so were the French Revolutionaries who used Rousseau's concept of "volonté general/popular sovereignty" to justify what W. Friedmann called "revolution without end or measure" (1967: 77). Interestingly, both Kant and Rousseau have helped introduce the legal transition from individualism to communitarianism. Using the concept of a cultural matrix, certainly the political rise of nationalism did not impede this evolution. America's birth benefited from this tide, as his emphasis of national sovereignty would soon be used to oppose the British colonists.

Kant's new vocabulary is often merged into a discussion of labels, which he uses to categorize various concepts. His opus, *The Critique of Pure Reason* (1781), is replete with them. Interestingly, Kant's conceptual craftsmanship has never been equaled. The Kantian concepts of space and time are so well defined that despite using the old terminology of "space" and "time" there is no fear of confusion associated with those perennial labels. For instance, there are two Kantian spaces: one subjective and one objective, one known from experience and the other merely inferred. The difference comes from the fact that space contains an impenetrable core at the level of "things in themselves," outside the world of physics, according to Kant. On the other hand, time has no dual existence. There is no time in itself outside our perception of time. This "pick-and-choose" dualism is not without irony, and Hegel was among the first to note it, though neither Hegel nor Kant had any well-documented influence on our Founding Fathers. Hegel's influence on Marx is well known. However, his influence on our Founding Fathers is nonexistent. One reason might be Hegel's and Kant's devotion to the divine, perhaps, was too foreign to our ingrained common law interests in circumstances and our case-by-case approach to normativity. Nevertheless, while Kant assumes human reason cannot decipher "the things in themselves," he is nevertheless able to tell us a lot about them (Schroeder 2002).

Within the larger conceptual frame of "antinomies of the reason," Kant's "things in themselves" become explained through the use of the binary terminology of "thesis" and "antithesis." This is another example where Kant's terminology remains utterly clear despite its ambivalent nature. The concepts identified as "thesis and antithesis" are not used to develop any type of dialectical view of the world, as Hegel would soon do. The concepts, thus labeled, are used to develop his theory about the dual reality, to which I have already alluded. Some things are perceptible to our senses, including reason, while others are opaque to our human abilities of "interpellation" using Althuser's terminology to describe the interaction between humans and their surrounding contingency. For instance, Kant's thesis of the first antinomy (1781) is defined as "the first conflict of the transcendental ideas" and it states: "The world has a beginning in time, and is also limited as regards space" (1998: 470). While the proof, its antithesis, opposes it because "the world has no beginning in time, [...] and no limits in space" (id.).

I cannot be sure whether the Kantian methodical deductions, and his use of philosophical argumentation, or his irony, and/or his penchant for ambivalence are the roots of his dualism. While I argued that Kant elucidates some abstract concepts despite vague or ambiguous labels, it is possible that by choosing ambiguous terminology, Kant reveals a fundamental ambivalence toward their subject matter – time, space, and similar intangibles – and by extrapolation, his ambivalence toward the possibility of philosophy itself (Gadris 2016). His ambivalence resonates with Marx's and the pragmatist's distrust of conceptual vagaries. Kant resists a straightforward rejection of philosophy while remaining quizzical about metaphysical speculation, as Stelios Gadris suggests. This ambivalence perhaps liberates Kant and allows him to reach the conclusion that reason leads to fallacies, and then minimize the impact of that conclusion with something even harder to achieve than exercising reason: virtue. Morality is what Kant thinks can save us from our fallible senses and reason. That is ironic coming from Kant, because morality, almost infinitely far more than reason and senses, is highly uncertain, largely knowable, and as a Marxian, I have to add, highly contextual.

More problematic for a legal scholar is Kant's introduction to "justice," which takes place in the same opus in which he introduces the call for "moral ends," in his *Critique of Practical Reason* (1788). If we were to accept that both morality and justice are Kantian ends, and the view that they are in perpetual tension because one is forlorn and the other optimistic, how can we establish the role of each?

The self-critical tendency of reason, upon which Kant based his approach to philosophy and which made scholars (Waggoner 2014) call him "the first real Modernist," seems to be the cause of the split ends. In light of this self-examination, Michel Foucault (1984) described Kant as the first to incorporate into his philosophy a self-conscious sense of "presentness," which is ironic at so many levels. However, this is easily understood if we read Kant's philosophy as an abstract painting which, instead of capturing reflected objects (metaphysics), captures the possibility of reflection. And when nothing else can be added, then morality and justice come to mind. Though Kantianism has inspired some American legal scholars, its jocular irony might have proved too unsuitable for the self-righteous nature of any scholarship to make a lasting impact. Luckily, Hegel came along, subsequently, resurrecting dialectics and saving philosophy from the burdens imposed by Kant's willingness to employ irony in his philosophy.

If much is known about dialectics through Hegel's work, Jean Jacques Rousseau perhaps is wrongfully neglected. His *Social Contract* (1762) is a classic example of dialectics in a Hegelian sense of thesis and antithesis followed by their negation through a solution. Rousseau's social contract is a label for a solution to a problem:

> The problem is to find a form of association which will defend and protect with the whole common force the person and goods of each associate, and in which each, while uniting himself with all, may still obey himself alone, and remain as free as before. This is the fundamental problem of which the Social Contract provides the solution.
>
> Book 1: 90

From a possible solution, Rousseau's social contract becomes the solution.

> The social contract is a sacred right which is the basis of all other rights. Nevertheless, the right does not come from nature, and must therefore be founded on conventions.
> *Book I*: 3–4

The rest of the book is Rousseau's demonstration that there is no other solution to the problem earlier identified. His contractarian demonstration goes back to the state of nature, but the contract is a give-and-take between a Prince and his People, thus ingrained in positive law. The Founding Fathers liked this hybrid perception of the law: its natural legitimation and its procedural positivism, ingrained in our checks in balances.

5   Jeremy Bentham's Common Sense and Grotius' Technocratic Approach to Law

The last body of scholarly work summarized here belongs to two legal ideologues. Grotius promoted the Rule of Law of a victorious capitalism seeking global reach, while Bentham attempted to slow it down, by pointing to the danger of legal vagueness which sounded progressive while enabling vicious legal abuse.

Grotius, a Dutch lawyer, wrote his legal narrative at a time of economic development, when Dutch entrepreneurs were establishing New Netherland and New Amsterdam, to legitimize the new era of capitalist globalization. The world was expanding by making more land and goods susceptible to being commonly and privately owned. Grotius clarified the rules of acquiring, enjoying, and transferring property, as well as the rules of defending it. The second book of *Iure Belli Ac Pacis* (1646) focused on property in a logical discursive manner, logically explaining the limits of what could be owned. The main question for him was explaining how both individuals and nations could share the material world. He found help in Roman law, for instance, and used Cicero's simile to explain how new lands could be acquired like empty theater seats that are for all to grab, but once a seat occupied, it belonged to the user alone.

Grotius' popularity has grown in parallel with the importance of law as an efficient tool to govern people in a perceived "non-ideological," rational, if supra-national in manner. To most legal scholars, "Grotius" stands for international law. For instance, the Grotius Lectures are a series of annual lectures sponsored by the American Society of International Law since 1999. Bertrand

Russell mentions him once in his *History of Western Philosophy* (1945: 630), and that may be because Grotius is a scholastic innovator. As the French legal philosopher Simone Goyard-Fabre argues (2003), Grotius created the field of legal theory, carving it out of philosophy (17–23).

In *Critique de la Raison Juridique* (2003), Goyard-Fabre explains Grotius' *De iure belli ac pacis* (1625) as a work of legal scholarship. Since law is a human creation, legal theory shares that quality too. In addition, Goyard-Fabre clarifies, it is legal knowledge obtained methodologically through deduction and discursive thought (id.: 20). Grotius aimed to clarify concepts he thought mislabeled then organize them according to a set of principles which Descartes had called *modern rationalism* (id.: 19). He aimed to create a body of knowledge which would present the law as what a Marxist might call, detached superstructure. I believe this approach is responsible for Grotius' legal influence and widespread acceptance throughout generations, and the different civil and common law systems.

His attitude towards law was almost mathematical. His theory of government was directed at people and nations of the same powerful status, as if nations were equal numbers in some mathematically conceived game of chess. As the world was just being colonized, Holland was an international player, alongside, France, England and Spain. In other words, there was enough for all to share, and if peoples disregarded the rules of making and preserving peace – what he termed "peace etiquette" – Grotius (1913) proposed a codification of the rules in what could be called a "war etiquette" (id.: 21–23).

According to Grotius, people could acquire property rights and transfer them through contracts. Contractual responsibility equalized the field among propertied people: everybody (who was landed in some way) could engage in contractual relations and be bound by them. Kings were bound by the same contractual principles as their subjects. More than legitimizing an existing state of affairs, he legitimized an optimal, harmonious, status quo. This was done by ensuring that his theory of social change was palatable to economic growth in both times of war and peace. Moreover, Grotius was introducing rules for acquiring and maintaining peace by managing the most disruptive possible change: war.

Focusing on the larger picture of modernity, Grotius engaged in a global project. He resurrected Roman principles to validate his heroic narrative: everybody could both own and share, and thus prosper. In this rational world of few details, he introduced a subversive Roman idea: the regime of property had little influence on the type of government. Grotius used Cicero's work as support for his theory of property. Through this interpretation, Grotius focused on elevating physical possession, including looting, over title. By relying on

Roman law and its dual regime of property – personal and communal – Grotius was separating law from the form of government, making personal property irrelevant for a republic, monarchy or dictatorship. Ironically, in his quest to clarify legal rules, Grotius turned law into an amorphous label whose role was to make palatable the mercantilism of the day – in times of peace as well as in times of war.

The influence of Jeremy Bentham extends far beyond what H.L.A. Hart (1982) refers to dismissively as a "spectacular non sequitur," discussing Bentham's argument about legal excuses nullifying or reducing criminal liability. Jeremy Waldron perfectly demonstrated Bentham's "rights" to influence today's American jurisprudence when he used Bentham's own diatribe against natural rights as "nonsense on stilts" to sum up Bentham's work (Waldron 1987: 29). Interestingly, Marx's opinion of Bentham was far from flattering: In the first volume of *Das Kapital*, in a footnote to Chapter XXII, Marx references the English philosopher, "I should call Mr. Jeremy a genius of bourgeois stupidity." I find many similarities between Marx and Bentham. Among them, I would argue that their distrust of vague legal terminology produced a scholarship of contextuality and relativism: Bentham's utilitarianism and Marx's dialectical materialism.

In *Anarchical Fallacies*, Bentham objected vigorously against the "terrorist language," "mischievous," and "dangerous nonsense" of the *Declaration of the Rights of Man and of the Citizen*. He found any talk about rights useless by their unenforceable nature, which exceeded what a state could do (id.: 52). On the first article of the Declaration, Bentham stated:

> *Men (all men) are born and remain free, and equal in respect of rights. Social distinctions cannot be founded, but upon common utility...*
>
> All men born free? Absurd and miserable nonsense! When the great complaint-a complaint made perhaps by the very same people at the same time, is-that so many men are born slaves. Oh! but when we acknowledge them to be born slaves, we refer to [positive] laws [being] contrary to those laws of nature.
>
> WALDRON 1987: 59; emphasis in the original

Bentham criticized "natural rights" as mortal enemies of the law. He saw them as subverting the work of the government. He viewed natural rights "stark" nonsense, and a "contradiction in terms." In *Supply without Burthen or Escheat Vice Taxation: being a proposal for a saving of taxes by an extension of the law of escheat including strictures on the taxes on collateral succession, comprised in the budget on 7th December, 1795,* Bentham further clarified his position:

> What a legal right is I know. I know how it was made. I know what it means when made. To me a right and a legal right are the same thing, for I know no other. Right and law are correlative terms: as much so as son and father. Right is with me the child of law: from different operations of the law result different sorts of rights. A natural right is a son that never had a father.
> WALDRON 1987: 73

Here, Bentham's view of natural rights would have a broader appeal if presented in its surrounding contingency: the bloody aftermath of the French Revolution.

> When I hear of natural rights ... I always see in the background a cluster of daggers or of pikes introduced into the National Assembly.
> WALDRON 1987: 29

In that light, Bentham's reasoning becomes broadly persuasive: why confuse and contradict when clarity is also an option? Furthermore, all rights come with qualifications. Think only about American constitutional law, for instance. The BILL OF RIGHTS could be called the *Bill of Qualifications*. So, Bentham seems to argue, if there are no absolute rights, why label them as such?

Rather than address the irony ideology creates, Bentham sermonizes. When he notes that the French *Declaration of Human Rights* contains both the recognition of the absolute (natural) right to liberty or property, and qualifies its limitations a few lines below, Bentham seems furious. His outburst of disillusionment, in hindsight, seems apt. Both the French Revolution and American Independence did not have the benefit of using similar historical events to know how to evaluate their legal language. The lack of historical perspective may be a reason the legislator in each of these political situations shows dogmatism and a lack of trust, as Bentham correctly noted. The language of natural rights is the language of mistrust, the mistrust of one government about the wisdom of future governments. But change cannot be stopped, and vague language in its attempt to mask it does not inspire respect for the law. In fact, it can be argued that legal language so dogmatically vague can easily be used to cover up atrocities. And one may argue that the natural law language of the

American Declaration of Independence, ironically, made it possible for a minority of white men to enslave a majority.

6 American Jurisprudence and Marx: Strange Bedfellows ... Not

This brief historical survey of what philosophical ideas inspired American jurisprudence should further emphasize the deep theoretical connection between Marx and us (American jurists), a connection interrupted only by our different ideologies and contingency. Furthermore, some thinkers discussed here engaged irony with various degrees of success. Plato was able to see Socrates' use of irony, but he ignored the irony embedded in his own philosophy. Plato, like Marx, could not see how his thinking becomes fodder for other thinkers. Relevance is co-dependent of a work's temporality.

Ironically, I credit Marx for this clarifying lens with which to view scholarship. I credit him for making it easier to see the limits of scholarship, and thus of jurisprudence, in a way that does not limit its aspirations for meaning or impact. Ironically, it increases the pressure because all scholarship comes with a limited relevance-built-in mechanism. Scholarship has a lifespan as if it were human: the more you aspire to achieve the more you can potentially achieve.

Marx's body of work is acutely political, even when it presents an argument in a dialectical debate keenly aware of its historicity. A dialectical approach to systemic contingency when studying any given legal issue, while acknowledging its ideological bias, should be a welcome legal training of all future jurists. This is in addition to the current pluralist approach, which has been the liberal standard for debate and difference within the last half a century.

When pluralism rejects universalism, it loses sight of the system and the socio-economic downtrodden with no other liberal identifier making them worth catering to. More ideologically conservative movements, such as *Law and Economics*, has misused its utilitarian bent by encouraging an a-historical efficiency in view of some out-of-context empiricism. This lens has come to support a conservative, austerity-embracing, agenda which hurts the same large, but often ignored socio-economic sector.

Whereas *Critical Legal Studies* (CLS) delves into the internal contradictions imminent to any legal system, it offers no viable societal solutions. *Critical Race, Queer, and Feminist studies*, with their accent on the fractional, tribal *Other*, as opposed to the socio-economic despondent Other, has missed its chance of becoming a systemic theory focused on the common good of all. Thus it remains a second-level, reformist theory. Some legal theories embrace specific social problems, such as *Law and Society*, which is prone to investigate discrete issues, like the death penalty. While not apologetic for the current political system, this attempt to discover the truth in law has a limited usefulness by its very own nature.

More interesting is the *Law and Philosophy* approach for the same reason other scholars have criticized it: its abstraction. As shown here, the Kantian legal theory, as espoused by George Fletcher (1987), is remarkable for its analysis of human agency, something with which all legal theories struggle. In a Kantian vein, Fletcher explains law as a tool which reconciles the subjective choices of different agents and makes them compatible with each other. Understanding law as the normativity that "acknowledges our concrete particularity and seeks to harmonize our divergent purpose" (1987: 543), it is easier to pose the question of political primacy and answer within a philosophical primacy paradigm.

Humans position themselves in the surrounding world using knowledge, whether it is Gadamer's meta-knowledge, which incorporates preconceptions and unfiltered beliefs about society and how it works, or more sophisticated subjectively filtered theories. According to Gadamer (1986), the primitive Greek meaning of *theoria* (theory) was that of "participation in the delegation sent to a festival for the sake of honoring the gods" (Scheibler 2000: vii). We might have come a long way from that early representation, but theories do remain subjective interpellations of reality. Legal theories limit that social interpellation to social interaction governed by specific norms whose compliance is ensured by state institutions, and known as legal norms. The result of an act of authorship, legal theories mirror both their author's set of values and beliefs and the cultural values and traditions of the subject embracing the theory. As such, when acted upon, legal theories are deeply subjective and imbued with multiple sets of beliefs.

Marx's work has been derided for having been co-opted by politicians promoting lofty goals focused on otherness and the integrity of the world (Cohen 2017). Critics note how those goals of human betterment and global peace have failed and their promoters-turned-dictators in control of the economy, and the party of government (Pumar 2009). Perhaps, *Tovarich Stalin*, a Darth Vader for the ages, has conquered our academic imagination to such a degree that we refuse but a superficial acquaintance with Marxist theory. While this disinterest has been discussed in the case of French intelligentsia by Verena Andermatt Conley (2005), the retreat from Marx is not without nuances. As Gary Minda stated, *Critical Legal Studies* (CLS):

> attempted to recreate a 'left intelligentsia' in American law. Except for the legal realists of the thirties and forties, and a handful of sixties Marxists,

> there has never been a serious 'leftist' presence in American legal education. To establish a left intelligentsia in American law one would have to break free from the consensus orientation which has dominated American jurisprudence for this and much of the last century, and in fact of the century before that, too. To do this, CLS had to hold itself out as a 'radical dissident movement' within the legal academy.
>
> MINDA 1997: 10

Like the recipient of the 2004 Pulitzer Prize for general non-fiction, *Gulag: A History*, whose success could be viewed in its author's legal brief-like writing skills, Marxian-flavored knowledge has little to do with Marxian texts and very much with the interpellator's prejudice. *Gulag* reads like a lawyer's product: a winning conclusion replete with arguments and chosen facts to stress its inevitability (Neacşu 2004). Like that book, the American refusal to engage with Marxian thought is a conclusion foretold. It is replete with imagery of bearded, old white men and concentration-like labor camps (id.), rather than objective, Marxian text.

Sadly, or merely ironically, CLS's exhibition of disregard for Marx is mostly based on gross generalizations and thoroughly unexamined assumptions that other liberal schools of jurisprudence have shown. For instance, Judge Richard Posner calls CLS a reminder of 1960s infantile leftism. Posner's pseudo-analysis has caught the eye, especially with those who lack any contextualism, having not experienced the 1960s:

> This [1960s] skepticism has fueled, along with political radicalism and sheer infantilism, the contemporary movement in legal scholarship known as 'critical legal studies.'
>
> POSNER 1987: 768

With so much to lose by being seen as progressive, the pantheon of American jurisprudence has been most thoroughly hegemonic in its output. One might say that since the ascent of Justice Felix Frankfurter, no legal mind had associated itself with hefty goals similar to those of the late Harvard Law Professor and U.S. Supreme Court Justice. Among Justice Frankfurter's many achievements, it is of import to mention that he founded The American Civil Liberties Union (ACLU), as well as worked on the defense team in the Sacco-Vanzetti case about the wrongfully accused Italian immigrant anarchists, and backed the third party, Progressive candidate Robert M. La Follette for President in 1924 (Presser 2017).

If the survey helps legal scholars see my point, one way to avoid the sarcasm of wildly different readings would be recognizing the meaning-making role of ideology, and acknowledge its inherent presences. That law is a *Gallerte* of sorts, as was noted centuries ago by Justice Holmes when he emphasized the need to understand history and political thought when attempting to understand what law is. American jurisprudence, scholarship about law, reflects the structure of scholarship and the content of its object of study, which makes it so vibrant, interesting, and rich in meaning. This brief survey about common intellectual roots shared by Marxian thought and American jurisprudence might point out the unfortunate uniformity of thought in the current schools of jurisprudence, and might even encourage a break from the current penury of jurisprudential imagination.

CHAPTER 10

Irony, Jurisprudential Meaning-Making, and Ideological Camaraderie

Like Buñuel's film, this book too employs irony. Using Marxian theory is ironically viewed through the lens of his thoroughly bourgeois life. Stressing the difference of meaning stemming from the ideological clash between the textual instigator (S_1) and the textual interpellator (S_2), which I contend irony actuates, it becomes obvious that my ideology is different than Marx's, and also different than that of today's establishment scholars. Meaning also fluctuates with the contingency of the Regime of Truth of each moment, and this book is, first of all, a call for academic diversity, and then, an ironic demonstration that the best way to teach liberal jurisprudence is to include theories based on Marxian, as well as other, points of view.

Today, American legal theories work with the ideological umbrella of liberalism. As a result, their criticism of the Rule of Law is not that different, though, ironically, they do criticize its tenets. For instance, classical legal liberalism is much reviled by *Critical Legal Studies* (CLS, *the Crits*) philosopher Roberto Mangabeira Unger, as shown below. Understandably, Unger's is a solid criticism because there are perhaps as many strands of liberalism as there are of Christianity (albeit, for clarity purposes, the liberal savior is private property, not Jesus). Furthermore, classical liberalism promotes an idealized relationship between the individual and the state, where individual human beings were independent agents, able to provide for most of their needs. In this scenario, the state could become more and more emaciated in its welfare role, as Duncan Kennedy, another CLS co-founder, actually imagined at little cost to this Greek-like statuesque image of a well-fed patrician posing for the anonymous individual. The problem is that though the state has been emaciating for the last half of a century to the point of barely standing, individual agency has also eroded for the 99% of the population to a point that the masses are barely standing either.

Thus, ironically, the establishment diversity of legal scholarship seems to have one voice. This voice unanimously supports the hegemonic Rule of Law, and the letter of our democratic Constitution – a democracy of rich men, an oligarchy. As a result, the spirit in which our federal Constitution is applied could not be further removed from Aristotle's definition of democracy in

Politics, and is closer to the spirit of his description of the despotic Athenian Constitution, which prevailed until the time of Solon:

> Not only was the [application of the] constitution at this time oligarchical in every respect, but the poorer classes, men women, and children, were in absolute slavery to the rich.
> ARISTOTLE 2008: §2

If we were to use Aristotle's definition of democracy from his *Politics*, then today's America is an oligarchy ruled by the few for the benefit of the few.

> Tyranny is [like] monarchy exercising the rule of a master over political society; oligarchy is when men of property have the government in their hands; democracy, the opposite, when the indigent, and not the men of property, are the rulers.
> ARISTOTLE 1905: 115

Assuming that there is value in a democracy where the indigent, irrespective of race, gender, age, sexual orientation, enjoys as much dignity as a corporation does today, then can our current jurisprudential models rooted in *Liberal Formalism* – whether they are *Law as Science, Realism, Critical Legal Studies* (*"CLS"*), and their off-shoot theories – help imagine a way to promote such a society? And to the extent that our establishment is critical – and I signal here *Law and Literature* in its Fergusonian vision (Ferguson 2016) and Sarat's *Studies in Law, Politics, and Society* (Sarat 2017) – they of Formalism, these models all chip off at classical liberal theory, but themselves do little else other than legitimize the current corporatist system.

Continuing with Aristotle's definition of democracy and the Rule of Law, because the defender of any form of government is hegemony in action, none of the schools mentioned above can go for the irony of our democracy. Where is the government of the masses? And if democracy is said to be the government of the many, what about the situation when the many are all propertied and have the power in their hands, as Aristotle asked two thousand years ago – would that still be a democracy (Aristotle 1905: 115–116)? What if Aristotle is right, and that the number of the governing body, whether the greater or the smaller, is an accident? What if the real difference between oligarchy and democracy is not the number of people who benefit from the Rule of Law, but whether the indigent do, because the "real difference between democracy and oligarchy is poverty and wealth" (id.). And this is not discussed by any of the schools of jurisprudence because, I argue, none, unlike political theorists, have ever pointed out to their ironic ideology (Dardot and Laval 2016a).

Perhaps that is because, deeply Rortian in their fear of employing any final truths, ironically they do not see the effects of their statements: legitimizing the system. While ironists are "always aware of the contingency and fragility of their final vocabularies and thus of their selves" (Rorty 1989: 73–74), liberal theorists have turned a deaf ear to historical class struggle of the twenty-first century. The current liberal theories see no alternative to the liberal system, and worse, while they engage the system and promote limited, "second-level" changes which do not affect the system's major structure, they ignore the surrounding seismic social-economic change that has occurred in the American society in this century; the downtrodden, the have-nots have turned against the liberal leftist ideology and embraced right-wing ideology.

1 Classical Liberalism and Marx

Half of a century ago Unger (1975) explained the power of competing theories to predict events or to control them. But that was an illusion, Unger added. Such standards eliminated the need for justification and proof. He brilliantly exposed the political purpose behind all theories, but he only viewed the flaws of the grand theories. Only grand theories seemed flawed because they carried the inherent riddle of all theories to a higher level of abstraction. "The more general the theory, the clearer the inadequacy of the solution becomes" (34), Unger wrongly postulated, forgetting that the smaller a theory is, despite its smaller flaw, that does not maximize its truthfulness, only the ease with which it can be ignored or discarded.

In *Knowledge and Politics* (1975), Unger's attempts "total criticism" as an elaborate theoretical tantrum against classic liberal theory. His project is hard to ignore because he is superbly fluent in philosophy. His theory matches Ocham's nominalism, Descartes' epistemology, as well as the writings of Thomas Hobbes, Grotius, and Bodin. Inasmuch, Unger's theory worked to support the foundations of classical metaphysics in its scholastic form by the time legal liberalism matured. Much like liberal thought had been before, he wanted his approach to be viewed as a repudiation of the existing theories. In building this attempt, Unger managed to paint legal liberalism, the large umbrella, into which all current legal theories take refuge.

Unger called liberalism obsolete. Unnecessary, I would argue. Recently, Kessler and Pozen (2016) demonstrated how theories tend to cannibalize themselves over time, thus making the issue of obsoleteness moot. Drawing on prescriptive legal theories in the field of originalism, textualism, popular constitutionalism, and cost-benefit analysis, Kessler and Pozen remark how theories first gain popularity and momentum. But then they distance themselves from their original roots, and thus, destroy themselves like an elite athlete who starts using performance-enhancing drugs to keep up while destroying all chances of any future career. That is not Unger's obsoleteness. It is a political choice authors often make. Unger probably thought that theories often became incomprehensible in time because of the antinomy of theory and the surrounding socio-economic reality, whose dynamics move theories to a point of no-compliance. Under these circumstances, criticism becomes inevitable. A new framework evolves. The new contingency puts pressure on S_2 to come up with something more relevant. If liberalism is T_1, what could pressure S_2 to develop a different theory?

Social order stands on rules. Rules mirror social values. Values are dynamic, as they translate cultural traditions and political interests. Within the Western liberal world, one of the most cherished social values is qualified freedom. This is the freedom sanctioned to individuals by the liberal state through what we call the Rule of Law, as well as by their religious institutions and moral beliefs.

Legal rules have their long history of legitimacy in the surrounding natural order and in the secular power of governments, as positive law. When positivism is the guiding principle, legal norms embrace a certain level of formality. They have to be promulgated following a specific procedure so they become publicly acceptable, and thus, binding and freely obeyed. This point of view is of little consequence to engage in the debate of natural versus positive law, as well as to address the implications of the view that society has no inherent order. Or, to the contrary, society has an intrinsic order which can be discovered if only studied. It becomes obvious that irrespective of the origin of this normative order, the liberal state has the ultimate power of coercive enforcement when free obedience fails. What matters is that the liberal society is a society governed by laws that respect a certain procedure. This is another way of saying that the liberal society is governed by legal norms which are general, uniform, public, and enforceable, and as such form the Rule of Law.

However, if this is a great achievement by twentieth-century standards, it should have seemed rather mediocre by twenty-first century standards. In other words, to be mesmerized at the procedural goal of the liberal Rule of Law seems rather limited. Much more interesting would be to build a harmonious communal life for the entire society. That would mean for legal theories to stop being descriptive and begin to take risks in making suggestions to become normative. However, the risk is becoming derisory. As we will see below, Rawls proposed justice as fairness, and when analyzed, his justice became similar to charity or benevolence.

That the classical liberal theory cannot promote a communal goal rests in the ideology of the liberal state – the enabler of the liberal order – which has in mind individual ends and social values to the extent that individual ends allow it. Liberal theory is uncomfortable with communal social values. Unger explains it scientifically: the individual, and individual interaction, rather than social groups, and social interaction, form the primary unit of liberal societies. Again, the irony of such a position is that it is very hard to find out the individual position of marginalized people more than once every four years for a presidential election. As a result, the consequences are so blunt and disastrous that many individually refuse to resurface for years to come.

The teachings of liberalism have always been uncompromisingly hostile to the classic idea of objective good, where objective good is the communal, social good, Unger continues. That hostility, as we shall discuss, is also common to all liberal theories, including those of latter-day liberalism. The doctrinal objective value is incompatible with the premises of liberalism. Unger believes that people accept only goals that embrace choice as an expression of personality. Furthermore, he proposed that objective goods come as commands or are perceived as commands rather than understood as the necessity. For Unger, that means objective goals are incompatible with individually accepted goals. While Unger's position seems reasonable, it rests on the assumption that people's behavior is unchangeable irrespective of the social economic reality surrounding them. For instance, it assumes that the value that is subjective today will remain subjective tomorrow, and that objective goods cannot ever be experienced as subjective values.

But these are exceptional times. Todd Gitlin explained them best:

> Public reason has plunged into a state of emergency. Dishonesty, non sequiturs, and distortions of fact (the president prefers the term "truthful hyperbole") are the disorders of the day. As under the totalitarianisms of the 20th century, the key institutions of public enlightenment – higher education and journalism – are impugned as "elitist," "enemies of the people" that transmit hoaxes and "fake news." Truth is condemned at the wave of a tweet. (2017)

Even Richard Posner, a conservative, calls for a change in the legal regime, so "private incentive is aligned with the goal of wide-spread prosperity" (2010: 2). Personally, I would have called on fairies to spread golden dust on the downtrodden.

Nevertheless, there is widespread consensus that the values of our society need to be recalibrated. The disagreement starts with the need for other political and legal theories to provide guidance. Maybe the binary "individual" versus "communal," or "subjective" versus "objective," do not aptly describe our new reality, where the "communal" contains the mass of individuals representing the 99 percent of the population. We are past the point where vague values of right and left could meaningfully represent reality.

Let's think about the environment. Posner looks at climate change and sees inevitable capitalist crises (id.: 3). From another angle, fossil fuel is a natural richness, which, when exploited, employs a large population with no other means of subsistence. But burning fossil fuel negatively affects individuals and communities. Temporarily, the effect can be denied in the short run. But in the long run, unless individuals can escape the destruction of the environment, they will be destroyed with it.

In other words, when fighting climate change is the most immediate political goal today, liberalism demands that each individual sees it as subjectively important in order for the liberal state to make it into an achievable goal. According to Unger, stating that this is in everybody's interest would deny that possibility because it would take it from a freely chosen option to an imposed objective command. Sure, Unger's objections can be bypassed if all individuals have access to unadulterated scientific data without media distortions or ideological misrepresentations. Or, following procedural prescriptions as in environmental law litigation, we could engage in something called "balancing of the equities," a process which requires enormous work to understand what it takes to explain the virtues of objective, scientifically sound, and publicly beneficial goals then reach the same results.

However, when politics are the creatures of corporate lobbying promoting corporate interests by maximizing short-term benefits at the expense of the public, communal goal, being formal and inflexible becomes short-sighted. Indeed, there is a danger of bypassing a meek individual freedom, almost inexistent for the masses, in the name of an objective good. But more realistic is to bypass the enormous lobbying power of corporations interested in immediate gratification, and give the community some respite from exploiting its richness, which here is fossil fuel.

Think only about the history behind the passing and then the implementation of such pieces of environmental legislation as the *Endangered Species Act*, or the *Comprehensive Environmental Response, Compensation, and Liability Act*, known also as *Superfund* or CERCLA. More to the point, think about the current executive orders defunding such agencies as the Environmental Protection Agency. Unger noticed this internal contradiction of liberal theory and he still rejected the possibility that communal goals could become a matter of free choice, or even that communal goals may become primordial values to protect society as a whole. The fear of Marx(ism) translated into emasculating reason, and much of the theoretical debacle we face now is a consequence of a lack of irony. Posing a question, if no theory is objective, and if promoting a theory in the name of a societal good is unattainable because it ignores individual choice, what happens to the reverse? Is society just an amalgam of individual choices? Is there no hierarchy of those choices, because if there is, then how are the primary choices decided?

The inner antagonism liberalism has at its core, between individual and collective, has run its course. The social life liberalism has represented "in the language of speculative thought" (Unger 1975: 145) is far removed from reality. In the twentieth century, this antagonism was very much on display, and liberal thinkers attracted large audiences when they talked about the individual in danger of being overcome by faceless social forces. Today, there is a new antagonism, that between ignored individuals and omnipotent über-individuals. Liberal theory does not seem well-suited to address it. Liberal thought is the matrix of democratic government, where individuals participate in government through elected representatives continues to have its attraction. Certainly, there is hope that democracy is not in peril. Reality seems to demand a more sophisticated theory; especially where the balance between the role of the individual and the community has been markedly uneven. Interestingly, a weak democracy where individuals do not participate in a meaningful way – either because their choices are uninformed or because they refuse to participate – negatively impacts the community at large. Individuals cannot dissolve in communities and communities will never become small groups of one. The question unadressed by liberalism is the creation of the Uber-individual at the expense of the masses of faceless individuals.

At the same time, no one can dispute that individual values, goals and desires will always retain some degree of autonomy from communal values. From this perspective, perhaps the distinctions have been drawn wrongly all along. There is no need to talk about antagonistic individual and communal views, but about their symbiotic interdependency. Communal goals, those essential to surviving, which Marxism deemed social-economic because it viewed survival primarily as a social-economic issue – safe housing, meaningful education, and basic healthcare – need not to be treated as such any longer. Safe housing, meaningful education and basic healthcare enable individuals to reach their emotional, physical and intellectual potential. There is no antagonism between the individual and the community. The antagonism is between the Uber-individual and what is left of our freedoms.

This brings us to the idea of freedom in liberal theory. Much has been discussed under its name. Under this label, *Lockner* was decided. So was *Griswold v. Connecticut,* 381 U.S. 479 (1965). Freedom is often used to protect individual liberty, and there is nothing more attractive about the task of the state than to impose a standard of legislation and adjudication so only the social arrangements most conducive to the flourishing of individual talents should be allowed. Interestingly, though, classical liberal theory has never been able to implement this goal. Only a theory that would recognize the value of community would be able to bring about the much-needed freedom to engage in action benefitting the individual for the immediate and further future. Basic human dignity is a value that depends on strong communities supportive of individual development, which requires access to health care, good education and good employment prospects. Rawls' justice talks about leveling the playing field. That is possible if we strengthen communities.

Every type of social life has two complementary perspectives: one is a theoretical reflection and the other is the political-legal order. Both are reflections of a social-economic and political reality, much like what Marxian theory calls the primary and secondary level of social structure. The distinction is useful only to the extent that social life needs order and its order is justification. And both are imperatives to engage the members of a given society.

The liberal state established by the decisive social and cultural changes of the seventeenth century culminated in the French and the Industrial Revolution. It is a category that describes the characteristics of many Western and assimilated societies and the emergence of the welfare–corporate and the socialist state (Unger 1975: 151). There are two main elements in the traditional definition of the liberal state. One has to do with the character of economic organization. The other reflects the relationship between society and the state: government.

The liberal state relies on an industrial and capitalist society. Its distinctive mode of economic activity is industrial production for mass consumption. Unger stresses the type of economic organization, such as its private ownership of property. With respect to social and political organization, liberal society is defined by the dissolution of the post-feudal, aristocratic system of estates, or fixed social ranks, and by the consequent distinction between political status and social circumstance. Social position no longer defines political status. All persons in principle achieve formal equality as citizens and as legal persons. They acquire similar political and civic duties and entitlements. But a relatively broad range of inequities in social and economic circumstances is tolerated and treated as a matter different from legal political equality. The reach of politics is restricted to be more or less explicit constitutional measures that replace the implicit "fundamental law" of feudal and post-feudal societies. There is a range of programs like, economic and moral, into which government may not intrude. And finally, physical organization tends to be democratic as well as constitutional. Power is exercised through electoral representation.

So, theories do not become obsolete. The ideology behind them makes them appear as such. The irony – and Unger strikes me as immune to irony – is that their subjectivity is no longer able to encourage a relevant explanation for the specific problems they tackle. The same goes for legal theories confronting legal problems.

The only way to disqualify a theory is by looking at its power of explanation, which is how a theory subjectivizes or interpellates reality. All theories are biased, as Foucault, for instance, reminded us not too long ago, and to the extent that we use theories to decipher reality, we use them to subjectivize reality. Some theories attempt to build a grand picture. Others focus on a corner of reality in a piecemeal approach to understanding. For Unger, he is attracted to classical liberal political theory because it is a grand dame of theoretical enterprises. To that extent, his critique could have been, as well, directed against Marxism. But liberalism comes in so many flavors, just to focus on its classical version is to have missed all the other theories the academe has embraced since the nineteenth century.

Certainly, arguing that a theory has become obsolete makes its critique more manageable. What easier way to disqualify a pageant contestant than to divulge her advanced age? But what better way to make pageantry more interesting than embracing each contestant's history? By refusing to see historical contingency in the value of classical liberalism, for instance, Unger is closer to Rawls' theorizing than perhaps he ever anticipated. Similarly, by refusing historicity, Unger is closer to Law and Philosophy and its embrace of final, philosophical truths.

Liberalism is a way of thinking. Liberalism is a way of life. But what is its value? That answer contains as much ideology as the theory itself. However, it is not much if it does not engage its perils.

2   Law as Science or the Rejection of Ideology

If ostriches were jurists, one could say that this school of thought – Law as Science – was as dedicated to keeping things detached from the surrounding existence as ostriches are to hiding their eggs. Its promoters seemed to have desired to decipher the meaning of law in the same way ostriches check their nests when they bury their heads in the sand, probably pretending that no one around can tell what they are doing.

Historically, Law and Science can be regarded as the first school of American legal thought. It was introduced to Harvard Law School in 1870 by Christopher

Columbus Langdell when he became Harvard's Dane Professor. Ironically, it took legal teaching to a new level of seriousness and risked to forget the essence of what was supposed to be taught: the messiness of life. Even today, many current schools of legal thought continue in this vein.

The problem with this jurisprudential approach to law, according to Oliver Wendell Holmes, Jr. is its view of teaching law, or teaching "legal theology" (1897). Holmes criticized Langdell's syllogistic approach for its lack of appreciation for experience. "The Life of the Law," wrote Holmes, "is not logic, but experience" (1881: 1).

> The life of the law has not been logic; it has been experience. The felt necessities of the time, the prevalent moral and political theories, intuitions of public policy, avowed or unconscious, even the prejudices which judges share with their fellow men, have had a good deal more to do than the syllogism in determining the rules by which men should be governed. The law embodies the story of a nation's development through many centuries, and it cannot be dealt with as if it contained only the axioms and corollaries of a book of mathematics. In order to know what it is, we must know what it has been, and what it tends to become. (Id.)

American law schools continue to be renowned for their approach to law as science and continuing to use Langdell's Socratic method, which makes students learn as they publicly espouse their ignorance. When Langdell introduced what would become the Harvard "method," he wrote and published what became the modern law school casebooks (Langdell 1871):

> The day came for its first trial. The class gathered in the old amphitheater of Dane Hall – the one lecture room of the School – and opened their strange new pamphlets, reports bereft of their only useful part, the headnotes! The lecturer opened his.
> "Mr. Fox, will you state the facts in the case of Payne v. Cave? [3 T.R. 148, 3 Burr. 1921 (1789)]"
> Mr. Fox did his best with the facts of the case.
> "Mr. Rawle, will you give the plaintiff's argument?"
> Mr. Rawle gave what he could of the plaintiff's argument.
> "Mr. Adams, do you agree with that?"
> And the case-system of teaching law had begun....
> WARREN 1908: 372

Ironically, Langdell's method was originally flawed because it encouraged what it attempted to cure: a fictionalized view of the law. Pretending that jurisprudence is science and the teaching of law can be achieved in the same way science was taught, Langdell attempted to create social engineers. In turn, the focus was to produce professionals that were adept at solving social problems in their individuality, with the existing legal norms. Langdell's students were not taught about systemic problems or how to imagine different norms better suited for the types of social issues they encountered.

Proof of further irony is the evolution of the legal textbook method, Langdell conceived to help his students see how law is applied to specific cases and controversies. What used to be remarkable about Langdell's method, as then Harvard President Eliot remarked, was his reliance on the authentic version of the case law (an accurate version of a decision). Professor Langdell taught law by asking his students to go to the original sources, the court of opinion. And indeed, *Payne v. Cave*, the case that started the Harvard educational revolution, was reproduced in its entirety in a case book (Davis and Neacşu 2014: 498). Langdell did not ask his students to approximate the law or recite definitions and rules: "When and by what statute were lands made alienable in England after the conquest?" (id.), nor "What is the difference between an action of trespass and an action of trespass upon the case" (id.)? Langdell believed and taught his students that learning law was possible by reading and analyzing the original sources that were understandable and available – both printed in the case book and in the library, to a limited extent – thus permitting the deconstruction of the text and its reconstruction through analysis.

Langdell used case-books as an anthology, a collection of cases presented in their entirety to the student to read and analyze because, as he remarked in his first casebook available in the Harvard Law Library, it was there to supplant the scant availability of print copies of the reported cases he thought necessary to use in class. Langdell only wanted to use primary sources, the law itself in its original authoritative form, to teach students "what the law is" (Warren 1908: 361). By analogy to chemistry, Harvard University President Eliot explained Langdell's methodology:

> [Langdell] told me that the way to study [law] was to go to the original sources. I knew it was true, for I had been brought up in the science of chemistry myself; and one of the first rules of a conscientious student of science is never to take a fact or a principle out of second-hand treatises, but to go to the original [source]. (Id.)

Langdell aspired to teach law as a "science" which was supposed to be studied inductively, through primary sources. He thought that some inherent, basic principles of American common law could have been discoverable through close analysis of the opinions of courts in appellate cases (Presser 2017: 63), because, as Lawrence Friedman aptly described it, Langdell believed in the "the genius of the common law" residing in judge-made law (Friedman 1973: 531). Langdell believed in approaching law teaching methodically. However, he ignored the subjectivity inherent to his object of study: the judge-made law, which mirrors the judges ideology, philosophy, and politics even as they were coached in as-neutral-as-possible presentations.

Langdell did not ignore contingency in his study of the law. He assumed that law could incorporate it, and in a way, dominate it. Within the same time frame and within the same scientific vein of thought that legal institutions could be studied in an ahistorical manner, Oliver Wendell Holmes studied the law clearly within cultural perimeters, unlike Langdell. Talking about property and possession, Holmes referred to the existing schools of German law and invoked Kant and Hegel as well as Savigny and Ihering (Holmes 1881: 206). Certainly, legal institutions undergo changes when they adapt to what Holmes called "modern times" (id.: 247). Nevertheless, when it comes to property, and especially possession, there is nothing historic or political in his definition, but a scent of scientific technicality: "every right is a consequence attached by the law to one or more facts which the law defines" (id.: 214). In 1881, Holmes viewed differences between possession according to Roman law, German law, and even American common law. But those distinctions were mostly philosophical, explaining the reason for giving physical possession the role it had in proving ownership: the external manifestation of one's freedom (Kantian principle) or one's intent, the revered *animus domini* (in common law) (id.). They stemmed from the object of property, rather than the social relationship of property, making distinctions of little consequence.

By 1844, decades before Llewellyn and Holmes, Karl Marx, also well versed in Roman and German law, wrote something totally novel. He situated his argument in British political economy, and was perhaps thus able to view that private property started to spring out of the social relations of labor and capital, the two facets of the industrial economy of that time (Marx 1907: 91). Private property acquired a "subjective essence," it became activity, labor. It became two persons, the waged worker and the capitalist, acting together for opposite interests: wages and capital. These two forms of private property defined the latter half of the 19th century and the entire twentieth century.

If the original casebook supported a literate approach to law on the assumption that a close reading of the judge-made law was the key to understanding the law, today the approach is a mere travesty, and the impossibility of raising questions that do not fit the allowed paradigm is certainly even fewer. As many legal scholars know all too well (Farnsworth 1988; Bodie 2007; Corbin and Dow

2007), casebooks today are not what they used to be when Langdell promoted their use to teach law. If they used to reproduce judge-made law, today, they are so heavily edited and shortened versions of the original cases they mimic, that their purpose cannot be Langdell's: teaching students "to never take a fact or a principle out of second-hand treatises, but to go to the original [document for] that fact or principle" (Davis and Neacşu 2014: 498). Under the guise of adherence to Langdell's principle that law is science, casebooks are currently serving the students a goulash of definitions, rules, and contextual information: in other words, secondary sources. Ironically, this is what Langdell wanted to end because something like this potpourri method is what law students were taught in the pre-Langdell years.

Today, such shorthand study of the law mirrors, perhaps unintentionally, a technological culture, which panders to the limited attention span inculcated and fostered by videogames and social media interactions. But, this legal ersatz, in addition to chipping away at our professional reverence for the original source of the law, is also a dangerous way of masking the political nature of the law, presenting it in a manner akin to laws of nature. Critical Legal Studies (*Crits*) adherents have long ago noted this feature of American Legal Education; especially Duncan Kennedy (1983) in his *Legal Education and the Reproduction of Hierarchy: A Polemic against the System* (1983), also known as the "Little Red Book." Nevertheless, casebooks seem here to stay. Also, the discussion about their print or digital presentation is only technical.

As complained earlier, all these schools of thought have little meaning if meaning comes from difference. Pretending that law is science and cases can be discussed in their autonomous existence to the extent that they resemble each other, they direct legal progress in that area. This fits the description for both law as science and the formalist school of law.

3   Formalism and Realism: Two Sides of the Same Coin

Formalism and Realism can be seen as the two sides of one jurisprudential coin. Formalism, as a political school of thought, embraced its liberal ideology to such an extent that in the spirit of Mills' free-market of ideas, it appeared with its so-called opposite: Realism, riding its coattails.

Formalism has often been presented as tautological. Insofar as formalism has a unifying vision, Lyrissa Barnett Lidsky (1995) wrote, that is a vision of an autonomous body of ascertainable rules. Formalism, as a school of legal thought, rests on a political desire to maintain the status quo. In a democratic system the general Rule of Law has special claim to organizing society. First, there is a hierarchy within the law viewed as the product of the branch of government most responsive to the people. Second, executives and judges are supposed to handle individual cases within the confines of the law. Statutes, which are seen as establishing rules of inadequate clarity or precision, are thus criticized and amended by judges. Thus, students are taught that in a judicial system such as ours judges constrained not only by the text of the Constitution but also by the decisions of superior courts and even by the prior decisions of their own court courts.

The late Justice Antonin Scalia employed a similar formalism not unlike the one that produced *Lochner v. New York*, (1905) – in his decisions. While a congratulatory use of the word formal or formalism seems almost a linguistic error, Frederick Schauer (1988) duly noted there is more to this legal system than its pejorative connotation. Its pejorative connotation is in large part due to Justice Peckham's language, which suggested that he was merely explaining a precise statutory scheme rather than expounding his conservative political views in *Lochner*. Most legal thinkers condemned *Lochner* (1905) as formalistic because Justice Peckham talked about the legal concept of contracting away one's life for mere subsistence, as if it were a privilege equal only to the privilege of accepting that nineteenth-century version of indentureship. Added restricted contracting is not liberty unless concepts have no specific meaning, as Justice Holmes noted in his now famous observation in his *Lochner* dissent "general propositions do not decide concrete cases" (198 U.S. 45, 76).

While often a highly abstract form of thinking, law is not a collection of some vacuums' legal concepts floating about society. Marxian schools of thought might place law in the superstructure. But even that would be disingenuous.

When Roscoe Pound dismisses formalism, he does it as any realist would: on the basis of the methodology used. Formalists see course decisions as the conclusion of a deductive syllogism in which the major premise is the pre-existing general law and the minor premise is a statement of the fact establishing the case.

Certainly, legal concepts, the rules of logic, and analogical reasoning are all useful tools, as Holmes and the other realists, such as Judge Jerome Frank, noted. However, the main question is not what law ought to be but what law is, and both formalists and realists have avoided that question. Thus, as interesting as the discussion between formalists and realists is, their differences pale to a large degree if one pays attention to the larger school of thought they belong to: legal liberalism.

4 The Limits of Rawls and Dworkin: Justice and Historical Contingency

Scholarly meaning is more than ideological. It mostly stems from its textuality, from their narratives. Some legal theories, for instance, start from an ideal of justice as the explanatory purpose for their narrative. Justice has been long-used as a corrector for various legal explanations. In the late twentieth century, in his *A Theory of Justice* (1972), John Rawls wrote that

> Justice is the first virtue of social institutions, as truth is of systems of thought. A theory however elegant and economical must be rejected or revised as it is untrue; likewise laws and institutions no matter how efficient and well-arranged must be reformed or abolished if they are unjust. (Id.: 3)

So, let's see what *untrue* and *unjust* represented for Rawls, an uncompromising legal writer. Unlike other theories, he accepted the limits of his influence *ab initio*.

> The only thing that permits us to acquiesce in an erroneous theory is the lack of a better one; analogously, and injustice is tolerable only when it is necessary to avoid an even greater injustice. Being first virtues of human activities, truth and justice are uncompromising. (Id.)

Rawls intuitively understood the need for hierarchy and organization in human activity, ergo thoughts and scholarship. Our legal institutions exist because they are legitimized by a primary rule, the Constitution, which establishes the type of society the American people should live in: representative democracy with a three-branch government of quasi-equal governing role. Social cooperation is the reason stable democracies exist, and social cooperation requires a set of interests mirrored in the basic norms organizing our society. Our Constitution gives voice to those set of interests, and recognizes the right to liberty of thought, as well as to corporeality, and by extension, the right to private property. Our Constitution does not establish how much private property an individual or corporation should amass. Additionally, it does not establish what proportion of the population should live in poverty in order to secure unlimited private property for few individual entities. Rawls discarded such details because of "our intuitive conviction [in] the primacy of justice" (id.: 4). While the historic record since its inception might have impacted the relevance of Rawls' theory of justice, nevertheless, let us continue our adventure in Rawlsland.

First, it is interesting to understand Rawls' view of justice because historically, there is a parallel between 1971 and 2019 America. Then the United States of America were at war in Vietnam. At the time of the Vietnam conflict, the war disproportionately killed the poor; especially the African American youth. Today, many African-American poor end up in the military and in jail, as if our concept of justice is to keep the perceived troublemakers under heavy surveillance and silent. In other words, when Rawls wrote his opus, justice was multifold, and the social, political, and legal institutions of the time were more interested in promoting order than justice. Nevertheless, social order cannot survive without some public acceptance of the official time of justice that society sanctions at one point or another. The way this basic social justice exists is by arrangement between major social political and legal institutions.

> Taken together as one scheme, the major institutions define man's rights and duties and influence their life prospects, what they can expect to be and how well they can hope to do. The basic structures the primary subject of justice because it's effects are so profound and present from the start. (Id.: 7)

Since 1971, economic inequality has increased steadily despite the fact that representatives of various non-economically identified social groups have improved their social status. More women are in the workforce. As well, more immigrant women toil in the homes that the American women of the workforce have abandoned so that these career women can fulfill their American dream. Our world is functioning more and more like an urban place or sanctuary city where borders are porous, but the social promotion depends heavily on the starting point, whether it is a citizenship or trust fund. Rawls looked at the concept of justice for the basic structure over a functioning society where social cooperation still existed. To make his work easier, he imagined the American society isolated from its neighboring countries. The fallacy of this arrangement is made obvious by ever-thriving globalization. But, Rawls' main idea remains pertinent: for him, justice cannot exist outside society, outside rules establishing that order, which includes legal norms.

Rawls' world is well structured. Justice belongs in the social arrangements to fulfill the ideal of order (id.: 9). Social cooperation is part of the social structure Rawls imagines, as there are many types of justice. But Rawls is most fond of justice as fairness, which is very strange because he connects it to instinct and posits it outside the social system, except that it resembles a charity of sorts. We cannot measure fairness. We are supposed to go to a state of nature: to a primitive condition of culture: to a purely hypothetical situation where individuals are moral persons able to see their own ends, as well as the ends of others. As such, they politely recognize when they are wrong and yield to persuasive argument.

Could morality be viewed as a luxury of the middle-class? Could someone make the argument that an empty stomach has little time for reflection? Poverty is a relative construct depending on the surrounding economy; nevertheless, to expect polite reflexivity is to ignore reality and to attempt to mask it. Think about contract law, and the bargaining power it requires, and all the fictions surrounding enforceable contracts. The economic position of the parties has always mattered, sometimes so much that economic duress cancels all contractual binding, and we understand there cannot be any contract at all. So, going back to Rawls' theory of justice, justice as fairness exists only for those situations where the parties can be rational and parties can be rational almost always only when they are mutually disinterested, ergo their social economic status is quasi-equivalent. In other words, justice, a theoretical construct as primary as Rawls sees it, and only secondary to truth is a construct of luxury.

The current social crisis is the result of a lack of fairness, or better said, of the impossibility of achieving justice as fairness. But can it be that a different type of justice, a utilitarian justice, is a more appropriate standard? Rawls aims to discredit utilitarianism. Indeed, at first blush it seems that each man who realizes his interests is certainly free to balance his losses against his gains. Additionally, some are willing to sacrifice some needs and associate with others in order to find a way to other needs. No doubt usefulness works as sticks and carrots. However, what happens when the social economic realities are so divergent that usefulness has no common meaning among various members of society? Rawls answers that question when he dismisses utilitarianism as a thing that "does not take seriously the distinction between persons" (id.: 27).

Remarkably, Rawls shares Aristotle's view that man possesses a sense of justice, and that sharing a common understanding of justice makes a polis. Rawls' theory of justice is attractive because it talks about "weightings" and balancing ends. Also, it emphasizes the connection between the political and legal: a constitutional democracy rests on our common understanding of justice as fairness (id.: 243). Thus, rather than a common understanding of justice, a polis requires a social structure where interests are balanced and procedures are set in place to handle "contingencies of particular situations." Irrespective of how things turn out, all polis needs some level of distributive justice achieved (id.: 274).

Rawls knows all too well that there is no scheme of procedural political rules which guarantees that unjust legislation will not be acted upon. Moreover, "[i]n the case of a constitutional regime, or indeed of any political form, the ideal of perfect procedural justice cannot be realized" (id.: 198). Like Thomas Paine, Rawls was able to note the systemic problem, and the theoretical flaws in other systems, such as Bentham's. However, because he seems to believe that his justice as fairness is an objective concept, the limits of his own theories escape him.

In the intuitionist approach of the aggregative-distributive dichotomy, Rawls perhaps creates a straw man. But, the idea of priority is what matters, more than the intuitionist's two principles of justice: (1) the basic structure of society is to be deigned first to produce the most good in the sense of the greatest net balance of satisfaction and (2) to distribute satisfactions equally.

> [T]here is nothing necessarily irrational in the appeal to intuition to settle questions of priority no doubt in the conception of justice will have to rely on intuition to some degree nevertheless we should do what we can to reduce the direct appeal to our considered judgments. [...] For if men balance final principles differently, as presumably they often do, then their conceptions of justice are different. The assignment of weights is an essential and not of minor part of a conception of justice. If we cannot explain how these weights are to be determined by reasonable ethical criteria, the means of rational discussion of complement and intuitionist conception of justice is, one might say but half a conception. We should do what we can to formulate explicit principles for the priority problem, even though the dependence on intuition cannot be eliminated entirely. (Id.: 41)

Then Rawls goes on to explain how justice as fairness also relies on a primordial position. Although it limits the role of intuition in favor of rationality, because in adjudicating claims, one needs guiding principles, which for Rawls springs out of justice. Rawls also considers morality in justice and notices the difficulty of using such a strategy because it is too subjective: the person making the judgments is presumed to have the ability, the opportunity, and the desire to reach a correct decision (id.: 48). But Rawls does not seem to entertain the opposite possibilities: that people do not have the inclination to develop intuition (or be in touch with their intuition, so beloved by another ironist, Henry Bergson). Nor do they have the ability to be moral, because morality is not part of the human essence – it is acquired and often exercised as an element of "noblesse oblige" of material abundance.

Furthermore, could people be more inclined to reach judgments that mirror their moral norms? If so, how should society react to that? In the same way that the core of Rawls' liberalism was justice, for Dworkin it was equality. In 1978, Ronald Dworkin wrote in favor of the separation of political decisions from particular constructions of the good in order to achieve equality. A government that chooses among notions of good and then sets policies based on one or more of them fails to treat citizens equally, Dworkin believed (1978: 127). In his earlier writings, Dworkin (id.: 134), like Rawls in *Political Liberalism*, demarcated a clear line between political values and personal preferences. If Rawls stressed the importance of moral bracketing to guarantee societal stability, Dworkin criticized the incorporation of majoritarian morality into the formulation of public policy. For instance, in the context of race, Dworkin argued that

> [l]egislation based on racial prejudice is unconstitutional not because any distinction using race is immoral but because any legislation that can be justified only by appealing to the majority's preferences about which of their fellow citizens are worthy of concern and respect, or what sort of lives their fellow citizens should lead, denies equality.
> DWORKIN 1985: 68

Rawls explained his principles of justice and through a thorough analysis of formal justice. He defined "formal justice" as "the impartial and consistent administration of laws and institutions, whatever their substantive principles" (Rawls 1971: 58). The only equality formal justice requires is that "in their administration laws and institutions should apply equally" (id.). For more justice is "obedience to system" (id.). Certainly, treating similar cases the same is not a sufficient guarantee of substantive justice. Actually, it is a guarantee of the opposite because the facts may be similar; consequences of those facts need to be judged differently. In other words, formal justice is all about appearances and social order, which can be seen as social justice.

Rawls does not stop with formal justice. He espouses two primordial principles of substantive justice. First, he states that each person is to have equal rights to the most extensive basic liberty that is compatible with a similar liberty for others. Second, he states that social and economic inequalities are to be arranged so that they are both (a) reasonably expected to be to everyone's advantage, and (b) attached to positions of offices open to all. The basic liberties of citizens are political liberty such as the right to vote and to be eligible for public office. This is together with freedom of speech and assembly, liberty of conscience and freedom of thought, freedom of the person along with the right to hold personal property, and freedom from arbitrary arrest and seizure, as defined by the concept of the Rule of Law. The second principle means that the distribution of wealth and income, while not equal, is available to all. Briefly put, Rawls believes in equal citizenship and equality of opportunity (id.: 61), and besides the subject of justice, to the basic structure of society.

Correctly, Rawls explained the reason for this assignment is that its effects are profound, pervasive, and "present from birth" (id.: 96). This reasoning correctly explains that in his theory of justice, each person holds to relevant positions that of equal citizenship defined by their place in the distribution of income and wealth (id.). Additionally, Rawls notes with remarkable accuracy that members of the society are different because some benefit from undeserved inequalities that called for redress. Rawls identified birth and national endowment as such inequalities. When all these observations are done, Rawls goes into prescriptive mode and asserts that society must give more attention to those with fewer native assets and to those born into less favorable social positions. "The idea is to redress the bias of contingencies in the direction of equality" (id.: 100–101).

One way to address this bias is by spending on the education of the less rather than the more intelligent, at least at a certain time of life, save the early years of school. This is how Rawls wants to avoid a callous meritocratic society (id.: 100) and move in favor of a more equal society where efficiency and technocracy are not promoted values. Sensing that he is losing the battle with reason, Rawls goes back to intuition in explaining that some people cannot obtain everything they want. Rather, they have to accept as just, partial fulfillment, what is called equilibrium, "the result of agreements freely struck between willing traders" (id.: 119). This is for, when the natural state of things cannot ensure justice, the man-made state may do just that in a relative manner with the use of rights. In this, it sanctions private or public interests, rights conveyed only by a society where the Rule of Law is recognized and the general applicability is publicly accepted legal norms.

Perhaps, the more interesting part of Rawls' theory of justice refers to the main institutions of a constitutional democracy, which for him are necessary in order to obtain justice. Justice for him requires a specific structure that enables liberty of conscience and freedom of thought, as well as liberty of the person and equal political rights.

In a similar way, when Dworkin refers to constitutional intention, he was careful to establish that despite the relativism that surrounds even the most basic legal institutions, some meaning becomes well accepted in time; even if it has to be created artificially as "a term of art."

> Even though the concept of constitutional intention is a contested concept, legal practice might nevertheless settle, by convention, some aspects of this concept which ordinary language leaves open, so that constitutional intention becomes partially a term of art.
> DWORKIN 1981: 481

This jurisprudential debate about justice and public policy has had a great tradition, and I would like to end it with the brief filed in *State of Washington et al. v. Glucksberg* et al. 521 U.S. 702 (1997). There, six legal philosophers (including John Rawls, Ronald Dworkin and Robert Nozick) argued in favor of a Constitutional right to make the "most intimate and personal choices central to personal dignity and autonomy" (Fletcher 1997). Discussing the right to exercise some control over the time and manner of one's death, the philosophers equated the patient's action of refusing treatment with the patient's action of asking a willing doctor to help them reduce the time between the moment of the expiration of treatment and the expiration of life (id.). The Court did not recognize that individuals have a constitutionally protected interest in making those grave judgments for themselves, free from the imposition of any religious or philosophical orthodoxy by court or legislature. Denying that opportunity to terminally-ill patients who are in agonizing pain or otherwise doomed to an existence they regard as intolerable, the Supreme Court changed the conversation into a Constitutional right to assisted suicide. As such, it held that it was not a "fundamental liberty interest" and thus not protected by the Fourteenth Amendment.

That the six philosophers could not compel other jurists equally interested in the debate over terminology, about something so basic as the right to have professional help in exercising some control over the time and manner of one's own death, points to the poverty of liberal discourse. Chief Justice Rehnquist wrote the majority decision and found the English common law penalties associated with assisted suicide particularly significant. For example, at early common law, the state confiscated the property of a person who committed suicide. Like Blackmun in *Roe v. Wade*, Rehnquist used English common law to establish American tradition as a yardstick for determining what rights were "deeply rooted in the nation's history." Indeed, if *Roe v. Wade* and *Planned Parenthood v. Casey*, which held that other decisional moments in one's life benefit from constitutional protection, can be used as precedent in a case that negates them, I find myself wondering about the role of dissent in liberal jurisprudence – much like Duncan Kennedy wondered about the value of dialectical transformation.

> What looks to you like a whole is "really" just a temporary synthesis of previously discordant parts, about to develop an internal "contradiction." The contradictory elements, thesis and antithesis, will at first appear as holes in their own right. But then there will be "transcendence" or "going beyond" the opposition to a new synthesis, in a process that is simultaneously analytic and temporal, and is, obviously, a lot "bigger than the both of us." The process turns out to be a path–toward the self-transparent harmony of the whole and its parts–and Spirit turns out to be both the driving force and the underlying logic of the process/path.
>
> KENNEDY 2001: 1156

In the same way, I find myself realizing that what looks like differences among legal philosophers, there is nothing but just temporary disagreement. This is because the previous discordant parts about liberty, or justice, or public interest and morality, are going to develop into an internally monolithic account of wholes. The changes will be minimal. Whether we have the right to terminate a pregnancy or to terminate one's life in a humane manner depends on more fundamental rights, such as the right to healthcare, which as of today is hailed a social-economic fundamental right only by those of a particular critical ideology.

5   Critical Legal Studies and Marx

With one notable exception – *Critical Legal Studies* (CLS, or the *Crits*) – each latter-day liberal theory, pragmatic or postmodern, has embraced one community and one category of "other." Nevertheless, despite Unger's (2015) political position, the *Crits* tried hard to distance themselves from Marxian thought. They were selling out their integrity in a popularity context, so they would be more palatable to the American legal academe. Ironically, the *Crits* – a label commonly applied to CLS scholars (Minda 1989) – were so successful that they witnessed their own school's relevance diminish to oppositionist. However, their success almost succeeded in destroying the Marxian socio-economic otherness: the economic power struggle was replaced by social and political struggle for a specific group.

As opposed to all-encompassing ideologies from the right and left, neopragmatism shares with postmodern Europeans the interest in sex, minorities, traditions, religious struggles, etc. In that, this traces new forms of understanding of communities, their practices, laws, standards of acceptance of morality, political judgments, etc. (Molano 1999). Their approach to the studied phenomena is imbued with relativism, skepticism, and philosophical subjectivism, which are lenses used to study the individual and the community.

The attention to diversity is welcome, but its formal dogmatism has gone unchecked by reality. How much does it really matter for a teaching environment with 100 well-off white students, where 10 equally well-off students come from 10 different, but racially, ethnically, sexually, religious, age and gender-construed marginalized groups? None of the students could possibly understand what welfare state means or why it is necessary. And the same goes for the members of Congress or the Administrative agencies' management who cannot relate to public education, public infrastructure, or public healthcare. Horizontal diversity may be more important to any accurate narrative, but admitting the failure of how political identity diversity has been construed would require massive scholarly changes.

The *Crits* started as a leftist movement within the Ivy League legal academia (Kelman 1987; Gregory 1987; Turley 1987; Williams 1987; Kennedy and Klare 1984; Altman 1990; Balkin 1991). Since then, it has undergone so many changes that CLS no longer seems to possess a voice comprehensible to anyone outside its own small circle. Also, CLS has suffered many, often self-inflicted, injuries. So much so that, by now, there seems to be more flash than substance in its existence.

About two decades ago, I was writing that CLS might rediscover its own voice and agree that legal systems, as a product of the societies they purport to govern, and rights distribution often mirror social-economic structures (Neacşu 2000). In many ways, Duncan Kennedy's infamous 1983 "little red book," *Legal Education and the Reproduction of Hierarchy: A Polemic Against the System* captured the essence of CLS and appears to have contained the seeds of its future. The Polemic encouraged the legal community to "[r]esist!" and to avoid, or at least to postpone, becoming innocent ideological instruments (Kennedy 1983: ii) employed and exploited for the illegitimate reproduction of hierarchy (id.: 36).

By 2000, Duncan Kennedy's infamous *Polemic* manifested both the climax (1982–83) and the downfall of the *Crits*. Unfortunately, Kennedy's extraordinary sense of social injustice (Krever et al. 2015) did not serve him to seek solutions. For example, his refusal to adopt a clear and unique position, as observed by Peter Gabel and Duncan Kennedy (1984), could have probably sent a message of weakness to followers who decided, in response, to separate and focus on concrete action rather than on a definably indeterminate indeterminism (Boyle 1985; Kennedy 1976; Tushnet 1984; Singer 1984; Dalton 1985; Frug 1984; Heller 1984; Davis 1981).

Two decades ago, I could have written about the "salvation" of the CLS movement that was to abandon its almost cartoonish popular hype in favor of an authentic leftism. However, today I cannot make the same argument. CLS has been replaced by other liberal movements critical of illegitimate social power being exercised over their constituencies. (Cornell 1985; Minda 1997).

> [While the Fem-Crits keep] reminding us about the central importance of gender in framing our analysis of law[,] African-Americans, in turn, brought to the surface the importance of race consciousness in framing how the law dealt with race issues. The affinity between CLS and the legal feminist and critical race theory movements arose from the fact that these movements shared an 'outsider status' defined by the personal observation on what it was like to be 'outsider.'
> MINDA 1997: 9

For instance, critical race theorists became a "newly-organized splinter group" separating from CLS because their core belief was that "race was the real cause of disadvantage in society, and [not the] critical legal studies movement['s] debunking of liberalism" (Pyle 1999: 799).

Looking back, it seems that despite the enormous social transformations of the 1960s, the dominant theory of law remained unchanged, and, with what must have been increasing difficulty, continued to present law as neutral and above, or at least autonomous of, politics (Parker 1981; Peller 1988). CLS has successfully exposed the contradictions and incoherence of both left and right liberal theories (Moran 1997; Boyle 1985) while adding its voice to legitimizing the current hierarchies of "social power" (Hunt 1986). CLS sought to rectify social injustice when it viewed "legal scholarship [as] a kind of transformative political action" (Trubek 1984: 591) meant to change the organization of American society (Unger 1987a: 371). But then, something happened and somewhere along the way CLS continued to attack legal "formalism" (id.: 565) and "objectivism" (id.), all the while encouraging the instrumental use of legal practice and legal doctrine to advance leftist aims (Trubek 1984).

> By placing a belief in indeterminacy squarely at the center of judicial rhetoric, CLS challenged the importance of the vindication of rights, especially constitutional rights. CLS emphasized "the legal system's deviations from rules" and from that concluded, quite correctly, that this "demonstrates a crisis of liberalism." As a result, perhaps, CLS focused too much on language and too little on substance.
> NEACŞU 2000: 423–434

Roberto Mangabeira Unger, perhaps the leading voice for societal transformation in the critical school, attempted to "transform legal doctrine into one more arena for continuing the fight over the right and possible forms of social life" (Unger 1987: 579). According to Unger, two main tendencies can be distinguished in the critical legal studies movement.

> One tendency sees past or contemporary doctrine as the expression of a particular vision of society while emphasizing the contradictory and manipulable character of doctrinal argument. Its immediate antecedents lie in antiformalist legal theories and structuralist approaches to cultural history.
> Id.: 561

Another tendency grows out of the social theories of Marx and Weber and the mode of social and historical analysis that combines functionalist methods with radical aims. Its point of departure has been the thesis that law and legal doctrine reflect, confirm, and reshape the social divisions and hierarchies inherent in a type or stage of social organization such as capitalism (Trubek 1977; Unger 1984).

Unger viewed that transformation as taking place through an "internal development," in which the ideal conflicts of law are exploited to transform the actual law bit by bit. First, law changed and then the ideal conceptions were revisited in light of that change (Unger 1987; Bilsky 1997).

As Morton Horwitz pointed out, the *Crits'* most substantial achievement was their exposé of legal formalism as a disguise for the political and distributive functions of law has had a measurable impact on legal education (Horwitz 1977a). Another achievement is their showing in post-modern schools of jurisprudence (Kennedy 1980; Gordon 1984). In the process, however, it gave birth to division instead of unity among its cadre, thus, rendering it impossible to act as the phalanx of anything but its own internal disputes.

Whatever the cause, it seems that CLS has stopped short of answering its own questions about the law's lack of neutrality or about its failure to function with any kind of reason or logic. David Kairys observed this general preference for "debating other issues" instead of answering questions or even of acknowledging the fact that law functions to legitimate existing social and power relations.

> If law is not determinate or neutral or a function of reason and logic rather than values and politics, government by law reduces to government by lawyers, and there is little justification for the broad-scale displacement

of democracy. The extraordinary role of law in our society and culture is hard to justify once the idealized model is recognized as mythic.
KAIRYS 1998: 6

Perhaps this, or perhaps CLS's lack of coherent political objectives (Fletcher 1998: 690), might be the cause for it splitting into other schools of thought and to a large extent ending up forgotten. The lack of coherent political objectives in the CLS program induced many groups, such as feminists and critical race theorists, to spin off with their own particular programs for social justice (id.).

6 Feminism, Queer Theory and Marx

More than a decade ago, I was writing about the danger of pitting "particularism" – viewed as a discourse of the particular subject – against "essentialism" – viewed as a discourse of the universal subject. What caused that concern was what I perceived to be, ironically in retrospective, the unaddressed critique of the perils of particularism as a "new form of fixity" jurisprudentially (Neacşu 2005b), unlike other disciplines (Dallmayr 1987; Stychin 1994, Laclau and Mouffe 1985). I saw a specter of fear haunting America's Left, which included feminism and queer theories. The specter of fear, the fear of being perceived as "mediocrely petty-bourgeois and vaguely social-democratic," (Bourdieu and Wacquant 1992: 58), is the fear of participating in "any enterprise aimed at building against all forms of particularism" (id.). I called that the fear of "essentialist" meta-narratives, which was a euphemism for yet another reason to reject anything Marxian or Marxist. Although I did not notice its irony, the debate looked rigged. Martha Minnow best summarized that era's view of essentialism as intellectual sloppiness:

> [the] tendency to reduce a complex person to one trait–the trait drawing that person into membership in a particular group–and then to equate that trait with a particular viewpoint and stereotype.
> MINNOW 1997: 34

Sloppily, the *New Left* was creating intellectual straw men to easily dispose of them. This latter-day Left believed that they could resurface free of any Soviet blame. They embraced postmodernist thought and irrational French philosophers, who, confused by historical rigidity and bourgeois morality, succeeded in being interestingly ambiguous and saying whatever the American left wanted to hear in translation. But,

> [l]ike any theory born toward the end of a century, postmodernism nurtured a *fin de siècle* atmosphere, based on derision, disillusion, and parody of style. "Reason" became a metaphor, which ridiculed "the man who wishes to be taken seriously as a philosopher." Thus, the Left embraced postmodern and poststructural French thought as its theoretical foundation to explain the "other" and such universal social problems as those posed by gender and sexual orientation discrimination.
> NEACȘU 2005b: 125–126

It has often been clarified that Marx did not address either gender or sexual orientation discrimination in his theory of capitalism (Kellner 1995). Rather, Marx focused on the public sphere where the worker's alienation and self-alienation took place, of which a public sphere famously encroached the globe:

> The bourgeoisie has subjected the country to the rule of the towns. It has created enormous cities, has greatly increased the urban population as compared with the rural, and has thus rescued a considerable part of the population from the idiocy of rural life. Just as it has made the country dependent on the towns, so it has made barbarian and semibarbarian countries dependent on the civilized ones, nations of peasants on nations of bourgeois, the East on the West.
> GRUSKY 2001: 81; citing *The Communist Manifesto*

Marx famously explained how workers felt at home only in their leisure time. While at work, they felt homeless. However, he missed to explicitly point out that the inhuman plight that poor women and children were exposed, which made them homeless, both at home and in the public sphere – though he did describe it for his readers' own interpretation. In *Capital*, for instance, Marx described the predicament of pauper women and children across Europe from the Danube to the Atlantic Ocean. The Danubian Principalities, which are now Romania, embraced the corvée system during the second half of the nineteenth century. Under this system, entire peasant families – which included, of course, women and children – had to work three days a week "gratis for the capitalist," who was the owner of the land. Similarly, in England, the "cotton-spinning" industry employed children as young as seven years old, from six o'clock in the morning to nine o'clock at night, six days a week. Women, presumably, were exposed to similar or worse treatment (Marx 1887: 219–228).

Nevertheless, Marx was neither a feminist nor a queer theorist. To my knowledge, he ignored both gender and sexual orientation discrimination. He was concerned with commodification, with the never-ending process of the creation of new wants that were, by their nature, impossible for the working class to satisfy, causing alienation that begged for wages and further exploitation. Capitalist exploitation may well be the result of the exercise of power in a patriarchal society, but he ignored such an analysis. Obviously, he did not deal with that scenario because he thought that the most meaningful group identity was economic: neither genetic, age-related, or cultural. Certainly, there is a difference in degree between a child-worker's exploitation and that of her parents. Marx chose to let the liberals, often identified as "liberal cretins," (Marx 1887: 221) theorize nuances.

Marx did not engage in the politics of the personal. He was ages away from "'if you lick my nipple,' [as Michael] Warner remark[ed], 'the world suddenly seems comparatively insignificant'" (Morton: 35). But, if we look at identity as "the performance of desire" (id.: 36), as a place of "ideological and material contestation over need" (id.), then Marx too talked about identity when he analyzed desire; albeit as the result of the never-ending production of commodities (Elster 1986: 44).

By the end of the twentieth century, any legitimation that might have ever existed for a meta-theory, an "essentialist" discourse, has been displaced by what has come to be known as "identity politics," which focus on non-economic "identity" features. It is dominating the left-leaning public discourse. But, despite the opposing stance of Marx(ism) and identity politics, identity politics do rely on "essentialist" points of view. For instance, to become a member of a group, to some degree, all members' identity is "essentialized." Also, postmodern thought, despite its aspirations, is strikingly modernist. It assumes "a grand narrative to make sense of it all."

> For example, Catharine MacKinnon–who acknowledged that "[f]eminism has no theory of the state"–also recognized that feminist literature relies on either a liberal or a Marxist understanding of society. Thus, to the extent that identity politics does not use "redemptive human projects," as Fredric Jameson noted in 1984, and does not care about the world around it, it may be perceived as socially reactionary. Identity politics endorses the existing order, which epistemologically relies on essentialist assumptions that Aldous Huxley's Brave New World describes so well.
> NEACŞU 2005b: 128–129

In 2005, I was thoroughly ignored because I was calling for an examination of the regressive nature of postmodern politics: "identity politics seems to breed more identity politics" (Minow 1997: 56). All the while, essentialist theories, like Marx's, continued to provide the grounds to unify the disparate political movements. Marx could "provide values and ideals that might unite specific movements for specific goals" (Kellner 1995: 40). Back then, the economic times were too good and there was plenty to go around and satisfy various individual rights demands.

Then, I thought it a bold move for identity politics, which had distanced itself from the masses, seemingly in a desire to be beyond Left and Right (Kagarlitsky 2000). However, such distancing is hard to achieve and is often perceived as undemocratic. For instance, both gay and feminist activism in the former Soviet bloc arrived with "right-wing neo-liberal ideology," and the horrible anti-gay backlash we have witnessed needs to be partially explained ontologically.

> Current cultural politics discuss two forms of postmodernism: one of "reaction" and one of "resistance." The reactionary form "would seem to be [an example] of pure commodification and involves 'an instrumental pastiche of pop- or pseudo-historical forms.'" Conversely, the resistant form is "concerned with a critical deconstruction of tradition … with a critique of origins, not a return to them." Feminist and queer theories belong to the latter form of postmodern theories.
>
> NEACȘU 2005b: 131–132

The irony of identity politics remains in the constraints imposed by their often-unacknowledged liberalism, which comes in various shades of newness. Marx's work is, to a large degree, an ideological discourse about the downtrodden "others," the masses of others who are not part of any culturally identified groups, other than rednecks, possibly. Ironically, in America, the social group Marx's work talks to are totally ignorant and aggressively opposed to any of its explanations. And the (now defunct) *New Left* totally ignored them, and continues to do so, as if holding onto an ideological view is what matters most.

7 Intersectionality – Pragmatic Bridge between Theory and Reality

Marx wrote in *The Communist Manifesto* that "history of all hitherto existing society is the history of class struggles" (Marx and Engels 2012: 74). Without getting into any argument, if we continue reading his accounts of history, his summary seems accurate:

> Freeman and slave, patrician and plebeian, lord and serf, guild master and journeyman, in a word, oppressor and oppressed, stood in constant

opposition to one another, carried on an uninterrupted, now hidden, now open fight, that each time ended, either in the revolutionary reconstitution of society at large, or in the common ruin of the contending classes. (Id.)

Unlike in Marx's times, exploitation today has become more difficult to pinpoint, so the very idea of class struggle seems outdated or outright wrong. Today, there is no clear exploiter and exploited, because the terms have a nineteenth-century connotation. Instead, there is a myriad of intermediaries: some human, others automated. Since they are dispersed all over the globe, that makes it difficult for those working for a wage to perceive themselves as exploited. The workforce has lost its gendered outlook; women added layers of work interaction to their domestic and agricultural fiefdom.

In America, the bottom of the social ladder is a racially diverse mix, incorporating immigrants as well as many-generation American-born whites and blacks. Exploitation may be a vertical relationship, but without looking at its intersectionality, it cannot be properly described, because work and value have changed their outlook. Exploitation explained as subordination and vulnerability may be more accurate because it comes at the end of a long hierarchical chain, whose higher end cannot be easily perceived. The decades of blurring the lines between the private and public spheres and their current overlapping has made any discussion of exploitation in Marxian terms seem incomprehensible. This is a moment of theoretical discomfort, and it is an invitation for a new normativity. The moment is ripe for a theory to describe the existing social structures and their intersectional hierarchical organization.

In 1989, Kimberlé Crenshaw described the experiences women encountered in their daily lives as routine violence, and a broad-scale system of domination that affected them as a group, or a gendered class. She started the conversation about recognizing what was social and systemic with what had formerly been perceived as isolated and individual. Crenshaw situated her discourse within the identity politics of African-Americans, other people of color, gays and lesbians, and other minorities, which represented a source of strength. She became aware of the growing dissonance between classical liberal politics and the needs of various minorities to change dominant conceptions of social justice. Social power delineating differences among identity groups needed to cease being just that. Instead, it should become a source of empowerment and social reconstruction. As identity politics became absorbed by mainstream liberal politics, their goal became twice removed. Paradoxically, Crenshaw noted, identity politics did not transcend difference and failed to build alliances, although they frequently conflated intergroup differences. However, alliances could not be built ignoring or minimizing the import of race, class, or both (id.). Crenshaw noted the intersection of patterns of violence due to racism and sexism, and the reality of women of color who have been thus situated in at least two subordinated groups that frequently pursue conflicting political agendas.

> The problem with identity politics is not that it fails to transcend difference, as some critics charge, but rather the opposite – that it frequently conflates or ignores intragroup differences. In the context of violence against women, this elision of difference in identity politics is problematic, fundamentally because the violence that many women experiences is often shaped by other dimensions of their identities, such as race and class.
> CRENSHAW 2008: 279

By pointing out the need for an integrated, dialectical, perspective in describing and addressing subordination, Crenshaw forcefully interpellated reality. Her dialectics incorporate the gains made by the politics of identity and go a step further. The complex reality of gender, race, and economic subordination can be both analyzed through its separate impact and presented as a unifying experience, that of routine, daily, violence.

Through her visionary work, Crenshaw liberated our imagination. If exploitation ceased to mirror a reality experienced by the majority of the masses, it is perhaps because the profit that comes with it is not obvious any longer. However, the intersectionality of violence, the vulnerability thus created, does. Social work relationships are becoming so complex that the value created by work is no longer easily perceived as the source of profit. Before, the source came out of a somewhat clear equation: profit, the product of supervalue, was caused by the capital invested and in partial exchange for the worker's wage.

In *Capital*, Marx (1887) explains how the correlation between wage, capital, and profit worked in the first half of the nineteenth century. Imagine employees who live off of a wage received for eight hours of work, then turnaround to spend the remaining sixteen hours creating free content for Amazon and Wikipedia. They continue to provide free labor by investing capital in web hosting places and creating more content for search engines, thus enabling them to exist. While also clicking on Facebook and other social media postings exposing their and their acquaintances' vulnerabilities, which then are processed into wants that they would then work to satisfy with wages garnered from the next eight-hour day of paid work.

If you wonder how the production engine keeps working: the sixteen hours of previous family and relation time are now invested in a diffuse economy, whose only purpose is to motivate the worker to outperform themselves in those eight hours of wage producing work so that they can satisfy wants they never knew they had and to which they would be unaware if they did not engage the surrounding virtual reality. In itself, virtual reality is a space of possibility and alienation, a place of personal re-configuration, which cannot happen without a perpetual assemblage of what has been discarded so something new can replace it. This is violence at its most subtle embodiment. This violence is subtly individualized according to geography, but also age, gender, sex, race, and class.

This brief review was meant to underscore the value of transparency in legal meaning-making. Furthermore, in a monolithically liberal environment, only irony can set up differences. But irony is hard to notice unless scholarly communication expands to include scholars with different views.

In the current environment, it seems that Marx, a cultural creature of his historical time and cultural milieu, may be an unappetizing figure in the #MeToo era. But, his scholarship remains a blueprint of highs and lows of what one can aspire to produce and what one can reach if honest about their private and public subjectivity. While not always obvious, irony is imbedded in jurisprudence as it is in social scholarship. Let's unearth it so we can figure out the politics behind the present knowledge production and Regime of Truth.

• • •

This brief summary of some of the most resonant schools of American thought (of course, there are many others I have not touched upon, such as Law and Economics, or Experientialism) should point out the ironic ideology of meaning-making. Their presentation was to exemplify differences in content due to their topical interests, but also ideological constraints: whether they were due to their anti-essentialist, or (anti)-economic views.

More generally, I brought those schools of thought into attention because they help build my argument about the scholarly presence of irony and ideology. To the extent that jurisprudence is social scholarship, I argue that it embodies meaning-making incorporating the author (S_1) and audience's (S_2) ideology, which, in the process of meaning-making, actuate T_1's embedded irony.

While this book contends that ironic ideology belongs to all scholarship, its significance is larger because it comprises all theoretical explanations whose meaning is negotiated by their instigator and interpellator. Case in point is, for example, Jeffrey Toobin's (2018) popularization of Justice Anthony Kennedy's jurisprudence for the *New Yorker* audience in *After Kennedy*. Toobin's article was about the impact that Kennedy's retirement would have for the socially liberal minded. Ironically, that meaning escaped my textual interpellation. Let's see how that was possible.

The title itself, *After Kennedy*, clearly directed the reader's gaze to the Justice's replacement by President Trump. As Toobin wrote, it sounded ominous. Unexpectedly, to make his point, Tobin referenced *Janus v. AFSCME*, 585 U.S., 138 S.Ct. 2448 (2018), a case where Justice Kennedy sided with the conservative majority of the Court, and thus, in light of Trump's conservative replacement, would indicate continuity rather than disruption. *Janus* inflicted unions a deadly blow, because Kennedy sided with the majority. The holding in *Janus* created a new negative right for public employees covered by union-negotiated contracts. Due to *Janus*, public employees applying for a union position, once successful in their application, have a new right. That right is to change their mind and refuse to pay union dues. One may argue that employment outside the union is a different employment from that the one for which they applied, because the original employment benefitted from union-negotiated entitlements that came when they entered into that contractual relationship. Rather than making it a case about individual rights, *Janus* is about bad faith negotiations when a party is allowed to renege on part of its obligations. The Court described it as a matter of free speech, much practiced by elected judges who promised to abstain from judicial activism before Senate confirmation and do the opposite when invested with judiciary powers. *Janus* is so corrupting in its outreach – a case about freedoms and individual rights – that Toobin himself, ironically I would say, had to quote the dissent opinion written by Justice Elena Kagan.

> Justice Elena Kagan wrote in a dissent, this is "weaponizing the First Amendment, in a way that unleashes judges, now and in the future, to intervene in economic and regulatory policy." She added, "Speech is everywhere – a part of every human activity (employment, healthcare, securities trading, you name it). For that reason, almost all economic and regulatory policy affects or touches speech. So the majority's road runs long."
>
> TOBIN 2018: 20

To add another layer of irony: if Kennedy's jurisprudence is so destructive to liberal (union) values, is Toobin's ironic when he wrote about missing him? Ideologically, I would say Kennedy's voting with the majority in *Janus* was also an expression of his own free speech.

Toobin's ideology, his set of beliefs about power structure in society, is somewhat similar to Anthony Kennedy's, otherwise, Toobin could not have valued Kennedy's jurisprudence. Noteworthy, Toobin makes dignity the fulcrum of his argument. He states that with the loss of Kennedy, the Court's dignified lawmaking will disappear with Kennedy's retirement. However, dignity is a concept not without irony. It can easily mean so many things.

> There is no mystery about Supreme Court Justice Anthony Kennedy's favorite word. It is "dignity," which he invoked repeatedly in his opinions. The word appears three times in his 2003 decision in Lawrence v. Texas, which established the principle that gay people could not be thrown in jail for having consensual sex. He mentions it nine times in his most famous opinion, Obergefell v. Hodges, from 2015, which guaranteed the right to same-sex marriage in all fifty states. Lawyers, hoping to appeal to the Court's swing vote, sprinkled their briefs and arguments with "dignity," even as critics on both the left and the right found Kennedy's infatuation with the word (which does not appear in the Constitution) maddening, because it was never quite clear what he meant by it.
> TOOBIN 2018: 19

So, Kennedy's dignity appears in terms of one' sexuality, and that is better left to the private realm. And what better guarantee that one's sexuality remains a private matter than confining it to the bourgeois institution of marriage? If so, would not Kennedy's jurisprudence become less of an expression of distributive dignity and more of the desire of a prude to keep uncomfortable discussions outside the public realm? Luckily for us, and progress in general, Kennedy failed in what I perceive to be another facet of his conservatism – gender and sexuality have become now, more than ever, issues of public debate.

Ideology is not a monolithic block of ideas. For instance, Toobin's ideology, like Kennedy's, is liberal. Toobin's is less conservative than Kennedy's. But ironically, their common liberalism makes Toobin blind to Kennedy's and muddles the clarity of his argument. Ironically, Toobin can bemoan Kennedy's human conservatism not because it would be missed, but because something worse might come (and it came in the form of Justice Brett Kavanaugh). Toobin adheres to a set of beliefs about the role of government, and that includes the judiciary, to protect the status quo. He worries that "a new [Supreme Court] majority can and will bestow those rights and take them away, in chilling new ways." Toobin's ideology makes him unable to see that for almost half a century, the Supreme Court engaged in a counter-revolution of sorts, emptying out rights of any substantive common-sense meaning. For instance, in American history, unionization implemented the benefits that social democracies ensured elsewhere, but with various levels of social service according to the years of unionized work. As Willy Forbath would say,

> Progressives have forgotten how to think about the constitutional dimensions of economic life. In the thick of a grave economic crisis, that is unfortunate. Work, livelihoods, and opportunity; material security and insecurity; poverty and dependency; union organizing, collective bargaining, and workplace democracy: for generations of American reformers, their constitutional importance was self-evident.
>
> FORBATH 2011: 1116

Toobin could not have written this article had he been aware that Justice Kennedy was an active member of the American judiciary-led, counter-revolution. For Kennedy's legacy, *Janus* is not an exception. *Obergefell* is the exception because it could be interpreted as more than a straight man's desire to keep what he viewed as private, private. After Kennedy will be what has been with Kennedy, and Toobin refused to write that essay. The more recent Supreme Court incarnations have been using chilling new ways to dismantle the pre-existing rights bestowed on the American people by their predecessors.

We are in the midst of dismantling the jurisprudence of the first three-quarters of the twentieth century. The new ways have become entrenched by now, implemented by Republican appointees with Republican views about the demise of the administrative, regulatory state, who are opposed to social justice and supportive of rampant economic inequality. The irony of Toobin's writing is his disappointment that the American type of hillbilly oligarchy has forgotten that even indentured apprentices have rights and voted for the French Bourbon crass display of "let them buy cake if they don't want to pay union fees for bread."

This imbedded irony by the author, willingly or not, is what I call here the irony of meaning. It is where meaning is the meeting place of the author's perspective and the reader's. Irony, for me, comes out of the author's plowing of the soil of meaning and the reader sowing its seeds. While both have clear expectations about the harvest, trees or bushes, much of the details often surprise both.

And here comes Marx and his body of work.

There is a way of writing about government and lawmaking limiting ourselves to specific aspects of government and lawmaking. Or, one could focus on one government branch, such as the judiciary, or on one specific institution of that branch, the Supreme Court, for instance. Even more precisely, one could write about the work of one Justice in one term, or his most humanizing decision ever. Better yet, as with Kennedy, one could focus only on his concluding words in the 2015 decision in *Obergefell v. Hodges,* which recognized the right of same-sex couples to be married. "It would misunderstand these men and women to say they disrespect the idea of marriage" (135 S.Ct. at 2608), Justice Kennedy wrote, because "they do respect it, respect it so deeply that they seek to find its fulfillment for themselves," and "they ask for equal dignity in the eyes of the law" (id.) and "the constitution grants them that right" (id.). Another way to write about government and lawmaking is to proceed in the opposite way, so we do not miss the work of the text of law, a statute, a judgment, or a regulation, and start perceiving and conceiving its meaning not in a separate manner but as integral to a societal power code constantly weaving in and self-challenging the role and work of its constitutive institutions. But such a reading would be labeled dialectic, and most often a dialectical interpretation requires a historical positioning of any object of study in a particular set of socio-economic and political circumstances, which is an invitation to explore both its roots and consequences, and especially the ideology of that exploration.

I trace this type of integrated exploration to Karl Marx. It has been so discredited that one is inclined to believe that there is not a lot of value in this method of research. But, what if that discretization is mere rumor gone awry?

Marxian analysis comes in handy because of its ideological irony. Marx, whose work has been publicly used in a marvelous PR coup to give intellectual support to two Russian peasant revolts, in 1905 and 1917, had been dismissed as populist. However, if one reads his work, it becomes obvious that Marx wrote for his intellectual peers, well versed in Hegel, Greek drama, classical music, world history, and local politics. Marx, perhaps like the Toobins of today, tried to educate the rich, the strata of the German well-off population who found holding a newspaper, or, in today's world, a tablet with the *New Yorker* cartoons on display, a pleasant pastime. Out of his secular integrity, perhaps, Marx embraced the ideology of the exploited, and denounced the power structure bent against them. Fittingly, he devoted his intellectual prowess, and how mighty that was, to sensitize the powerful to the plight of the downtrodden. Marx saw the spectrum of misery coming out of European factories and feared for the future of his blind and deaf peers.

Surely, today the downtrodden have virtual spaces to let off steam, pursue a civil society engagement and exchange political opinions, or even send emojis to the powerful. Yet and still, hunger and dignity remain satisfied non-digitally. While the Marxian irony is that his peers ignored his message, his work, and especially the interaction with his work through the years, remain ours to explore and ponder. I sometimes find the modernity of Marx's work translated in his desire to build a society for the ages, which is the reason that makes his detractors discard it as populist and utopian. Still, that does not explain why destruction and square thinking has been so appealing to the post-postmodern intellectual in the last decades.

If we tend to give names to what we understand and what we do not because we need to make sense of the world, we need to reconsider what is liberal, what is not, and what is different and perhaps unknown. Only sometimes, we become so scared or unnerved that we choose ambiguity in hopes that our discomfort will go away. It does not. It only increases. This book is a call for reconsideration and rebirth. Meaning-making is its own phoenix. This cycle requires a return to Marx so something more fitting can be imagined.

SUMMARY AND CONCLUSION

Ideological Irony and Liberal Scholarship

After studying law in Soviet Romania at the end of last century, being a Civil Court trial judge, a researcher, and a law teacher there at a time where a Westernized hype of Hayek adoration was sipping through to take over academia, I studied EU and American law, went on to work on the Israeli-Palestinian peace process, and then promoted social and economic tolerance through my U.S.-based writing. I practiced law in New York City before settling into legal research and teaching at Columbia University and Barnard College. I could never understand one's attraction to Hayek's economic adventure except as an ideological choice. As explained by Edmund Phelps, whose unabashed Hayek admiration I use as an antidote to my aversion, Hayek's most impressive innovation is his "growth-in-knowledge" concept. It combines formal, as well as, personal or "tacit" knowledge. Hayek's knowledge theory, ironically, reminded me of Henry Bergson's intuition. Stuart Hall called it difference. Without making sure that there is difference within the academe, little knowledge can be added to the existing paradigm.

When, I started my doctoral studies at Rutgers University, School of Communication and Information (2007–2011), with the desire to aquire the tools to understand the difference between the Marx I read and the Marx everyone else was reading. At that time, I was thinking in Kessler and Pozen's terms: how did Marx work himself impure? Instead, I demystified fake news, apparently right on time for the new era of collusion between the third and fourth estates.

Somewhat, my quest to apply Marx to Marx, and to the liberal academia has only increased. Asserting my ideological identity I was able to find that Marx missed acknowledging ideological limits in his own scholarship. As a result, he set no margins of error for the inevitable irony of subsequent interpellations of his text. He wrote as if no subsequent meaning-making negotiation of his text could happen. It took me almost another decade to understand the ideological irony in this Marxian flaw.

Cornel West once said, "America is in the midst of a massive social breakdown" (West 1991: xi). I believe that we have only deepened that crisis, and the re-evaluation of our knowledge production and Regime of Truth are imminent. My contribution to this process is ideological irony as structural parts of meaning-making. Marx and his works have provided the sounding board for my argument.

Perhaps my openness to the irony of meaning comes from my attitude towards scholarship. Hume did not see any necessary obligation in scholarship production as revelatory writing that delivered the spoken word of God. However, interpellating reality in a desire to articulate a problem that is suddenly visible within the existing theoretical paradigm, scholarship is in demand, especially when it articulates it into a descriptive or normative narrative. Having its premise in reality, as Marx correctly understood its starting point, scholarship is contingency and interpellation. Not a God's creation, scholarship reflects the S_1's private and public subjectivity; ergo it is biased and transient.

As private subjectivity, alienation is S_1's objectification, while ideology expresses S_1's public attitude about their personal and social cultural baggage, which reflects S_1's subservient or critical attitude toward the surrounding power structure. The reasoned narrative, then communicated, opens itself for meaning-making negotiation. The text interpellates the audience, S_2, transforming the public into engaged readers, critics, and commentators. Their own private feelings and emotions, as well their cultural baggage and public attitude toward it, plays a role in the meaning negotiation. Even their own ideology plays a role, though it is are rarely mentioned. Furthermore, during this phase of meaning-making, the interaction of S_1's ideology and alienation with S_2's alienation and ideology may add meaning that is different or even opposite to what is expressed in the narrative. The dormant meaning of scholarship is thus actuated. I call this scholastic irony. In the case of jurisprudence, for instance, ideology is highly political because the object of jurisprudence is law, a rule of behavior issued then sanctioned by political (legislative) bodies. Ideology gives meaning an ironic turn: it influences meaning-making in unexpected ways. Irony is independent of ideological falsehood, but it magnifies the falsehood or morality contained in the text.

As a long-time student of Marxian works who grew up in Soviet Romania and engaged in quixotic battles with the liberalism of Hayek and Foucault in the American academe, I have noticed both ideology and irony in academic meaning-making. Using my privileged position, I employ Marx and his works to point out the structure of scholarship. Both the young and the adult Marxian works are referenced here eluding the dismissiveness of "Marxism," or even the more seditious, "Marxism-Leninism." The usefulness of Marx results from his enormous intellectual roots, because what is Marx without Hegel, Ricardo, Feuerbach, Smith, Proudhon, or even Engels? Hopefully, it becomes clear that in the same way Marxian work was an ironic ideological response to the liberalism of his day, today's western scholarship since Marx is an ironic ideologically oriented response to his work.

Edward Said's (1996) analysis in "The Limits of the Artistic Imagination and the Secular Intellectual" offers six axes of activity and thought "orienting intellectual activity" (6). They are intended to (1) provide counter-information in an age where the media have the resources to manage and manipulate reality; (2) represent a reinterpretive function at the level of communicating ideas; (3) demystify and articulate the basic issues of justice and human good or evil surrounding these issues; (4) disrupt all attempts to privatize knowledge; (5) prevent consensus on the basis of domination; and (6) "exercise a moral function of deploying the irreconcilable and irreducible oppositions between ideas, peoples, societies, histories, and claims" (Davies 2008: 9).

The project undertaken here is meant as an alternative to the overall thinking, or lack of it, in the face of the unstoppable flood of information. Through Marx's work, we could gather perspective over our own act of scholarship production. In the process, we can also learn how to parse through old and new meaninglessness. Paraphrasing Walter Benjamin, as well as, through the folly of our times, this process attempts to satisfy the desire to always find ourselves in the knowing.

> "Knowledge" is the [defense] in an argument to win, [so we] may assert mastery over it. As Walter Benjamin wrote in one of his earliest essays, "the philistine, you will have noted, only rejoices in every new meaninglessness. He remains in the right."
> SUTHERLAND 2011: 111

But, what if this tendency to always be accepted, to be "in the right," and thus avoid confronting the unfamiliar is what keeps us from acknowledging that the current social cataclysm is a sign of structural oppression gone too far? Bringing attention to irony as an unavoidable, intrinsic element of scholarship should humble us and free our intellectual ambition to reach new heights. We will stumble no matter what, but paraphrasing Norman Vincent Peale, without dreaming we cannot build anything worth dreaming.

Could this project be seen as a call to dream backwards in the past? Why today, promote the work of Marx, a bearded, misogynistic, European man? First, his contingency and ours are similar. Like him, we are witnessing a profound cultural crisis. Marx's theory marks an emancipatory moment in Western scholarship because of its breath and dialectic interdisciplinary roots, along with Marx's open embrace of his subjectivity. Marx's genius was his ability to synthesize existing theoretical accumulation, and to thereby lend a new direction to the dialectical methodology of investigation, as if implementing Hegel's words:

> But it is here as in the case of the birth of a child; after a long period of nutrition in silence, the continuity of the gradual growth in size, of quantitative change, is suddenly cut short by the first breath drawn – there is a break in the process, a qualitative change and the child is born. In like manner the spirit of the time, growing slowly and quietly ripe for the new form it is to assume, disintegrates one fragment after another of the structure of its previous world. That it is tottering to its fall is indicated only by symptoms here and there. Frivolity and again ennui, which are spreading in the established order of things, the undefined foreboding of something unknown – all these betoken that there is something else approaching. This gradual crumbling to pieces, which did not alter the general look and aspect of the whole, is interrupted by the sunrise, which, in a flash and at a single stroke, brings to view the form and structure of the new world.
>
> HEGEL 2003: 6

Second, there is so much to learn from Marxian interpellation. He ignored the private sphere, where the political became personal, but his subjectivity marked his scholarship perhaps more because of his inability to include the private sphere into his scholarship. At this junction, in "the midst of a massive social breakdown" (West 1991: xi), when alienation has become our state of being, "pork chop tribalism," paraphrasing Huey Newton (id.: xviii), the scholarship of the status quo cannot continue. At a minimum, we need to acknowledge our tribalism. Furthermore, Marxian theory, with its focus on democratically shared power, has enriched progressive scholarship with its analytical reasoning. Kimberlé Crenshaw's theory of intersectionality (1989), for instance, which addresses our multilayered contingency in a dialectical, inclusive, and deeply ideological manner, incorporates a micro-level Marxian theory of race and gender issues, addressing only the complex facets of our present-day reality.

In mapping the intersections of race and gender, the concept does engage dominant assumptions that race and gender are essentially separate categories. But, what if we disrupt the tendencies to see race and gender as exclusive or separable, especially if we factor in issues such class, sexual orientation, age, and color (Crenshaw 1995)? Let's bring that map forward. Let's work on leadership, on issues which can be representative of everybody in the gutter.

Finally, Marx's work was his ideologically ironic response to the scholarship of his time. This is mine. The irony surrounding all scholarship reminds us that all knowledge production is transient. Ironically though, by embracing our subjectivity, we can control its meaning, and with it, its relevance.

This book calls for interpellating Marx's works with an acknowledged ideological lens. As such, it also becomes an attempt to oppose technocratic, and merely cosmetic managerial changes at a time when more is needed. The era introduced by Thomas Paine's *Common Sense* (1776) promoted the capitalist commoner's revolt against British aristocracy (Knapp 2013). Its binary structure remained unchanged when Marx dissected the power structure a century later, though the entrepreneurial bourgeois had replaced the aristocrat, and the wealth production required both the capitalist and the wage earner to actively engage in its production. Since, inequality between employers and employees changed only superficially. Most of the bitterly gained socio-economic entitlements, such as healthcare and pension benefits that unionized jobs used to offer until not long ago, have been lost.

Politically, 2016 may go down in history as the year when less educated, politically ignored commoners became united in their distrust of the liberal establishment irrespective of its minimal deviations towards right or left. How did that happen? For almost a decade, the have-nots have been becoming the majority of the electorate, as a recent Pew Research Center report, "A Nation of 'Haves' and 'Have-Nots'?" shows:

> In 1988, far more Americans said that, if they had to choose, they probably were among the "haves" (59%) than the "have-nots" (17%). Today, this gap is far narrower (45% "haves" vs. 34% "have-nots"). (http://www.pewresearch.org/2007/09/13/a-nation-of-haves-and-havenots/)

What can the Future Guardians of the Law do? Shall they continue in the same existing vein, or shall they try something different?

Given the theoretical vacuum of the contemporary left, I wish I could write that all it took was the election of the 45th President, Donald J. Trump (a marginal political neophyte) to awaken U.S. legal academe to the importance of the writings of Karl Marx (another misunderstood outsider, although at the opposite end of Trump's political and intellectual spectrum). This has not been the case. The one hundredth anniversary of the Bolshevik Revolution, "one of the great events of human history," as the famous reporter John Reed described it, has come and gone (Reed 1919). With it, we have missed out on another chance to re-evaluate Marx(ism), both the label, and especially, the brilliance of his writings, as Marcuse often described his body of work (Marcuse 1966).

But, missed chances are only opportunities to start anew, as this book wants to be. And again, history has lessons for us. Today's rise of Trumpism is very much similar to the rise of Jacksonian democracy. Both point out the ironic relationship between the literal political theory of a democratic government they pretend to use and the figurative political performance, the actuation of that demagogy. While some scholars believe that this gap has only increased since Jackson first used it (Mercieca 2008), it has rarely appeared so clear to the uninitiated. Today, like then, the word "democracy" is highly used to explain the reasons for political actions, "to benefit the people." Nonetheless, it is more and more unclear who the people are. As Jennifer Mercieca (2008) explains, Jacskon invoked democracy and behaved like a despot, but as his Farewell Address shows, the country he left behind remained what it was when he inherited: a mere republic (id.).

Noah Webster noted in 1837, American republican political theory had developed between 1764 and 1824. As Mercieca observed, that was in opposition to monarchy, aristocracy, and democracy:

> America's first generation of political leaders had distrusted democracy as the rule of the worst. They viewed the government of all overall as tumultuous, short lived, and violent; neither property nor liberty, they feared, were secure under democracy.
>
> MERCIECA 2008: 442

The Founding Fathers gifted America with a particular type of republicanism. Through representation, it filtered the will of the people and preserved hierarchy in order to prevent equality. As well, it provided stability at all costs (id.: 446). Part of that project, the Rule of Law, ensured that property became a form of liberty. Property ensured stable hierarchy, because it prevented equality. Furthermore, due to its duality, shackle and freedom, as a form of liberty property became protected and protectable by all – even those non-propertied. That is the irony of our democratic stability.

The rise of Jacksonian Democrats, like the Trumpian Republicans today, rested on a tension between the meaning of democracy and its actuation. The Jacksonian Democrats were able to rise to power, Mercieca explains, because they promised the people participation and equality. In other words, their rise was made possible by them getting rid of the pretense and the growing gap between the literal political theory of a democratic government and its figurative political performance. In time, Mercieca continues, Jackson reversed to the earlier status quo, and embraced the previously derided pretense. Moreover, his administration reverted to the original role of the government, hence her claim that America's democratic style is primarily ironic. Persuasively, Mercieca explains how our democratic style figuratively negates its literal political theory; it allows politicians to occupy the realm of democratic appearances by eliding the fact that the American government is merely a republic.

Inspired by this argument, I thought adding to it with a book about scholarly meaning-making. I used Marxian work welcoming its many contradictions: while reviled, it is easily accessible. Maybe different, sometimes marginalized, his work however made it through the various regimes of truth into the world of Knowledge (K) (Figure 1). Because it is ironic, I started looking into the role of irony and the journey has been spellbinding. Irony influences meaning not only when the scholar, the textual instigator S_1, incorporates it textually. As shown here, irony is also in the eye of the beholder, being actuated by the textual interpellator (S_2) in the process of understanding.

The meaning-making negotiation between the textual instigator (S_1) and the textual interpellator (S_2) is even more dramatic when the scholars' ideology dramatically diverges from the hegemonic normativity. Ironically, the well-established "King of America," metaphor, as Thomas Paine (1922) dubbed "the law" in *Common Sense*, enables different meanings when interpellated by scholars with different ideologies.

> But where, say some, is the King of America? I'll tell you, friend, he reigns above, and doth not make havoc of mankind like the Royal Brute of Great Britain. Yet that we may not appear to be defective even in earthly honors, let a day be solemnly set apart for proclaiming the charter; let it be brought forth placed on the divine law, the word of God; let a crown be placed thereon, by which the world may know, that so far as we approve of monarchy, that in America the law is king. For as in absolute governments the king is law, so in free countries the law ought to be king; and there ought to be no other. But lest any ill use should afterwards arise, let the crown at the conclusion of the ceremony be demolished, and scattered among the people whose right it is.
> PAINE 1922: 35–36

Paine's metaphor (T_1) has had the same meaning for centuries: "The American Rule of Law" acts as if King, because ours is a government of rules duly adopted by duly elected representatives that repealed the monarchy of a king's whims. In 1989, the late Supreme Court Justice Antonin Scalia (S_2) incorporated Thomas Paine's metaphor (T_1) in his Chicago Law Review article (T_2). The expectation was that T_1's meaning would remain unchanged, as mentioned above. Unexpectedly, Scalia's T_2 proved our expectations wrong. Scalia (S_2) negated the core of Paine's meaning. Scalia negotiated a meaning where indeed there was no King George, but instead of a government of laws adopted by duly elected representatives, Scalia's meaning was a government of nine justices, appointed for life, as if kings (Scalia 1989: 1176).

The Rule of Law is supreme, but its High Priests are above, Scalia, a self-proclaimed originalist, advocated within the existing Paradigm of Knowledge. His was a disruptive interpretation of Paine's work, but it still fit the republican label. His High Priests (Justices) had no inherited power, and his negotiated meaning remained unnoticed – perhaps because everyone seems busy dining with ideological friends, as if a character in Buñuel's *Discreet Charm of the Bourgeoisie*. Nevertheless, Scalia proposed a startlingly different meaning of Paine's work. His negates the very republican (*res publica*) core of our Rule of Law. His meaning replaces a government of rules with one of Nine Justices. Not denying the impact of contingency, the difference between the long-accepted view of the American King as the Rule of Law, and Scalia's view of the Justices replacing the Rule of Law, stems from the ideological clash between Scalia's reading of Paine and my (S_3) interpellation of Scalia's view of Paine's words. All things considered, that is the ideological irony of meaning, generally, and of American jurisprudence, specifically: treacherous fluidity. And this why this book is a call for academic diversity, as the only form of intellectual checks and balances.

References

Abrams v. United States. 1919. 250 U.S. 616 (United States Supreme Court).

Ackerman, Bruce. 1991. *We the People: Foundations*. Cambridge, MA: Belknap Press of Harvard University Press.

ACTL, and IAALS. 2008. *Interim Report on the Joint Project of the American College of Trial Lawyers Task Force on Discovery and the Institute for the Advancement of the American Legal System*. http://perma.cc/6VD6-7Y93.

Adorno, Theodor W. 1973. *Negative Dialectics*. New York, NY: Seabury Press.

Althusser, Louis. 1971. *Lenin and Philosophy and Other Essays*. London, UK: New Left Books.

Althusser, Louis. 1972. *Politics and History. Montesquieu Rousseau, Hegel and Marx*. London, UK: NLB.

Althusser, Louis. 1984. *Essays on Ideology*. London, UK: Verso.

Althusser, Louis. 2006. *Philosophy of the Encounter: Later Writings, 1978–1987*. New York, NY: Verso.

Altman, Andrew. *Critical Legal Studies. A Liberal Critique*. 1990th ed. Princeton: NJ: Princeton University Press.

Amis, Martin. 2017. "Martin Amis on Lenin's Deadly Revolution." *The New York Times*. https://www.nytimes.com/2017/10/16/books/review/martin-amis-lenin-russian-revolution.html.

Anders, Günther. 2016. "On Promethean Shame." In *Technology, Digital Culture and Human Obsolescence*, ed. Christopher John Müller. London, UK: Rowman & Littlefield International, 29–95.

Arendt, Hannah. 1951. *The Origins of Totalitarianism*. New York, NY: Harcourt, Brace.

Arendt, Hannah. 1998. *The Human Condition*. 2nd ed. Chicago, IL: University of Chicago Press.

Aristotle. 1818. *The Rhetoric, Poetic and Nichomachean Ethics*. http://www3.nd.edu/~powers/ame.20231/aristotle.ethics.pdf.

Aristotle. 1905. *Aristotle's Politics*. Oxford, UK: Clarendon Press.

Aristotle. 2008. *The Athenian Constitution*. Project Gutenberg.

Arruzza, Cinzia, ed. 2008. *Pensare Con Marx, Ripensare Marx: Teorie per Il Nostro Tempo*. Roma, IT: Alegre.

Arthur, Christopher J. 2004. *The New Dialectic and Marx's's Capital*. Leiden, NL: Brill. https://libcom.org/files/Arthur%20-%20The%20New%20Dialectic%20and%20Marx%E2%80%99s%20Capital.PDF.

Asiai, Philippe. 2002. "Foucault croise Marx. Ou les assonances entre Foucault et Althusser entre 1965 et 1976 [24/04/2002]." In *Groupe d'études « La philosophie au sens large »*, Paris, FR. https://philolarge.hypotheses.org/files/2017/09/24-04-2002_Asiai.pdf.

Atkinson, Charles, and John Hughes. 1972. "Russell's Critique of Socialist Theory and Practice." In *Essays on Socialist Humanism in Honour of the Centenary of Bertrand Russell, 1872–1970*, ed. Ken Coates. Nottingham, UK: Spokesman Books, 13–31.

B, a Rhinelander [Karl Marx]. 1842. "Proceedings of the Sixth Rhine Province Assembly. Third Article. Debates on the Law on Thefts of Wood, May 23 to July 25, 1841." *Rheinische Zeitung,* No. 298 (Supplement, October 25). https://www.marxists.org/archive/marx/works/download/Marx_Rheinishe_Zeitung.pdf.

Bajerski, Michal. 2016. "'I Understand You, So I'll Not Hurt You with My Irony': Correlations Between Irony and Emotional Intelligence." *Psychology of Language and Communication* 20(3): 235–254.

Bakshy, Eytan, Solomon Messing, and Lada A. Adamic. 2015. "Exposure to Ideologically Diverse News and Opinion on Facebook." *Science* 348(6239): 1130–1132.

Balibar, Etienne. 1989. "Foucault et Marx: La Question Du Nominalisme." In *Michel Foucault Philosophe: Rencontre Internationale Paris, 9, 10, 11 Janvier 1988*, ed. Association pour le Centre Michel Foucault Georges Canguilhem. Paris, FR: Éditions du Seuil, 54–76.

Balkin, Jack M. 1991. "Ideology as Constraint." *Stanford Law Review* 43(5): 1133–1169.

Banaji, Jairus. 2010. Theory as History: Essays on Modes of Production and Exploitation. Leiden, NL: Brill.

Banks, Glenn, et al. 2016. "Conceptualizing Corporate Community Development." *Third World Quarterly* 37: 254–263.

Barbe, Katharina. 1995. *Irony in Context*. Amsterdam/Philadelphia: John Benjamins Pub. Co.

Barrett, Michèle. 1991. *Politics of Truth*. Stanford, CA: Stanford University Press.

Barthes, Roland. 1989. "The Death of the Author (1968)." In *The Rustle of Language*, Berkeley, CA: University of California Press, 49–55. http://www.tbook.constantvzw.org/wp-content/death_authorbarthes.pdf.

Bentham, Jeremy. 1891. *Fragment on Government*. Oxford, UK: At the Clarendon Press.

Bentham, Jeremy. 1998. "Anarchical Fallacies; being and examination of the Declaration of Rights issued during the French Revolution (Selection) – 1796." *Headline Series* (318): 56–68.

Bentham, Jeremy. 2002. *Rights, Representation, and Reform: Nonsense upon Stilts and Other Writings on the French Revolution*. Oxford, UK: Oxford University Press.

Berger, Arthur Asa. 2006. *50 Ways to Understand Communication. A Guided Tour of Key Ideas and Theorists in Communication, Media, and Culture*. New York, NY: Rowman & Littlefield Publishers, Inc.

Berlin, Isaiah. 1959. *Karl Marx: His Life and Environment*. New York, NY: Oxford University Press.

REFERENCES

Berlin, Isaiah. 2016. "The Artificial Dialectic." In *The Soviet Mind: Russian Culture under Communism*, ed. Isaiah Berlin Henry Hardy. Washington, DC: Brookings Institution Press, 92–111.

Berman, Marshall. 1999. *Adventures in Marxism*. New York, NY: Verso.

Bielefeldt, Heiner. 2003. *Symbolic Representation in Kant's Practical Philosophy*. Cambridge, UK: Cambridge University Press.

Bilsky, Eric A. "Metaphysical and Ethical Skepticism in Legal Theory." *Denver University Law Review* 75(1): 187–227.

Blackledge, Paul. 2006. *Reflections on the Marxist Theory of History*. Manchester, UK: Manchester University Press.

Blumenau, Ralph. 2017. "Kant and the Thing in Itself." *Philosophy Now* 120 (June/July). https://philosophynow.org/issues/31/Kant_and_the_Thing_in_Itself.

Boag, Keith. "Money Man." *CBC, Canada*. http://www.cbc.ca/news2/interactives/sh/wex94ODaUs/trump-robert-mercer-billionaire/.

Bodie, Matthew. 2007. "The Future of the Casebook: An Argument for an Open-Source Approach." *Journal of Legal Education* 57(1): 10–35.

Bond, Robert, and Solomon Messing. 2015. "Quantifying Social Media's Political Space: Estimating Ideology from Publicly Revealed Preferences on Facebook." *American Political Science Review* 109(1): 62–78.

Boucke, Oswald Fred. 1932. *Laissez Faire and After*. New York, NY: Thomas Y. Crowell Co.

Bourdieu, Pierre, and Loic J.D. Wacquant. 1992. *An Invitation to Reflexive Sociology*. Chicago, IL: The University of Chicago Press.

Bowers v. Hardwick. 1986. 478 U.S. 186 (United States Supreme Court).

Boyer, Dave. 2016. "Obama Slams Senate GOP for Blocking Garland Nomination as Supreme Court Begins New Term." *The Washington Times*. www.washingtontimes.com.

Boyle, James. 1985. "The Politics of Reason: Critical Legal Theory and Local Social Thought." *University of Pennsylvania Law Review* 133(4): 685–780.

Brennan, Patrick McKinley. 2002. "Realizing the Rule of Law in the Human Subject." *Boston College Law Review* 43(2): 227–349.

Bricker, Darrell, and John Ibbitson. 2018. "What's Driving Populism? It Isn't the Economy, Stupid." *The Globe and Mail*. https://www.theglobeandmail.com/opinion/what-is-driving-populism-it-isnt-the-economy-stupid/article37899813/.

Bridges, James. 1973. *The Paper Chase*. https://www.zotero.org/dananeacsu/items/collectionKey/3QEFNBBS/itemPage/movie_script.php.

Brown v. Bd. of Ed. of Topeka, Shawnee County, Kan. 1954. 347 U.S. 483 (United States Supreme Court).

Buñuel, Luis. 1972. *The Discreet Charm of the Bourgeoisie [Le Charme Discret de La Bourgeoisie]*. PG, Fantasy/Drama.

Burchell, Michael, and Jennifer Robin. 2011. *The Great Workplace: How to Build It, How to Keep It, and Why It Matters.* San Francisco, CA: Jossey-Bass.

Campbell, M. Stephen, and Sven Nyholm. 2015. "Anti-meaning and Why It Matters." *Journal of the American Philosophical Association* 1(4): 694–711.

Cardarelli, Albert P., and Stephen C. Hicks. 1993. "Radicalism in Law and Criminology: A Retrospective View of Critical Legal Studies and Radical Criminology." *Journal of Criminal Law and Criminology* 84(3): 502–553.

Chaffee, Steven M., and Jack M. McLeod. 1973. "Interpersonal Approaches to Communication Research." *The American Behavioral Scientist* 16(4): 469–499.

Champion, Justin. 2010. "Decoding the Leviathan: Doing the History of Ideas through Images, 1651–1714." In *Printed Images in Early Modern Britain: Essays in Interpretation*, ed. Michael Hunter. Burlington, VT: Ashgate, 255–275.

Cicero, Marcus Tullius. 1895. *The Speech in Defence of Cluentius.* London, UK: Macmillan.

Closen, Michael L., and Robert J. Dzielak. 1996. "The History and Influence of the Law Review Institution." *Akron Law Review* 30(1): 15–50.

Cohen, Gerald A. 2018. "Bourgeois and Proletarians." *Journal of the History of Ideas* 29(2): 211–231.

Cohen, Josh. 2017. "Terry Eagleton's Materialism Treats Its Arguments like Carelessly Piled Bricks." *NewStatesmanAmerica.* https://www.newstatesman.com/culture/books/2017/03/terry-eagletons-materialism-treats-its-arguments-carelessly-piled-bricks.

Comprehensive Environmental Response, Compensation, and Liability Act (Superfund or CERLCA). 1980. 42 U.S.C. § 9601 et seq.

Conley, Verena Andermatt. 2005. *Litterature, Politique et Communism. Lire "Les Lettres Francaises," 1942–1972.* New York, NY: P. Lang.

Copin, Julien. 2003. "Marx Dans Les Mots et Les Choses et l'Archeologie Du Savoir. Un Parcours de Michel Foucault." *Actuel Marx en Ligne* 19 (28/3/2003). https://actuelmarx.parisnanterre.fr/alp0019.htm.

Corbin, Anne M., and Steven B. Dow. 2007. "Breaking the Cycle: Scientific Discourse in Legal Education." *Temple Journal of Science, Technology & Environmental Law* 26(2): 191–221.

Cork, Jim. 1949. "John Dewey, Karl Marx, and Democratic Socialism." *The Antioch Review* 9(4): 435–452.

Cornell, Drucilla. 1985. "Toward a Modern/Postmodern Reconstruction of Ethics." *University of Pennsylvania Law Review* 133(2): 291–380.

Cotterrell, Roger. 2006. *Law, Culture and Society: Legal Ideas in the Mirror of Social Theory.* Burlington, VT: Ashgate.

Crenshaw, Kimberlé Williams. 1989. "Demarginalizing the Intersection of Race and Sex: A Black Feminist Critique of Antidiscrimination Doctrine, Feminist Theory and Antiracist Policies." *University of Chicago Legal Forum* 1989 1: 139–167.

Crenshaw, Kimberlé Williams. 1991. "Beyond Racism and Misogyny: Black Feminism and 2 Live Crew." *Boston Review* 16(6): 6–11.

Crenshaw, Kimberlé Williams. 2008. "Mapping the Margins: Intersectionality, Identity Politics, and Violence Against Women of Color." In *The Feminist Philosophy Reader*, ed. Chris Cuomo Alison Bailey. New York, NY: McGraw-Hill, 279–309.

Cripps [Samoiloff], Louise. 1997. *C.L.R. James. Memories and Commentaries*. New York, NY: Cornwall Books.

cunningham, e. christi. 2007. "Exit Strategy for the Race Paradigm." *Howard Law Journal* 50(3): 755–826.

Dallmayr, Fred. 1987. "Hegemony and Democracy: A Review of Laclau and Mouffe: Hegemony and Socialist Strategy: Towards a Radical Democratic Politics." *Philosophy and Social Criticism* 13(3): 283–296.

Dalton, Clare. 1985. "An Essay in the Deconstruction of Contract Doctrine." *The Yale Law Journal* 94(5): 997–1114.

Dardot, Pierre, Christian Laval, and El Mouhoub Mouhoud. 2007. *Sauver Marx?: Empire, Multitude, Travail Immatériel*. Paris, FR: Éditions La Découverte.

Dardot, Pierre, and Christian Laval. 2016a. *Ce Cauchemar qui n'en finit pas. Comment le néolibéralisme défie la démocratie* [*This Nightmare that Never Ends. How Neoliberalism Defies Democracy*]. Paris, FR: La DÉcouverte.

Dardot, Pierre, and Christian Laval. 2016b. *Marx, prénom: Karl*. Paris, FR: Éditions Gallimard.

David, Larry, and Jerry Seinfeld. 1989–1999. *Seinfeld*. NBC.

Davies, Carole Boyce. 2008. *Left of Karl Marx: The Political Life of Black Communist Claudia Jones*. Durham, NC: Duke University Press.

Davis, Julie Hirschfeld, and Mark Landlerjan. 2017. "Trump Nominates Neil Gorsuch to the Supreme Court." *The New York Times*. https://perma.cc/ZM97-97US.

Davis, Michael H. 1981. "Critical Jurisprudence: An Essay on the Legal Theory of Robert Burt's Taking Care of Strangers." *Wisconsin Law Review* 1981(3): 419–453.

Davis, Michael H., and Dana Neacşu. 2001. "Legitimacy, Globally: The Incoherence of Free Trade Practice, Global Economics and Their Governing Principles of Political Economy." *UMKC Law Review* 69(4): 733–790.

Davis, Michael H., and Dana Neacşu. 2014. "The Many Texts of the Law." *British Journal of American Legal Studies* 3: 481–506.

Debord, Guy. 1967. *La SociÉtÉ Du Spectacle*. Paris: Buchet/Chastel.

Destutt de Tracy, Antoine Louis Claude, comte. 1817. 1 *ÉlÉmens d'idÉologie*. Paris, FR: Courcier.

Dewey, John. 1916. *Essays in Experimental Logic*. Chicago, IL: University of Chicago Press.

Dewey, John. 1917. "The Need for A Recovery of Philosophy." In *Creative Intelligence: Essays in the Pragmatic Attitude*, ed. John Dewey. New York, NY: H. Holt, 3–69.

Dewey, John. 1920. *Reconstruction in Philosophy*. New York, NY: Mentor Books.

Dewey, John. 1929. *The Quest for Certainty: A Study of the Relation of Knowledge and Action*. New York, NY: Minton, Balch.

Dewey, John. 1935. *Liberalism and Social Action*. New York, NY: Capricorn Books.

Dewey, John. 1938. *Logic, the Theory of Inquiry*. New York, NY: H. Holt and Company.

Dewey, John. 1951. *The Influence of Darwin on Philosophy, and Other Essays in Contemporary Thought*. New York, NY: P. Smith.

Dewey, John. 1964. *John Dewey on Education: Selected Writings*, ed. Reginald D. Archambault. Chicago, IL: University of Chicago Press.

Dewey, John. 1978. "The Problem of Truth." In *The Middle Works, 1899–1924*, ed. Jo Ann Boydston. Carbondale, IL: Southern Illinois University Press, 12–68.

Dewey, John. 2003. "From Absolutism to Experimentalism." In *The Many Faces of Philosophy: Reflections from Plato to Arendt*, ed. AmÉlie Oksenberg Rorty. New York, NY: Oxford University Press, 385–393.

Dewey, John. 2016. *The Public and Its Problems: An Essay in Political Inquiry*, ed. Melvin L. Rogers. Athens, Ohio: Swallow Press.

Dickens, Charles. 1853. *Bleak House*. 1993rd ed. London, UK: Wordsworth Editions, Ltd.

Dorf, Michael C. 1999. "Create Your Own Constitutional Theory." *California Law Review* 87(3): 593–612.

Duberman, Martin Bauml. 1989. *Paul Robeson*. New York, NY: Knopf.

Dworkin, Ronald. 1978. "Liberalism." In *Public and Private Morality*, ed. Stuart Hampshire. Cambridge, UK: Cambridge University Press, 113–145.

Dworkin, Ronald. 1981. "The Forum of Principle Symposium–Constitutional Adjudication and Democratic Theory." *New York University Law Review* 56(3): 469–518.

Dworkin, Ronald. 1986a. *A Matter of Principle*. Cambridge, MA: Harvard University Press.

Dworkin, Ronald. 1986b. *Law's Empire*. Cambridge, MA: Belknap Pres.

Dworkin, Ronald, et al. 1997. "Assisted Suicide: The Philosophers' Brief." *The New York Review of Books* 44(5): 41–47.

Eastman, Max. 1934. *The Last Stand of Dialectic Materialism: A Study of Sidney Hook's Marxism*. New York, NY: Polemic Publishers.

Eastman, Max. 1955. *Reflections of the Failure of Socialism*. New York, NY: Devin-Adair.

Edgeworth, Brendon. 2003. *Law, Modernity, Postmodernity: Legal Change in the Contracting State*. Burlington, VT: Ashgate.

Eilperin, Juliet, and Mike DeBonis. 2016. "President Obama Nominates Merrick Garland to the Supreme Court." *The Washington Post*. https://perma.cc/J5RF-B3UE.

Elster, Jon. 1985. *Making Sense of Marx*. Cambridge, UK: Cambridge University Press.

Elster, Jon. 1986. *An Introduction to Karl Marx*. Cambridge, UK: Cambridge University Press.

Emmott, Bill. 2017. *The Fate of the West: The Battle to Save the World's Most Successful Political Idea*. New York, NY: The Economist in association with Profile Books Ltd. and Public Affairs.

Endangered Species Act. 1973. 16 U.S.C. ch. 35 § 1531 et seq.

Endicott, Timothy. 2013. "The Irony of Law." In *Reason, Morality, and Law: The Philosophy of John Finnis*, ed. Robert P. George John Keown. Oxford, UK: Oxford University Press, 327–345.

Engels, Frederick. 1940. *Dialectics of Nature*. New York, NY: International Publishers.

"Executive Order No. 13769, Protecting the Nation from Foreign Terrorist Entry Into the United States." 2017. *Federal Register* 82(20): 8977–8982.

Farnsworth, E. Allan. 1988. "Casebooks and Scholarship: Confessions of an American Opinion Clipper." *SMU Law Review* 42(3): 903–918.

Federal Election Comm'n v. National Conservative Political Action Comm. 1985. 470 U.S. 480 (United States Supreme Court).

Ferguson, Robert A. 2016. *Practice Extended: Beyond Law and Literature*. New York: Columbia University Press.

Fernback, Jan. 2002. "The Individual within the Collective: Virtual Ideology and the Realization of Collective Principles." In *Virtual Culture: Identity and Communication in Cybersociety*, ed. Steven G. Jones. London, UK: SAGE Publications Ltd, 36–54.

Feuerbach, Ludwig. 1855. *The Essence of Christianity*. New York, NY: C. Blanchard.

Fletcher, George P. 1987. "Law and Morality: A Kantian Perspective." *Columbia Law Review* 87(3): 533–558.

Fletcher, George P. 1997. "'The Philosopher's Brief': An Exchange." *The New York Review of Books* 44(5): 45.

Fletcher, George P. 1998. "Comparative Law as a Subversive Discipline." *The American Journal of Comparative Law* 46(4): 683–700.

Foner, Philip S. 1967. *The Bolshevik Revolution, its impact on American radicals, liberals, and labor. A documentary study by Philip S. Foner*. New York, NY: International Publishers.

Foner, Philip S. 1983. *Karl Marx Remembered: Comments at the Time of His Death*. San Francisco, CA: Synthesis Publications.

Forster, Paul. 2011. *Peirce and the Threat of Nominalism*. Cambridge, MA: Cambridge, University Press.

Foucault, Michel. 1969. "What Is an Author? [Qu'est-Ce Qu'un Auteur?]." Presented at the Collège de France, 22 February, 1969. https://www.open.edu/openlearn/ocw/pluginfile.php/624849/mod_resource/content/1/a840_1_michel_foucault.pdf.

Foucault, Michel. 1970. *Les mots et les choses; une archÉologie des sciences humaines* [*The Order of Things: An Archaeology of the Human Sciences*]. Paris, FR: Gallimard.

Foucault, Michel. 1972. *The Archaeology of Knowledge and the Discourse of Knowledge*. New York, NY: Pantheon Books. https://monoskop.org/images/9/90/Foucault_Michel_Archaeology_of_Knowledge.pdf.

Foucault, Michel. 1980. "Truth and Power," *Power/Knowledge and The Archaeology of Knowledge*. New York, NY: Pantheon Books.

Foucault, Michel. 1984. "What Is Enlightenment?" In *The Foucault Reader*, ed. Paul Rabinow. New York, NY: Pantheon, 32–50.

Foucault, Michel. 1988. *Politics, Philosophy, Culture: Interviews and Other Writings, 1977–1984*. ed. Lawrence D. Kritzman. London, UK: Routledge.

Foucault, Michel. 1994. "Structuralisme et Poststructuralisme." In 3 *Dits et Ecrits*, Paris, FR: Gallimard/Seuil, 431–457.

Foucault, Michel. 2001. *Dits et Écrits, 1954–1988*. Paris, FR: Gallimard.

Forbath, William E. 1983. "Taking Lefts Seriously." *The Yale Law Journal* 92(6): 1041–1064.

Forbath, William E. 2011. "The Distributive Constitution and Workers' Rights." *Ohio State Law Journal* 72(6): 1115–1157.

Frank, Jerome. 1942. *If Men Were Angels: Some Aspects of Government in a Democracy*. New York, NY: Harper.

Frankenberg, Günter. 2011. "Down by Law: Irony, Seriousness, and Reason." *German Law Journal* 12(1): 300–337.

Frankfurt, Harry G. 2005. *On Bullshit*. Princeton, NJ: Princeton University Press.

Fraser, David, and Alan Freeman. 1987. "What's Hockey Got to Do With It, Anyway? Comparative Canadian-American Perspectives on Constitutional Law and Rights." *Buffalo Law Review* 36(2): 259–284.

Frears, Stephen. 1990. *The Grifters*. Cineplex-Odeon Films.

Freeman, Alan D., and John H. Schlegel. 1985. "Sex, Power and Silliness: An Essay on Ackerman's Reconstructing American Law Scholarship from inside the Movement." 6(3): 847–864.

Freeman, M.D.A. 2008. *Introduction to Jurisprudence*. 8th ed. London, UK: Thomson Reuters.

Friedman, Lawrence M. 1973. *A History of American Law*. 1st ed. New York, NY: Simon & Schuster.

Friedmann, Wolfgang. 1967. *Legal Theory*. 5th ed. London, UK: Stevens.

Frug, Gerald E. 1984. "The Ideology of Bureaucracy in American Law." *Harvard Law Review* 97: 1276–1388.

Fuchs, Christian. 2017. "Günther Anders' Undiscovered Critical Theory of Technology in the Age of Big Data Capitalism." *Journal for a Global Sustainable Information Society* 15. http://www.triple-c.at/index.php/tripleC/article/view/898/1022.

Fukuyama, Francis. 2006. *The End of History.* New York, NY: Free Press.
Fuller, Lon L. 1958. "Positivism and Fidelity to Law – A Reply to Professor Hart." *Harvard Law Review* 71(4): 630–672.
Funakoshi, Motoaki. 2009. "Taking Duncan Kennedy Seriously: Ironical Liberal Legalism." *Widener Law Review* 15(1): 231–287.
Gadamer, Hans Georg. 1986. *The Idea of the Good in Platonic-Aristotelian Philosophy.* New Haven, CT: Yale University Press.
Gabel, Peter, and Duncan Kennedy. 1984. "Roll over Beethoven." *Stanford Law Review* 36(1): 1–54.
Gadris, Stelios. 2016. "Two Cases of Irony: Kant and Wittgenstein." *KANT-STUDIEN* 107(2): 343–368.
Gay, Peter. 1969. *The Enlightenment. An Interpretation.* New York, NY: Knopf.
Geertz, Clifford. 1973. *The Interpretation of Cultures; Selected Essays.* New York: Basic Books.
Gitlin, Todd. 2017. "Promoting Knowledge in an Age of Unreason." *The Chronicle of Higher Education.* http://www.chronicle.com/article/Promoting-Knowledge-in-an-Age/239434?cid=trend_right.
Goethe, Johann Wolfgang von. 1882. *The Autobiography of Goethe. Truth and Fiction Relating to My Life.* Boston, MA: S.E. Cassino.
Goldstein, Warren S. 2006. "Introduction." In *Marx, Critical Theory, and Religion: A Critique of Rational Choice*, ed. Warren S. Goldstein. Leiden, NL: Brill, x–8.
Gordon, Robert W. 1984. "Critical Legal Histories." *Stanford Law Review* 36: 57–125.
Gordon, Robert W., and William E. Nelson. 1988. "Exchange on Critical Legal Studies." *Law and History Review* 6: 139–186.
Gorsuch, Neil M. 2014. "Law's Irony." *Harvard Journal of Law & Public Policy* 37(3): 743–756.
Goyard-Fabre, Simone. 2003. *Critique de La Raison Juridique.* Paris, FR: Press Universitaire de France.
Gramsci, Antonio. 1971. *Selections from the Prison Notebooks of Antonio Gramsci*, ed. Geoffrey Nowell, Smith Quintin Hoare. New York: International Publishers.
Gregory, David L. 1987. "A Guide to Critical Legal Studies, by Mark Kelman." *Duke Law Journal* 1987: 1138–1150.
Greenberg, Clement. 1961. *Art and Culture: Critical Essays.* Boston, MA: Beacon Press.
Griswold v. Connecticut. 1965. 381 U.S. 479 (United States Supreme Court).
Grotius, Hugo. 1913. *Iure Belli Ac Pacis – 1646.* Washington, DC: Carnegie Institution of Washington.
Grusky, David B., ed. 2001. *Social Stratification, Class, Race, & Gender in Sociological Perspective.* 2nd ed. Boulder, CO: Westview Press.
Grutter v. Bollinger. 2003. 539 U.S. 306 (United States Supreme Court).

Habermas, Jürgen. 1996. *Between Facts and Norms: Contributions to a Discourse Theory of Law and Democracy*. Cambridge, MA: MIT Press.

Hall, Jerome. 1949. "Concerning the Nature of Positive Law." *Yale Law Journal* 58(4): 545–566.

Hall, Stuart. 1974. "The Television Discourse – Encoding and Decoding." *Education and Culture* 25: 8–20. https://www.birmingham.ac.uk/Documents/college-artslaw/history/cccs/stencilled-occasional-papers/1to8and11to24and38to48/SOP07.pdf.

Hall, Stuart. 1997. *Representation and the Media*. Northampton, MA: Media Education Foundation.https://www.mediaed.org/transcripts/Stuart-Hall-Representation-and-the-Media-Transcript.pdf.

Hamilton, Alexander. 1787. "The Federalist, No. 1 & No. 9." In *The Federalist*, ed. Jacob E. Cooke. Middletown, CT: Wesleyan University Press, 3–7; 50–56.

Hart, H.L.A. 1958. "Positivism and the Separation of Law and Morals." *Harvard Law Review* 71(4): 593–629.

Hart, H.L.A. 1982. *Essays on Bentham. Studies in Jurisprudence and Political Theory*. Oxford, UK: Clarendon Press.

Hart, H.L.A. 1994. *The Concept of Law*. Oxford, UK: Oxford University Press.

Hauser, Gerard A. "Forum: The Nature and Function of Public Intellectuals." *Philosophy and Rhetoric* 39(2): 125–126.

Hayek, Friedrich August von. 1994. *The Economics of F.A. Hayek: Capitalism, Socialism and Knowledge*, ed. H. Hagemann M. Colonna and O.F. Hamouda. Brookfield, VT: E. Elgar.

Hegel, Georg Wilhelm Friedrich. 1952. *Hegel's Philosophy of Right*. 2015th ed. Ed. Sir Thomas Malcolm Knox. Oxford, UK: Oxford University Press.

Hegel, Georg Wilhelm Friedrich. 2003 [1817]. *The Phenomenology of Mind*. Mineola, NY: Dover Publications, Inc.

Heller, Michael A. 1998. "The Tragedy of the Anticommons: Property in the Transition from Marx to Markets." *Harvard Law Review* 111(3): 621–688.

Heller, Thomas C. 1984. "Structuralism and Critique." *Stanford Law Review* 36(1): 127–198.

Henry, Michel. 1976. *Marx. Une philosophie de la réalité*. Paris, FR: Gallimard.

Henry, Michel. 1983. *Marx: A Philosophy of human reality*. Bloomington, IN: Indiana University Press.

Henry, Michel. 2014. *From Communism to Capitalism: Theory of a Catastrophe [Du communisme au capitalism]*. London, UK: Bloomsbury Academic.

Hobbes, Thomas. 1929 [1651]. *Leviathan*. London, UK: Clarendon Press.

Hobsbawm, Eric J. 1962. *The Age of Revolution: Europe 1789–1848*. Cleveland, OH: World Pub. Co.

Høgsbjerg, Christian. "Karl Marx and the First International." *Socialist Review* (September 2014 (394)). http://socialistreview.org.uk/394/karl-marx-and-first-international.

Holmes, Oliver Wendell, Jr. 1881. *The Common Law*. 1946th ed. Boston, MA: Little Brown.

Holmes, Oliver Wendell, Jr. 1897. "The Path of Law." *Harvard Law Review* 10(8): 457–478.

Horton, John. 2001. "Irony and Commitment: An Irreconcilable Dualism of Modernity." In *Richard Rorty. Critical Dialogues*, Cambridge, UK: Blackwell Publishers, 15–28.

Horwitz, Morton J. 1977a. "The Rule of Law: An Unqualified Human Good?" *The Yale Law Journal* 86(3): 561–566.

Horwitz, Morton J. 1977b. *The Transformation of American Law 1780–1860*. Cambridge, MA: Harvard University Press.

"How Senators Voted on the Gorsuch Filibuster and the Nuclear Option." 2017. *The New York Times*. https://perma.cc/SS3E-G9QP.

Howarth, David. 1988. "Hegemony, Political Subjectivity, and Radical Democracy." In *Laclau: A Critical Reader*, ed. Oliver Marchart Simon Critchley. New York, NY: Routledge, 256–276.

Hunt, Alan. 1986. "The Theory of Critical Legal Studies." *Oxford Journal of Legal Studies* 6(1): 1–45.

Hutchinson, Allan. 1987. "Indiana Dworkin and Law's Empire." *Yale Law Journal* 96(3): 637–665.

Hutchinson, Allan, and Patrick Monahan. 1984. "Law, Politics, and the Critical Legal Scholars: The Unfolding Drama of American Legal Thought." *Stanford Law Review* 36(1&2): 199–245.

Hutchinson, Allan, and Patrick Monahan, eds. 1987. *The Rule of Law. Ideal or Ideology*. Toronto, CA: Carswell.

Hutcheon, Linda. 1995. *Irony's Edge: The Theory and Politics of Irony*. London, UK: Routledge.

Inkpin, Andrew. 2013. "Taking Rorty's Irony Seriously." *Humanities* 2(2): 292–312.

James, William. 1907. *Pragmatism, a New Name for Some Old Ways of Thinking*. New York, NY: Longmans, Green & Co.

James, William. 1912. "Pragmatism in Business and Politics." *Commercial & Financial Chronicle* 95: 1009–1010.

Janus v. AFSCME. 2018. 585 U.S. __ (United States Supreme Court).

Jinks, Derek P. 1997. "Essays in Refusal: Pre-Theoretical Commitments in Postmodern Anthropology and Critical Race Theory." *The Yale Law Journal* 107(2): 499–528.

Johnson, Gregory. 2002. "The First Founding Father: Aristotle on Freedom and Popular Government." In *Liberty and Democracy*, Philosophic reflections on a free society, ed. Tobor A. Machan. Stanford, CA.

Johnson, Phillip E. 1984. "Do You Sincerely Want to Be Radical?" *Stanford Law Review* 36(1/2): 247–291.

Jones, Richard A. 2008. "Philosophical Methodologies of Critical Race Theory." *Georgetown Journal of Law & Modern Critical Race Perspectives* 1(1): 17–40.

Judt, Tony (with Timothy Snyder). 2012. *Thinking the Twentieth Century*. New York, NY: Penguin Press.

Kagarlitsky, Boris. *The Return of Radicalism Reshaping the Left Institutions*. 2000th ed. London, UK: Pluto Press.

Kairys, David. 1998. "Introduction." In *The Politics of Law: A Progressive Critique*, ed. David Kairys. New York, NY: Basic Books.

Kant, Immanuel. 1788. *The Critique of Practical Reason*. Auckland, NZ: Floating Press.

Kant, Immanuel. 1890 [1781]. *The Critique of Pure Reason [Kritik Der Reinen Vernunft]*. London, UK: G. Bell and Sons.

Katznelson, Ira. 1998. *Liberalism's Crooked Circle. Letters to Adam Michnik*. Princeton, NJ: Princeton University Press.

Kaufmann, Eric. 2018. *Whiteshift: Populism, Immigration and the Future of White Majorities*. London, UK: Allen Lane, an imprint of Penguin Books.

Kekršytė, Nijolė. 2017. "Rethinking Ideology: Greimas's Semiotics, Neomarxism, and Cultural Anthropology." *Semiotica* 2017(219): 485–509.

Kellner, Douglas. 1995. "The End of Orthodox Marxism." In *Marxism in the Post-Modern Age: Confronting the New World Order*, ed. Antonio Callari et al. New York, NY: Guilford Press, 33–41.

Kelman, Mark. 1981. "Interpretive Construction in the Substantive Criminal Law." *Stanford Law Review* 33: 591–673.

Kelman, Mark. 1984. "Trashing." *Stanford Law Review* 36(1&2): 293–349.

Kelman, Mark. 1987. *A Guide to Critical Legal Studies*. Cambridge, MA: Harvard University Press.

Kennedy, David W. 1985. "Spring Break." *Texas Law Review* 63(8): 1377–1423.

Kennedy, Duncan. 1976. "Form and Substance in Private Law Adjudication." *Harvard Law Review* 89(6): 1685–1778.

Kennedy, Duncan. 1979. "The Structure of Blackstone's Commentaries." *Buffalo Law Review* 28: 205–382.

Kennedy, Duncan. 1980. "Toward an Historical Understanding of Legal Consciousness: The Case of Classical Legal Thought in America, 1850–1940." *Research in Law and Sociology* 3: 3–24.

Kennedy, Duncan. 1981. "Cost-Reduction Theory as Legitimation." *The Yale Law Journal* 90(5): 1275–1283.

Kennedy, Duncan. 1982. "The Stages of the Decline of the Public/Private Distinction, 130 U Pa L Rev 1349, 1349–50 (1982)." *University of Pennsylvania Law Review* 130(6): 1349–1357.

Kennedy, Duncan. 1983. *Legal Education and the Reproduction of Hierarchy: A Polemic Against the System*. Cambridge, MA: Afar.

Kennedy, Duncan. 1993. *Sexy Dressing Etc.* Cambridge, MA: Harvard University Press.

Kennedy, Duncan. 1997. *A Critique of Adjudication. Fin de Siècle.* Cambridge, MA: Harvard University Press.

Kennedy, Duncan. 2001. "A Semiotics of Critique." *Cardozo Law Review* 22(5): 1147–1189.

Kennedy, Duncan, and Karl E. Klare. 1984. "A Bibliography of Critical Legal Studies." *The Yale Law Journal* 94(2): 461–490.

Kennedy, Emmet. 1978. *A Philosophe in the Age of Revolution, Destutt de Tracy and the Origins of "Ideology."* Philadelphia, PA: American Philosophical Society.

Keršytė, Nijolė. 2017 "Rethinking ideology: Greimas's semiotics, neomarxism, and cultural anthropology." *Semiotica* 2017(219): 485–509.

Kessler, Jeremy K., and David E. Pozen. 2016. "Working Themselves Impure: A Life Cycle Theory of Legal Theories." *University of Chicago Law Review* 83(6): 1819–1892.

Kierkegaard, Søren. 1965. *The Concept of Irony with Constant Reference to Socrates.* Bloomington, IN: Indiana University Press.

King, Peter, Lord. 1864. *The Life and Letters of John Locke: With Extracts from His Journals and Common-Place Books.* London, UK: Bell & Daldy.

Kirchgaessner, Stephanie, and Jonathan Watts. Monday, May 11. "Catholic Church Warms to Liberation Theology as Founder Heads to Vatican." *The Guardian.* https://www.theguardian.com/world/2015/may/11/vatican-new-chapter-liberation-theology-founder-gustavo-gutierrez.

Kitching, Gavin. 1988. *Karl Marx and the Philosophy of Praxis: An Introduction and Critique.* London, UK: Routledge.

Knapp, Aaron T. 2013. "Law's Revolution: Benjamin Austin and the Spirit of '86." *Yale Journal of Law and The Humanities* 25(2): 271–358.

Kolakowski, Leszek. 1978. *Main Currents of Marxism: The Founders.* Oxford: Oxford.

Kolakowski, Leszek. 1983. "Marxism and Human Rights." *Daedalus* 112(4): 81–92.

Krever, Tor, Carl Lisberger, and Max Utzschneider. 2015. "Law on the Left: A Conversation with Duncan Kennedy." *Unbound* 10(1): 1–35.

Laclau, Ernesto, and Chantal Mouffe. 1985. *Hegemony & Socialist Strategy: Towards a Radical Democratic Politics.* London: UK: Verso.

Langdell, Christopher. 1871. *Selection of Cases on the Law of Contract.* Boston, MA: Little Brown.

Lasch, Christopher. 1966. "UnAmerican Activities." *The New York Review of Books*, October 6, 1966: 11–13.

Latham, Earl. 1966. *The Communist Controversy in Washington from the New Deal to McCarthy.* Cambridge, MA: Harvard University Press.

Laval, Christian, Luca Paltrinieri, and Ferhat Taylan, eds. 2015. *Marx & Foucault: Lectures, Usages, Confrontations.* Paris, FR: Éditions la Découverte.

Lawrence v. Texas. 2003. 539 U.S. 558 (United States Supreme Court).

Lear, Jonathan. 2011. *A Case for Irony*. Cambridge, MA: Harvard University Press.

Lehrer, Nicole, Thanassis Rikakis, and Aisling Kelliher. 2013. "Experiential Media and Digital Culture." *Computer* 46: 46–54.

Lemke, Thomas. 2004. "« Marx sans Guillemets »: Foucault, La Gouvernementalité et La Critique Du Néolibéralisme." *Actuel Marx* 36: 13–26. https://www.cairn.info/revue-actuel-marx-2004-2-page-13.htm.

Lenin, Vladimir Il'ich. 1973 [1913]. "The Three Sources and Three Component Parts of Marxism." In *Karl Marx and His Teachings*, Moscow, USSR: Progress Publishers, 7–13.

Lenin, Vladimir Il'ich. 1982. *On the Question of Dialectics*. Moscow, USSR: Progress Publishers.

Levinson, Sanford V. 1983. "Escaping Liberalism: Easier Said Than Done." *Harvard Law Review* 96(6): 1466–1488.

Levinson, Sanford V., and Jack M. Balkin. 2010. "Morton Horwitz Wrestles with the Rule of Law." In *Transformations in American Legal History : Law, Ideology, and Methods : Essays in Honor of Morton J. Horwitz. Volume I*, ed. Alfred L. Brophy and Daniel W. Hamilton. Cambridge, MA: Harvard University Press, 483–500.

Lichtheim, George. 1967. *The Concept of Ideology and Other Essays*. New York, NY: Random House.

Lidsky, Lyrissa Barnett. 1995. "Defensor Fidei: The Travails of a Post-Realist Formalist." *Florida Law Review* 47(4): 815–839.

Lind, Douglas. 1999. "Logic, Intuition, and the Positivist Legacy of H.L.A Hart." *SMU Law Review* 52(1): 135–166.

Ling, Trevor. 1980. *Karl Marx and Religion in Europe and India*. New York, NY: Barnes & Noble Books.

Lochner v. New York. 1905. 198 U.S. 45 (United States Supreme Court).

Locke, John. 1690. *An Essay Concerning Human Understanding. In Four Books*. London, UK: Printed for Tho. Basset, and sold by Edw. Mory.

Locke, John. 1884 [1689]. *Treatises on Government*. London, UK: George Routledge and Sons.

Locré, Jean Guillaume, baron de. 1827. *La Législation Civile, Commerciale et Criminelle de La France, …* Paris, FR: Treuttel et Würtz.

Lorenzini, Daniele. 2013. "Foucault News." *What is a "Regime of Truth"?* https://michel-foucault.com/2013/10/31/what-is-a-regime-of-truth-2013/.

Lukács, Georg. 1971. *History and Class Consciousness; Studies in Marxist Dialectics*. Cambridge, MA: MIT Press.

Lukacs, John. 1968. *Historical Consciousness or the Remembered Past*. New York, NY: Harper & Row.

Luxemburg, Rosa. 1999. *Rosa Luxemburg: Reflections and Writings*, ed. Paul Le Blanc. Amherst, NY: Humanity Books.

Luxemburg, Rosa. 2004. *The Rosa Luxemburg Reader*, ed. Kevin B. Anderson and Peter Hudis. New York, NY: Monthly Review Press.
Lydon, Christopher. 2017. "Noam Chomsky: Neoliberalism Is Destroying Our Democracy." *The Nation*, June 2, 2017. https://www.thenation.com/article/noam-chomsky-neoliberalism-destroying-democracy/.
Lyon-Callo, Vincent. 2010. "To Market, to Market to Buy a...Middle-Class Life? Insecurity, Anxiety, and Neoliberal Education in Michigan." *Learning and Teaching: The International Journal of Higher Education in the Social Sciences* 3(3): 63–90.
Mah, Harold. 1987. *The End of Philosophy, the Origin of "Ideology": Karl Marx and the Crisis of the Young Hegelians*. Berkeley, CA: University of California Press.
Mann, Geoff, and Joel Wainwright. 2008. "Marx Without Guardrails: Geographies of the Grundrisse." *Antipode* 40(5): 848–856.
Marcuse, Herbert. 1966. *One-Dimensional Man: Studies in the Ideology of Advanced Industrial Society*. Boston, MA: Beacon Press.
Marx, Karl. 1837. "Scorpion and Felix – A Humoristic Novel." https://www.marxists.org/archive/marx/works/1837-pre/verse/verse41.htm.
Marx, Karl. 1856. "Speech at the Anniversary of The People's Paper." *The People's Paper*. https://perma.cc/Y2P8-N7BS.
Marx, Karl. 1865. "On Proudhon." *Der Social-Demokrat* (17: February 3, 1865). https://www.marxists.org/archive/marx/works/1865/letters/65_01_24.htm.
Marx, Karl. 1867. "Vorschläge Für Das Programm Der Internationalen Arbeiterassoziation (IAA) [Proposals for the International Workers Association (IAA) Program]." In *Marx-Engels-Werke*. Berlin, DE: 1956.
Marx, Karl. 1887. *Capital: A Critical Analysis of Capitalist Production*, ed. Frederick Engels. London, UK: S. Sonnenschein, Lowrey & Co.
Marx, Karl. 1909. *Capital. The Process of Circulation of Capital*, ed. Frederick Engels. Chicago, USA: Charles H. Kerr & Co.
Marx, Karl. 1910. *The Poverty of Philosophy* [*Misere de La Philosophie*] (*A Reply to "La Philosophie de La Misere" of M. Proudhon*). Chicago, IL: Charles H. Kerr.
Marx, Karl. 1959. *Economic and Philosophic Manuscripts of 1844*. Moscow, USSR: Progress Publishers. https://www.marxists.org/archive/marx/works/download/pdf/Economic-Philosophic-Manuscripts-1844.pdf.
Marx, Karl. 1970. *Critique of Hegel's "Philosophy of Right."* Cambridge, UK: University Press.
Marx, Karl. 1973. *Grundrisse. Foundations of the Critique of Political Economy*. New York, NY: Random House.
Marx, Karl. 1975. *Early Writings*. New York, NY: Vintage Books.
Marx, Karl. 2001a. *The Eighteenth Brumaire of Louis Bonaparte*. London, UK: Electric Book Co.
Marx, Karl. 2001b. *Critique of the Gotha Programme*. London, UK: Electric Book Co.

Marx, Karl. 2006. "Letter from Marx to His Father [Berlin, November 10, 1837]." In *The First Writings of Karl Marx*, ed. Paul M. Schafer. Brooklyn, NY: Ig Pub. https://www.marxists.org/archive/marx/works/1837-pre/letters/letter-to-father.pdf.

Marx, Karl. 2007. *Economic and Philosophic Manuscripts of 1844*. Mineola, NY: Dover Publications.

Marx, Karl. 2012 [1844]. *On the Jewish Question*. Chicago, IL: Aristeus Books.

Marx, Karl, and Frederick Engels. 1998. *The German Ideology: Including Theses on Feuerbach and Introduction to The Critique of Political Economy*. Amherst, NY: Prometheus Books.

Marx, Karl, and Frederick Engels. 2012 [1848]. *The Communist Manifesto*. ed. Jeffrey C. Issac. New Haven, CT: Yale University Press.

Marx, Karl, and Frederick Engels. 2019. *Collected Works. Karl Marx: 1835–1843*. Institute of Marxism-Leninism, Moscow, eds. Margarita Lopukhina Natalia Karmanova and Lyudgarda Zubrilova Victor Schnittke. Chicago, IL: Alexander Street Press.

Mauco, Olivier. 2009. "The Ideology of the Self in Ludic Digital Worlds." In *Digital Technologies of the Self*, ed. Fred Dervin Yasmine Abbas. Cambridge, UK: Cambridge Scholars, 115–139.

McDermid, Douglas. 1998. "Pragmatism and Truth: The Comparison Objection to Correspondence." *Review of Metaphysics* 51(4): 775–811.

McDermid, Douglas. 2016. "Dewey, Naturalism, and the Problem of Knowledge." In *The Blackwell Companion to Naturalism*, ed. Kelly James Clark. Chicester, UK: John Wiley & Sons, Inc, 234–245.

McLellan, David. 1970. *Marx before Marxism*. New York, NY: Harper & Row.

McLellan, David. 1971. "Introduction." In *Marx's Grundrisse [Translation of Grundrisse Der Kritik Der Politischen Ökonomie]*, ed. David McLellan. London, UK: Macmillan, 1–15.

McLeod, Jack M., and Steven H. Chaffee. 1973. "Interpersonal Approaches to Communication Research." *American Behavioral Scientist* 16(4): 469–499.

McLuhan, Marshall. 1964. *Understanding Media: The Extensions of Man*. New York, NY: McGraw-Hill.

Menand, Louis. 2016. "He's Back. Karl Marx, Yesterday and Today." *The New Yorker* 92(32): 90. https://www.newyorker.com/magazine/2016/10/10/karl-marx-yesterday-and-today.

Mercieca, Jennifer R. 2008. "The Irony of the Democratic Style." *Rhetoric and Public Affairs* 11(3): 441–449.

Mill, John Stuart. 1870. *On the Subjection of Women*. Philadelphia, PA: J.B. Lippincott & Co.

Mill, John Stuart. 1947 [1869]. *On Liberty*. New York, NY: Harlan Davidson Inc.

Minda, Gary. 1989. "The Jurisprudential Movements of the 1980s." *Ohio State Law Journal* 50(3): 599–662.

Minda, Gary. 1997. "Neil Gotanda and the Critical Legal Studies Movement." *Asian American Law Journal* 4: 7–18.

Minow, Martha. 1997. *Only for Myself: Identity, Politics, and the Law*. New York, NY: New Press.

Mirfield, Peter. 1989. "In Defense of Modern Legal Positivism." *Florida State University Law Review* 16(4): 985–999.

Mises, Ludwig von. 2013. *Epistemological Problems of Economics*, ed. Bettina Bien Greaves. Indianapolis, IN: Liberty Fund.

Molano, Jose Olimpo Suarez. 1999. *Filosofia Politica Norteamericana : Dewey- Rawls- MacIntyre- Rorty- Nozick- Dworkin*. Medellin, BO: Universidad Pontificia Bolivariana.

Monaghan, Henry P. 1981. "Our Perfect Constitution." *New York University Law Review* 56(2–3): 353–396.

Monaghan, Henry P. 2004. "Doing Originalism." *Columbia Law Review* 104(1): 32–38.

Montesquieu, Charles de Secondat, baron de. 1758. "Lettres Persanes, No. 83." In *Œuvres Complètes*, ed. AndrÉ Masson. Paris, FR: Nagel, 169–170.

Montesquieu, Charles de Secondat, baron de. 1803 [1748]. *De l'esprit Des Lois*. Paris, FR: P. Didot et Firmin Didot.

Moran, Gerald P. 1997. "A Radical Theory of Jurisprudence: The 'Decisionmaker' as the Source of Law–The Ohio Supreme Court's Adoption of the Spendthrift Trust Doctrine as a Model." *Akron Law Review* 30(3): 394–468.

Morton, Donald. 1996. "Queer Consensus/Socialist Conflict." In *The Material Queer: A LesBiGay Cultural Studies Reader*, ed. Donald Morton. New York, NY: WestviewPress: A Division of HarperCollinsPublishers, 35–38.

Moseley, Fred, and Martha Campbell, eds. 1997. *New Investigations of Marx's Method*. Atlantic Highlands, NJ: Humanities Press.

Neacşu, Dana. 2000. "CLS Stands for Critical Legal Studies, If Anyone Remembers." *Journal of Law and Policy* 8(2): 415–453.

Neacşu, Dana. 2004. "Advocacy As History? That Takes the Prize!" *Santa Clara Law Review* 45(2): 213–231.

Neacşu, Dana. 2005a. "The Political Value of Knowledge and the Elite Schools' Curricula: To Ignore or Not to Ignore Marxism?" *University of Detroit Mercy Law Review* 82(2): 219–252.

Neacşu, Dana. 2005b. "The Wrongful Rejection of Big Theory (Marxism) by Feminism and Queer Theory: A Brief Debate." *Capital University Law Review* 34(1): 125–151.

Neacşu, Dana. 2014. "Technology, Alienation, and the Future of Litigation-Based Social Change." *Temple Political & Civil Rights Law Review* 24(1): 155–183.

Negri, Antonio. 2006. *Goodbye Mr. Socialism*. Milano, IT: Feltrinelli.

Newmark, Kevin. 2012. *Irony on Occasion: From Schlegel and Kierkegaard to Derrida and de Man*. New York, NY: Fordham University Press.

Nietzsche, Friedrich W. 1999. "Notebook 19 (Summer 1872–Early 1873)." In *Unpublished Writings from the Period of Unfashionable Observations*, The Complete Works of Friedrich Nietzsche: volume 11. Stanford, CA: Stanford University Press, 3–99.

Nogbou, Hyacinthe E. 2017. *Burke, Marx, Arendt et La Critique Des Droits de L'Homme*. Paris, FR: L'Harmattan.

Nowak, Piotr. 2014. *The Ancients and Shakespeare on Time: Some Remarks on the War of Generations*. Amsterdam/New York: Rodopi.

Obergefell v. Hodges. 2015. 576 U.S. __ (United States Supreme Court).

Paine, Thomas. 1922 [1776]. "Common Sense." In *The Complete Works of Thomas Paine*, New York, NY: Peter Eckler Pub. Co., 1–59.

Parekh, Bhiku. 1982. Marx's Theory of Ideology. Baltimore, MD: Johns Hopkins University.

Parker, Richard Davies. 1981. "The Past of Constitutional Theory--and Its Future." *Ohio State Law Journal* 42: 223–259.

Pavlik, John V. 2008. *Media in the Digital Age*. New York, NY: Columbia University Press.

Payne v. Cave. 1789. 3 Term Reports, 148 (King's Bench).

Peirce, Charles S. 1877. "The Fixation of Belief." *Popular Science Monthly* 12: 1–15.

Peirce, Charles S. 1997. *Pragmatism as a Principle and Method of Right Thinking: The 1903 Harvard Lectures on Pragmatism*. Albany, NY: State University of New York Press.

Peller, Gary. 1988. "Neutral Principles in the 1950s." *University of Michigan Journal of Law Reform* 21(4): 561–622.

Perez, Levi, and Brad Humphreys. 2013. "The 'Who and Why' of Lottery: Empirical Highlights from the Seminal Economic Literature." *Journal of Economic Surveys* 27(5): 915–940.

Perkins, Margo V. 2011. *Autobiography as Activism: Three Black Women of the Sixties*. Jackson, MS: University Press of Mississippi.

Piketty, Thomas. 2014. *Capital in the Twenty-First Century*. Cambridge, MA: The Belknap Press of Harvard University Press.

Planned Parenthood v. Casey. 1992. 505 U.S. 833 (United States Supreme Court).

Plato. 1992. *Republic*. 2nd ed. Indianapolis, IN: Hackett Publishing Co.

Poe, Edgar Allan. 1903. "The Spectacles." In *The Works of Edgar Allan Poe*. New York: P.F. Collier & Son, 315–352.

Posner, Eric. A., and Adrian Vermeule. 2013. "Inside or Outside the System?" *The University of Chicago Law Review* 80(4): 1743–1797.

Posner, Richard A. 1986. "Goodbye to the Bluebook Blues." *The University of Chicago Law Review* 53(4): 1343–1368.

Posner, Richard A. 1987. "The Decline of Law as an Autonomous Discipline: 1962–1987." *The Harvard Law Review* 100(2): 761–780.

Posner, Richard A. 1988. *Law and Literature: A Misunderstood Relation*. Cambridge, MA: Harvard University Press.

Posner, Richard A. 1995. *Overcoming Law*. Cambridge, MA: Harvard University Press.

Posner, Richard A. 2009. *A Failure of Capitalism: The Crisis of '08 and the Descent into Depression*. Cambridge, MA: Harvard University Press.

Posner, Richard A. 2010. *The Crisis of Capitalist Democracy*. Cambridge, MA: Harvard University Press.

Posner, Richard A. 2011. "The Bluebook Blues." *The Yale Law Journal* 120(4): 690–977.

Pozen, David E. 2008. "The Irony of Judicial Elections." *Columbia Law Review* 108(2): 265–330.

Pozen, David E. 2016. "Constitutional Bad Faith." *Harvard Law Review* 129(4): 886–955.

Preliminary Commission of Inquiry into the Charges Made Against Leon Trotsky in the Moscow Trials. 1937. *The Case of Leon Trotsky; Report of Hearings on the Charges Made against Him in the Moscow Trials, by the Preliminary Commission of Inquiry, John Dewey, Chairman, Carleton Beals (Resigned) Otto Ruehle, Benjamin Stolberg, Suzanne La Follette, Secretary*. New York, NY: Harper.

Presser, Stephen B. 2017. *Law Professors: Three Centuries of Shaping American Law*. St. Paul, MN: West Academic Publishing.

Pumar, Enrique S. 2009. "The Arduous Paths of Political Transitions: A Comparison of Cuba, China and Vietnam." *ASCE, The Association for the Study of the Cuban Economy*. https://www.ascecuba.org/asce_proceedings/the-arduous-paths-of-political-transitions-a-comparison-of-cuba-china-and-vietnam/.

Purdy, Jedediah. 1999. *For Common Things: Irony, Trust, and Commitment in America Today*. New York, NY: Vintage Books.

Pyle, Jeffrey J. 1999. "Race, Equality and the Rule of Law: Critical Race Theory's Attack on the Promises of Liberalism." *Boston College Law Review* 40(3): 787–827.

Quiniou, Yvon. 2013. *Retour à Marx: Pour Une Société Post-Capitaliste*. Paris, FR: Buchet Chastel.

Rahmatian, Andreas. 2007. "Friedrich Carl von Savigny's Beruf and Volksgeistlehre." *Journal of Legal History* 28(1): 1–29.

Ramachandran, Banu. 1998. "Re-Reading Difference: Feminist Critiques of the Law School Classroom and the Problem with Speaking from Experience." *Columbia Law Review* 98(7): 1757–1794.

Rawls, John. 1971. *A Theory of Justice*. Cambridge, MA: Harvard University Press.

Rawls, John. 2007. *Lectures on the History of Political Philosophy*. ed. Samuel Freeman. Cambridge, MA: Belknap Press of Harvard University Press.

Rehmann, Jan. 2013. *Theories of Ideology: The Powers of Alienation and Subjection*. Leiden, NL: Brill.

Reed, John. 1919. *Ten Days that Shook the World*. New York, NY: Boni and Liveright.

Regents of University of California v. Bakke. 1978. 438 U.S. 265 (United States Supreme Court).

Reich, Robert. 2008. "Why the Rich Are Getting Richer and the Poor Poorer." In *The Way Class Works: Readings on School, Family, and the Economy*, ed. Lois Weis. New York, NY: Routledge.

Reisman, W. Michael, and Aaron M. Schreiber. 1987. *Jurisprudence: Understanding and Shaping Law: Cases, Readings, Commentary*. New Haven, CT: New Haven Press.

Reyes, Antonio, Paolo Rosso, and Tony Veale. 2013. "A Multidimensional Approach for Detecting Irony in Twitter." *Language Resources and Evaluation* 47(1): 239–268.

Ricardo, David. 2000 [1817]. *Principles of Political Economy and Taxation*. London, UK: Electric Book Company.

Roe v. Wade. 1973. 410 U.S. 113 (United States Supreme Court).

Röpke, Wilhelm. 1979. *The Social Crisis of Our Time*. Westport, CT: Hyperion Press.

Rorty, Richard. 1982. *Consequences of Pragmatism: Essays, 1972–1980*. Minneapolis: University of Minnesota Press.

Rorty, Richard. 1989. *Contingency, Irony, and Solidarity*. Cambridge, UK: Cambridge University Press.

Rorty, Richard. 1990. "The Banality of Pragmatism and the Poetry of Justice." *Southern California Law Review* 63: 1811–1819.

Rorty, Richard. 2001. "Response to John Horton." In *Richard Rorty. Critical Dialogues*, Cambridge, UK: Blackwell Publishers, 29–32.

Rorty, Richard. 2009. *Philosophy and the Mirror of Nature*. Princeton, NJ: Princeton University Press.

Rousseau, Jean-Jacques. 1912. *Émile ...* Paris, FR: É. Mignot.

Rousseau, Jean-Jacques. 1920. *Social Contract and Discourses, Regnery Gateway, 1950*. London, UK: J.M. Dent & Sons.

Rowland, Christopher, ed. 2007. *The Cambridge Companion to Liberation Theology*. Cambridge, UK: Cambridge University Press.

Rubinstein, David. 1981. *Marx and Wittgenstein: Social Praxis and Social Explanation*. London, UK: Routledge & Kegan Paul.

Russell, Bertrand. 1945. *The History of Western Philosophy*. 4th printing. New York, NY: Simon and Schuster.

Ryan, Alan. 2014. *On Marx: Revolutionary and Utopian*. New York, NY: Liveright Publishing, Co.

Said, Edward W. 1975. *Beginnings: Intention and Method*. New York, NY: Basic Books.

Said, Edward W. 1996. "The Limits of the Artistic Imagination, and the Secular Intellectual." *Macalester International* 3: 3–34.

Sarat, Austin. ed. 2017. *Studies in Law, Politics, and Society*. Bingley, UK: Emerald Publishing.

Savage, Charlie. 2017. "Twitter Users Blocked by Trump Seek Reprieve, Citing First Amendment." *The New York Times.* https://perma.cc/LPM8-HQR9.

Savigny, Friedrich Karl von. 1848 [1803]. *Treatise on Possession: Or, The Jus Possessionis of the Civil Law [Das Recht Des Besitzes: Eine Civilistische Abhandlung].* 6th ed. London, UK: S. Sweet.

Scalia, Antonin. 1989. "The Rule of Law as A Law of Rules." *University of Chicago Law Review* 56: 1175–1188.

Schauer, Frederick. 1988. "Formalism." *Yale Law Journal* 97(2): 509–548.

Scheibler, Ingrid. 2000. *Gadamer: Between Heidegger and Habermas.* New York, NY: Rowman & Littlefield.

Schlegel, John Henry. 1984. "Toward and Intimate, Opinionated, and Affectionate History of the Conference on Critical Legal Studies." *Stanford Law Review* 36(1/2): 391–411.

Schroeder, Jeanne L. 2002. "The Stumbling Block: Freedom, Rationality, and Legal Scholarship." *William and Mary Law Review* 44(1): 263–374.

Schwartz, Louis B. 1984. "With Gun and Camera Through Darkest CLS-Land." *Stanford Law Review* 36(1/2): 413–464.

Sebok, Anthony J. 1995. "Misunderstanding Positivism." *Michigan Law Review* 93(6): 2054–2132.

Seidman, Louis Michael. 2014. "The Secret History of American Constitutional Skepticism: A Recovery and Preliminary Evaluation." *University of Pennsylvania Journal of Constitutional Law* 17(1): 1–113.

Selemeneva, Lioudmilia. 2007. "Balancing the Concrete and Abstract in Public Intellectual Reasoning: A Study of Hannah Arendt." PhD Dissertation. Carnegie Mellon University. http://ezproxy.cul.columbia.edu/login?url=https://search.proquest.com/docview/304884914?accountid=10226.

Shakespeare, William. 1906. *Shakespeare's Tragedy of Hamlet, Prince of Denmark,* ed. William J. Rolfe. New York, NY: American Book Co.

Shannon, Claude E., and Warren Weaver. 1949. *The Mathematical Theory of Communication.* Urbana, IL: University of Illinois Press.

Sheridan, Alan. 1980. *Michel Foucault: The Will to Truth.* London, UK: Routledge.

Shiffrin, Seana Valentine. 2014. *Speech Matters. On Lying, Morality, and the Law.* Princeton, NJ: Princeton University Press.

Singer, Joseph William. 1984. "The Player and the Cards: Nihilism and Legal Theory." *Yale Law Journal* 94(1): 1–70.

Sinnerbrink, Robert. 2014. *Understanding Hegelianism.* Hoboken, NJ: Taylor and Francis.

Sitaraman, Ganesh. 2017. *The Crisis of the Middle-Class Constitution: Why Economic Inequality Threatens Our Republic.* New York: Alfred A. Knopf.

Smith, Adam. 1993 [1776]. *An Inquiry into the Nature and Causes of the Wealth of Nations*, ed. Fred R. Glahe. Savage, MD: Rowman & Littlefield.

Smith, Kenneth. 2012. *A Guide to Marx's "Capital" Vols I–III*. London, UK: Anthem Press.

Smith, Steven B. 2016. *Modernity and Its Discontents: Making and Unmaking the Bourgeois from Machiavelli to Bellow.* New Haven, CT: Yale University Press.

Smolla, Rodney A. 1996. *Smolla and Nimmer on Freedom of Speech*. 3rd ed. Deefielf, IL: Clark Boardman Callaghan.

Somerville, Margaret A. 1994. "Labels versus Contents: Variance between Philosophy, Psychiatry and Law in Concepts Governing Decision-Making." *McGill Law Journal* 39(1): 179–199.

Springborg, Patricia. 2008. "The Paradoxical Hobbes: A Critical Response to the Hobbes Symposium." *Political Theory* 36(5): 676–688.

State of Washington et al. v. Glucksberg et al. 1997. 521 U.S. 702 (United States Supreme Court).

Stevenson, Bryan. 2014. *Just Mercy: A Story of Justice and Redemption*. New York, NY: Spiegel & Grau.

Stratton, Matthew. 2014. *The Politics of Irony in American Modernism*. New York, NY: Fordham University Press.

Strauss, Peter. 2014. *Legal Methods: Understanding and Using Cases and Statutes*. 3rd ed. St. Paul, MN: Foundation Press.

Stychin, Carl F. 1994. "Identities, Sexualities, and the Postmodern Subject: An Analysis of Artistic Funding by the National Endowment for the Arts." *Cardozo Arts and Entertainment Law Journal* 12(1): 79–132.

Sunderland, Edson R. 1939. "Discovery Before Trial Under the New Federal Rules." *Tennessee Law Review* 15(3): 737–757.

Sutherland, Keston. 2011. *Stupefaction: A Radical Anatomy of Phantoms*. New York: Seagull Books.

Swindler, William F., ed. 1979. *Sources and Documents of United States Constitutions: Massachusetts. Michigan. Minnesota. Mississippi. Missouri*. Dobbs Ferry, NY: Oceana Publications.

The Bluebook: A Uniform System of Citation. 2010. 19th ed. Cambridge, MA: Harvard Law Review Association.

Toobin, Jeffrey. 2018. "How Trump's Supreme Court Pick Could Undo Kennedy's Legacy." *The New Yorker*. https://www.newyorker.com/magazine/2018/07/09/how-trumps-supreme-court-pick-could-undo-kennedys-legacy.

Torrance, John. 1995. *Karl Marx's Theory of Ideas (Studies in Marxism and Social Theory)*. Cambridge, UK: Cambridge University Press.

Tourneux, Maurice. 1899. *Diderot et Catherine II*. Paris, FR: Calmann Lévy.

Trotsky, Leon. 1932. *The History of the Russian Revolution*. New York, NY: Simon and Schuster.

Trotsky, Leon. 1965. "An Open Letter to Comrade Burnham, Jan. 7, 1940." In *In Defense of Marxism (Against the Petty-Bourgeois Opposition)*. New York: Merit Publishers. 77–94.

Trubek, David M. 1977. "Complexity and Contradiction in the Legal Order: Balbus and the Challenge of Critical Social Thought About Law." *Law & Society Review* 11(3): 529–569.

Trubek, David M. 1984. "Where the Action Is: Critical Legal Studies and Empiricism." *Stanford Law Review* 36(1/2): 575–622.

Trump v. International Refugee Assistance Project. 2017. 582 U.S. __ (United States Supreme Court).

Turley, Jonathan. 1987. "Hitchhiker's Guide to CLS, Unger, and Deep Thought Introduction." *Northwestern University Law Review* 81(4): 593–620.

Tushnet, Mark. 1980. "Darkness on the Edge of Town: The Contributions of John Hart Ely to Constitutional Theory." *Yale Law Journal* 89(6): 1037–1062.

Tushnet, Mark. 1983. "Following Rules Laid down: A Critique of Interpretivism and Neutral Principles." *Harvard Law Review* 94(6): 781–827.

Tushnet, Mark. 1984. "An Essay on Rights." *Texas Law Review* 62(8): 1363–1403.

Tushnet, Mark. 1991. "Critical Legal Studies: A Political History." *Yale Law Journal* 100(5): 1515–1544.

Tushnet, Mark. 1999. "Review, The New Deal Constitutional Revolution: Law, Politics, or What?" *University of Chicago Law Review* 66(6): 1061–1080.

Twain, Mark. 1917. *Adventures of Huckleberry Finn (Tom Sawyer's Comrade)*. New York, NY: Harper & Bros.

Unger, Roberto Mangabeira. 1975. *Knowledge and Politics*. New York, NY: Free Press.

Unger, Roberto Mangabeira. 1983. "The Critical Legal Studies Movement." *Harvard Law Review* 96(3): 561–675.

Unger, Roberto Mangabeira. 1987a. *False Necessity: Anti-Necessitarian Social Theory in the Service of Radical Democracy*. Cambridge, UK: Cambridge University Press.

Unger, Roberto Mangabeira. 1987b. *Social Theory, Its Situation and Its Task*. Cambridge, UK: Cambridge University Press.

Unger, Roberto Mangabeira. 2015. *The Critical Legal Studies Movement: Another Time, a Greater Task*. New York, NY: Verso.

Vadim, Roger. 1956. *...And God Created Woman (Et Dieu ... Créa La Femme)*.

Waggoner, Matt. 2014. "Kant and the Perversion of the End." *Critical Horizons: A Journal of Philosophy & Social Theory* 15(1): 95–113.

Waldron, Jeremy. 1987. *"Nonsense Upon Stilts": Bentham, Burke, and Marx on the Rights of Man*. London, UK: Methuen.

Warner, Michael. 1996. "Tongues Untied: Memoirs of a Pentecostal Boyhood." In *The Material Queer: A LesBiGay Cultural Studies Reader*, ed. Donald Morton. New York: NY: WestviewPress: A Division of HarperCollinsPublishers, 39–44.

Warren, Charles. 1908. *History of the Harvard Law School and of Early Legal Conditions in America*. New York, NY: Lewis Pub. Co.

Warren, Frank A., III. 1966. *Liberals and Communism: The "Red Decade" Revisited*. Indiana, IN: Indiana University Press.

Watts, John L. 2014. "Tyranny by Proxy: State Action and the Private Use of Deadly Force." *Notre Dame Law Review* 89(3): 1237–1282.

Wax, Amy. 2018. "What Can't Be Debated on Campus." *The Wall Street Journal*. https://www.wsj.com/articles/what-cant-be-debated-on-campus-1518792717.

Wessell, Leonard P., Jr. 1979. *Karl Marx, Romantic Irony, and the Proletariat: The Mythopoetic Origins of Marxism*. Baton Rouge, LA: Louisiana State University Press.

West, Cornel. 1987. "Between Dewey and Gramsci: Emancipatory Experimentalism." *Northwestern University Law Review* 81(4): 941–951.

West, Cornel. 1991. *The Ethical Dimensions of Marxist Thought*. New York, NY: Monthly Review Press.

Wheen, Francis. 1999. *Karl Marx. A Life*. New York, NY: W.W. Norton & Co.

White, Neil. 2012. *Company Towns: Corporate Order and Community*. Toronto, CA: University of Toronto Press.

Williams, Joan C. 1987. "Critical Legal Studies: The Death of Transcendence and the Rise of the New Langdell." *New York University Law Review* 62(2): 429–496.

Williams, Joan C. 2017. *White Working Class: Overcoming Class Cluelessness in America*. Boston, MA: Harvard Business Review Press.

Williams, Michael. 1989. "Introduction." In *Richard Rorty's Contingency, Irony, and Solidarity*, Cambridge, MA: Cambridge University Press, xiii–xvi.

Williams, Patricia J. 1991. *The Alchemy of Race and Rights*. Cambridge, MA: Harvard University Press.

Wimsatt, William K., and Monroe Beardsley. 1946. "The Intentional Fallacy." *The Sewanee Review* 54(3): 468–488.

Windelband, Wilhelm, and Arnold Ruge, eds. 1913. *Encyclopaedia of the Philosophical Sciences*. London, UK: Macmillan.

Wittgenstein, Ludwig. 1969. *On Certainty*, ed. G.H. von Wright G.E.M. Anscombe. New York, NY: Harper & Row.

Wolff, Robert Paul. 2018. *Lecture 1*. Radical Political Economy – Blog hub of the Union for Radical Political Economics. https://urpe.wordpress.com/2018/05/20/robert-paul-wolff-on-karl-marx-lecture-series/.

Wolff, Robert Paul. 1988. *Moneybags Must Be So Lucky: On the Literary Structure of Capital*. Amherst, MA: The University of Massachusetts Press.

Woodley, Daniel. 2015. *Globalization and Capitalist Geopolitic : Sovereignty and State Power in a Multipolar World.* London, UK: Routledge, Taylor & Francis Group.

Yoshino, Kenji. 2005. "The City and the Poet." *Yale Law Journal* 114(8): 1835–1896.

Zhanga, Guangzi, et al. 2016. "Creativity and Social Alienation: The Costs of Being Creative." *The International Journal of Human Resource Management* 27(12): 1252–1276.

Zwart, Hub. 2017. *Tales of Research Misconduct: A Lacanian Diagnostics of Integrity Challenges in Science Novels.* New York, NY: Springer.

Index

Abrams v. United States 82
Adorno, Theodor 51–52, 94, 102
Adorno's (*Negative*) *Dialectics* 52
adulterating 85, 120, 144
Adventures of Huckleberry Finn 97
Alchemy of Race and Rights: Diary of a Law Professor 33
alienation (*see also* despondency) 2, 5, 6, 50, 53, 67–68, 71, 72–84, 85, 89, 92, 94, 102, 107, 111, 114, 118, 121, 149, 157, 164, 170, 218, 219, 223, 230, 232
Althusser, Louis 11, 89–90, 93, 113, 116, 168
Althusserian ideology 11, 89–90, 113
Althusserian interpellation 110
American jurisprudence 5, 12, 14, 29, 30, 48, 119, 123, 153, 154, 164, 168–169, 170, 173, 175, 176, 180, 181, 186, 188–191, 236
American King (Paine's) 12, 28, 96, 160, 236
American King (Scalia's) 160–162, 193, 235–236
Arendt, Hannah 78–79, 170
Aristotle 171, 173–175, 192–193, 208
Aristotle's dialectics 173–175
Arthur, Christopher 58–59
audience 2, 5, 6, 19, 30, 45, 116, 120, 135, 138, 160, 181, 198, 223, 224, 230
author (*see also* text-instigator) 2, 5, 6, 9, 12, 16, 17, 20, 21, 26, 35, 41, 50, 53, 65, 71, 90, 91, 99, 102, 114, 115, 116, 119, 125, 132, 133, 135, 136, 141, 143, 153, 156, 180, 189, 190, 195, 223, 226
author's ideology 35, 114
author's subjectivity 50, 99

Barrett, Michèle 36, 89, 90, 91, 93
Barthes, Roland 20, 21
Benjamin, Walter 41, 121–122, 231
Bentham, Jeremy 46, 116, 169, 176, 178, 184–188, 209
Berlin, Isaiah 7, 13
Big Capital 105
Black Freedom Movements 111
bourgeois (*see also* capitalism) 6, 13, 17, 18, 36, 37, 44, 75, 79, 89–90, 100, 102, 105, 106, 116, 118, 119, 126–127, 148, 149, 150, 186, 192, 217, 218, 225, 233

bourgeois charm 4, 13, 19, 100
Bowers v. Hardwick 152, 153
Brown v. Bd. of Ed. of Topeka, Shawnee County, Kan. 153
Buñuel, Luis 5–6, 7, 17, 30, 31, 32, 37, 84, 118–119, 192, 236

capital 20–21, 54, 57, 59, 63, 64, 67, 80, 88, 92, 101, 104–106, 122, 172, 203, 222
Capital (vol. I) (*see also* Das Kapital vol. I) 6, 56, 58, 59, 61, 75, 81, 175, 218, 222
Capital (vol. II) 56
capitalism 7, 10, 13, 14, 17, 18, 20, 30, 46, 48, 56, 58, 59, 61–62, 63, 64, 66, 67, 68, 74, 75, 79, 81, 88, 91, 126, 127, 149, 184, 216, 218
Chaffee, Steven 131–132, 134
Chomsky, Noam 33
classical liberalism 192, 194–200
CLS (*see also* Critical Legal Studies and Crits) 188, 189–190, 192, 193, 213–217
code civil des Français 64
Columbia University 24, 67, 97–98, 229
commodities 59, 64, 75–76, 100, 123, 175, 219
Common Sense 159–160, 233, 235
Communist Manifesto 11, 30, 31, 74, 104, 106, 126, 218, 220
Comprehensive Environmental Response, Compensation, and Liability Act (*Superfund* or CERLCA) 197
connectedness 103, 112, 113, 138
contingency 5, 7, 8, 9, 10, 11, 14, 15, 17, 19, 20, 23, 26, 28, 31, 35, 41, 46, 51, 54, 55, 56, 58, 60, 66, 67, 70, 84, 95, 103, 111, 120, 128, 129, 130, 132, 134, 138, 145, 160, 161, 180, 181, 182, 187, 188, 192, 194, 195, 200, 203, 206–213, 230, 231, 232, 236
contextualism 23, 25, 121, 190
contracts 12, 147, 165, 171, 185, 208, 224
creative alienation 5, 50, 71, 72, 73, 76, 77, 78, 81, 85
creative reification 74–78
Crenshaw, Kimberlé 102, 221–222, 232
Critical Legal Studies (*see also* CLS, and Crits) 5, 29, 188–190, 192, 193, 204, 213–217

INDEX

Critique of Hegel's Doctrine of the State   54
Critique of the Gotha Program   31, 61, 62
Crits   5, 32, 155, 192, 204, 213–217
cunningham, e. christi   34, 35

Das Kapital (*see also Capital*)   6, 61, 74, 186
Davies, Carole Boyce   46, 102, 231
Davis, Michael   8, 13, 111, 145, 164, 202, 204, 214
despondency (despondent) (*see also* alienation)   72, 79–80, 188
Dewey, John   16, 20, 22, 23–29, 35, 91
dialectical   15, 16, 25, 28, 43, 53, 54, 55, 58, 63, 69, 70, 83, 85, 90, 102, 103, 112, 121, 142, 169, 173, 178, 180, 182, 186, 188, 212, 222, 227, 231, 232
dialectical inquiry   25
dialectical laws   54
dialectical method (methodology)   54, 84, 180, 231
dialectical thinking   51
dialectical universals   173–175
dialectics   7, 10, 12, 16, 17, 31, 35, 39, 50–71, 79, 102, 118, 169, 175, 181, 183, 222
Diderot   108, 115
Discreet Charm of the Bourgeoisie   5, 31, 236
Dorf, Michael   23, 25
Dworkin, Ronald   206–213

Eastman, Max   25, 29, 30, 32, 49, 67, 68, 86, 111
Economic and Philosophical Manuscripts   70, 74, 77, 79, 81
eirōneia   119
Eleventh Thesis on Feuerbach   22
elite law schools   82–83, 95, 96, 99
Elster, Jon   7, 9, 50, 67–68, 77, 79–80, 89, 101, 219
Endangered Species Act   197
Engels, Frederich (Frederick)   7, 18, 28, 40, 41, 44, 45, 54, 61, 63, 66, 71, 75, 87, 89, 98, 104, 106, 127, 220, 230
Engels' dialectics   54
English political economy   9, 100
Enlightenment   40, 104, 105, 107, 109, 114–115, 116, 128, 196
Et Dieu créa la femme   20
experientialism   43, 223
exploitation   10, 18, 31, 46–47, 66, 102, 219, 221, 222

Facebook   105, 107, 109, 110, 222
feminine (scholarship)   17
feminism   111, 217–220
Feuerbach, Ludwig   24, 26, 78, 230
Fifth Thesis on Feuerbach   26
Fletcher, George   189, 212, 217
formalism   171, 193, 204–205, 215, 216
Foucault, Michel   1–3, 10, 20–21, 32, 36, 37, 73, 84, 90–92, 93, 98, 129, 183, 200, 230
Frankfurt School   39
French Revolution   86, 103, 181, 187
French socialism   9, 18, 100
Friedman, Lawrence   203
Friedmann, Wolfgang   7, 50, 72, 84, 167–168, 181

Gallerte   122–123, 167, 175, 191
Gay, Peter   104, 105, 108, 114, 115, 116, 117
Geertz, Clifford   87, 113, 141
German Ideology   26, 27, 61, 66, 79, 87
German philosophy   6, 9, 27, 100, 167
Gitlin, Tod   196
Gramsci, Antonio   7, 8, 14, 28, 60, 90, 147
Griswold v. Connecticut   199
Grotius, Hugo   184–186, 194
Grundrisse   40, 63, 74
Grutter v. Bollinger   95, 96

Hall, Stuart   2, 17, 19, 21, 35, 50, 90, 91, 120, 143, 170, 181, 229
Hamilton, Alexander   115–116
Harvard Law School   69, 98, 181, 200
Hegel, Georg Wilhelm Friedrich   6, 12, 30, 52–56, 60, 61, 67, 78, 131, 135, 136, 151, 181, 182, 183, 203, 227, 230, 231–232
Hegelian   11, 12, 18, 24, 26, 52, 53, 54, 55, 60, 61, 183
Hegel's dialectics   53, 55, 56
hegemony (hegemonic)   2, 5, 82, 85, 92, 105, 112, 147–153, 162, 190, 192, 193
hegemonic cluster of meaning   2
hegemonic normativity   3, 4, 235
high culture   6
Hobbes, Thomas   40, 115, 123–125, 126, 148, 155, 176–180, 194
Hobsbawm, Eric   63, 64
Holmes, Oliver Wendell (Jr.) (Justice)   53, 82, 150, 151–152, 167, 191, 201, 203, 205
Horwitz, Morton   154–155, 216

ideological   1, 2, 8, 10, 12, 13, 14, 15, 16, 19, 20, 24, 28, 31, 35, 36, 37, 43, 44, 45, 46, 47, 48, 49, 50, 51, 52, 55, 62, 68, 70, 78–81, 83, 84, 85, 86, 89, 90, 91, 93, 94–106, 107, 108, 110, 111, 113, 114, 115, 116, 118, 126, 130, 132, 141, 147, 148, 150, 151, 155, 157, 159, 160, 167–191, 176–180, 184, 188, 192, 197, 206, 214, 219, 220, 223, 229, 230, 232, 233, 236
ideological irony   1, 2, 5, 8, 9, 13, 18, 20, 43, 56, 72, 85, 99, 119, 120, 131–140, 141, 149, 150, 159, 227, 229–236
ideological meaning-making   113–117
ideology   2, 5–9, 10, 11, 12, 13, 14, 16, 17, 18, 20, 22, 31, 35, 36, 37, 41, 43, 44, 50, 51–53, 55, 56, 62, 65, 66, 67, 68, 72, 74, 76, 78, 79, 81, 84, 85–117, 118, 119, 120, 121, 123, 130, 131, 132, 133, 134, 138, 139, 141, 144, 145, 150, 151, 153, 159, 160, 161, 164, 170, 172, 175, 178, 180, 187, 191, 192, 194, 196, 200–204, 213, 220, 223, 225, 227, 230, 235
idiocy   75, 218
Idiotismus   75
inside/outside fallacy   15
Instagram   107, 110, 114
Institut de France   86
interdisciplinarity   9, 43, 53, 56, 79
interdisciplinary   16, 17, 31, 43, 51, 53, 56, 58, 60, 70, 83, 102, 112, 167, 231
interdisciplinary dialectical method   180
interdisciplinary dialectics   10, 35, 50–71
interpellate (interpellated)   2, 4, 11, 14, 25, 35, 51, 55, 60, 74, 76, 85, 113, 117, 118, 119, 127, 131, 143, 144, 160, 200, 222, 230, 235
interpellation   5, 9–16, 18, 51, 90, 99, 110, 118, 119, 130, 131, 132, 134, 137, 138, 142, 145, 182, 189, 224, 229, 230, 232, 236
interpersonal communication   131, 135, 137
intersectionality   102, 220–223, 232
ironic meaning-making   6
irony   5–9, 10, 11, 12, 13, 14, 16, 17, 18, 20, 29, 39, 41, 42, 49, 50, 53, 65, 67, 72, 74, 85, 91, 102, 106, 113, 118–130, 140–166, 167–191, 192–228
Ivy League   95–98, 99, 100, 104, 112, 163, 214
Ivy League Law Schools (academia)   95, 98, 99, 100, 104, 163, 214

Jacobs, Jack   53
Jacksonian Democrats   234

Jacksonian era   13
James, C.L.R.   47
James, William   23, 55, 168
Janus v. AFSCME   224
Jones, Claudia   46–48, 102–103, 159
judicial activism   224
Judt, Tony   138–139
jurisprudence   2, 5, 7, 8, 12, 14, 23, 41, 53, 63, 68, 69, 70, 82, 90–91, 98, 113, 141, 142, 145, 147, 149, 152, 153, 155, 156, 157, 158, 159, 167, 168, 178, 180, 188, 190, 192, 194, 202, 212, 216, 223, 224, 225, 226, 230
jurisprudential irony   141–166
jurisprudential meaning-making   5, 170, 192–228
just   48, 108, 154, 155, 170–173, 174, 211
justice   15, 30, 32, 33, 48, 91, 92, 105, 115, 154, 161, 162, 165, 170–173, 174, 175, 177, 183, 196, 199, 206–213, 217, 221, 226, 231
Justice (United States Supreme Court)   15, 53, 82, 95, 150, 152, 158, 159–166, 167, 190, 191, 205, 212, 223–227, 235, 236

Kagan, Elena (Justice)   224
Kant, Immanuel   25–26, 35, 105, 141, 169, 180–183, 203
Katzenelson, Ira   92
Kennedy, Anthony (Justice)   223–227
Kennedy, Duncan   22, 29, 69, 192, 204, 212–214, 216
Kessler, Jeremy K.   68–69, 131, 143–145, 194–195, 229
Kierkegaard, Søren   52, 135, 136, 137, 147, 154, 165
Kolakowski, Leszek   7, 67, 68, 120

labeling (self-labeling)   13, 43–49
label(s)   20, 30, 43–49, 58, 66, 90, 99, 105, 111, 169, 171, 172, 173, 174, 175, 178, 181, 182, 183, 186, 199, 213, 233, 236
labor   13, 26, 47, 54, 57, 58, 60, 61–63, 66, 71, 74, 75–76, 77, 79, 80, 81, 88, 101, 106, 122–123, 149, 151, 175, 203, 222
laissez-faire   13, 16, 30
Lawrence v. Texas   152, 225
Law and Literature   5, 151, 193
legal theory   18, 29, 30, 33, 142, 145, 148, 165, 167, 168, 173, 185, 189
Lenin (Vladimir Ilyich Ulyanov)   7, 8, 9, 13, 44, 46, 54, 89, 100

INDEX

Lenin's dialectics   54
liberal   4, 5, 7, 12, 13, 14, 15, 16, 17, 19, 20, 27, 29, 30, 36, 45, 47, 48, 49, 65, 67, 69, 82, 102, 103, 105, 106, 111, 112, 113, 116, 127, 128, 129, 130, 133, 139, 147, 148, 153, 173, 178, 179, 181, 188, 190, 192, 193, 194, 195, 196, 197, 198, 199, 200, 204, 212, 213, 215, 219, 221, 223, 224, 225, 228, 229, 233
Liberalism   12, 13, 16, 17, 30, 33, 36, 84, 92, 103, 104, 111, 116, 138, 139, 148, 157, 192, 194, 195, 196, 197, 198, 200, 205, 210, 215, 220, 225, 230
Liberation theology   39
Lochner v. New York   30, 53, 150, 151, 205
Locke, John   99, 105, 115, 125, 126, 169, 176–180, 181
Louis XVI   64
Lukács, György (Georg)   75, 89, 90, 101, 102, 103, 105, 113
Luxembourg, Rosa   47, 103

Madison, James   15, 115, 117
market (free market of ideas)   48, 82, 99, 204
Marx, Karl   1, 4, 5–9, 10, 11, 12, 13, 15, 16, 17, 18, 19, 20, 21, 22, 23–29, 30, 31, 32, 33, 35, 36, 37, 38, 39, 40, 41, 43, 44, 45, 46, 47, 48, 49, 50, 52–66, 67, 68, 70, 71, 74, 75–76, 77, 78, 79, 80, 81, 82, 84, 86–87, 88, 89, 90, 92, 94, 97, 98, 100, 101, 102, 104, 106, 107, 112, 118, 119, 121–123, 126–127, 130, 131, 148, 150, 153, 159, 169, 172, 175, 182, 186, 188, 189, 190, 194, 203, 213, 216, 217, 218, 219, 220, 222, 223, 226, 227, 228, 229, 230, 233
Marx's (interdisciplinary) dialectics   50–71
Marxian (theory)   1, 7, 8, 17, 18, 23, 35, 36, 43–49, 76, 79, 81, 83, 100, 101, 102, 167, 192, 199, 231, 232
Marxian dialectics   54, 67
Marxian ideology   36, 92, 103
Marxism   7, 8, 20, 25, 29, 30, 32, 43–49, 67, 68, 89, 97–98, 132, 198, 200, 230
Marxist-Leninist (Marxism-Leninism)   46–47, 230
McLuhan, Marshall   110, 132
meaning-making   1, 2, 4, 5, 6, 7, 8, 9, 12, 16, 17, 18, 20, 21, 29, 31, 35, 43, 44, 50, 66, 71, 72, 77, 81, 82, 85, 88, 93, 94, 96, 106, 110, 113–117, 118, 119, 120, 121, 122, 127, 130, 131, 132–134, 138–139, 143, 144, 159, 167, 170, 191, 192–228, 229, 230, 235
meaning-making negotiation   4, 16, 21, 31, 43, 113, 118, 120, 138, 144, 229, 230, 235
Menand, Louis   7
method of research   15–16, 50, 53, 63, 65, 66, 67, 68, 85, 99, 132, 227
Mill's free market of idea   48, 82, 99, 204
Mill, John Stuart   11, 30, 48, 82, 83, 96, 99, 128, 148, 204
Monaghan, Henry Paul   158–159
Montesquieu, Charles-Louis de Secondat, Baron de La Brède et de   115, 169, 180–181

Napoleon (Bonaparte)   64
Neacşu, Dana   8, 13, 80, 81, 82, 95, 97, 145, 190, 202, 204, 214, 215, 217, 218, 219, 220
negotiating meaning (*see also*, meaning-making negotiation)   5–9, 106, 143, 144, 161
Negri, Antonio   93
neoliberalism   5, 33
nomenclatura   13
nominalism   48, 194

Obergefell v. Hodges   225, 226, 227
On The Jewish Question   19
On the Subjection of Women   11
opium of the people   38, 39
originalism   15, 158–159, 195

Paine, Thomas   12, 23, 96, 159–162, 163, 164, 170, 209, 233, 235–236
Paradigm of Knowledge (Knowledge Paradigm)   1, 3, 4, 5, 10, 11, 13, 17, 26, 27, 32, 51, 68, 78, 82, 83, 91, 92, 94, 118, 131, 132, 236
Parekh, Bhiku   122, 175
Pavlik, John   108
Philosophy (particular type of intellectual enterprise)   6, 9, 18, 25, 27, 30, 40, 41, 46, 49, 50, 52, 53, 54, 60, 70, 72, 84, 88, 90, 99, 100, 102, 120, 123, 127, 128, 130, 132, 141, 167, 171, 173, 182, 183, 185, 188, 194, 200, 203
philosophy (reasoned narrative)   4, 5, 7, 8, 12, 21, 50, 62, 72, 106, 114, 131, 141
Plato   53, 54, 127, 135–136, 142, 146, 154, 169, 170–173, 175, 176, 188

Plato's dialectics   54
political consciousness   46
Posner-*fils* (*see also* Posner, Eric)   15
Posner, Eric   15
Posner, Richard (Judge)   14, 15, 150–151, 155–156, 169, 190, 196, 197
Pozen, David   68–69, 131, 143–145, 157–158, 194–195, 229
pragmatism   16, 19, 20, 23, 24, 25, 28, 43, 70, 151, 152, 179, 213
praxis   11, 24, 26, 27, 28, 29, 38, 39, 60, 90, 102
proletariat   10, 11, 13, 17, 56, 112
Proudhon, Pierre-Joseph   12, 230

Queer Theory   217–220
Quiniou, Yvon   112

Rawls, John   67, 70, 99, 195, 199, 200, 206–213
realism (and formalism)   204–205
realism (and nominalism)   48
reasoned narrative   4, 5, 12, 13, 14, 21, 43, 50, 72, 118, 128, 141, 153, 155, 159, 230
Reed, John   233
Regents of University of California v. Bakke   95
Regime of Truth   1–5, 10, 22, 53, 72, 82, 83, 91, 104, 105, 123, 139, 144, 170, 192, 223, 229
religion   12, 37–40, 52, 78, 87, 104, 115, 158
Ricardian political economy   18
Ricardo, David   6, 13, 21, 131, 230
Rorty, Richard   23, 51, 119, 126, 127–130, 134, 142, 150–153, 194
Robeson, Paul   46, 47
Roe v. Wade   153, 212
Rousseau, Jean-Jacques   99, 176, 180–184
Rule of Law   7, 12, 13, 28, 62, 65, 96, 99, 105, 142, 147, 150, 154, 155, 160, 161, 162, 164, 166, 173, 184, 192, 193, 195, 205, 211, 234, 235, 236
Russell, Bertrand   92, 173, 177, 178, 180, 181, 185
Russian Revolution   7, 29

Said, Edward   120, 231
Scalia, Antonio (Justice)   15, 159–166, 205, 235–236
scholarship production (*see also* theory production)   4, 5, 9, 16, 32, 33, 35, 41, 50, 65, 72, 77, 78, 118–130, 133, 135, 137, 230, 231

Scorpion and Felix   18, 121
Second Thesis on Feuerbach   25
Shakespeare, William   97
Smith, Adam   13, 230
Socrates   7, 127, 135–136, 146, 154, 171, 172, 188
Socrates' dialectics   7
Socrates' irony   135–136, 146, 188
Socratic Method   135, 136, 137, 145–147, 161, 169, 201
State of Washington et al. v. Glucksberg et al.   212
Stalin, Joseph (Stalinism)   8, 13, 25, 29, 45
storytelling   33–34, 35, 114
subjectivity   2, 5–8, 9, 10, 12, 13, 16, 21, 23, 25, 26, 27, 36–37, 43, 44, 50, 66, 71, 72–84, 85–117, 118, 119, 120, 126, 131, 132, 134, 138, 141, 142, 143, 151, 157, 159, 161, 164, 170, 200, 203, 223, 230, 231, 232
subordination   28, 33, 34, 46, 102, 163, 221, 222
superstructure (superstructural)   11, 89, 90, 91, 158, 185, 205
Sutherland, Keston   41, 122, 123, 175, 231
temps (temp underclass, temp workers)   66
text-instigator   2, 7, 12, 13, 16, 31, 43, 50, 51, 65, 71, 72, 76, 77, 81, 85, 94, 113, 119, 127, 131–132, 135, 138, 141, 143–145, 160
text-interpellator   2, 7, 9, 31, 43, 50, 51, 71, 72, 77, 81, 85, 116, 120, 126, 131, 132, 135, 138, 141, 144, 157, 159–161, 164, 235
textual instigation   9–16, 51, 120
textual interpellation   5, 9–16, 118, 119, 131, 132, 145, 224
The Critique of Pure Reason   26, 105, 181
The Discreet Charm of the Bourgeoisie   5, 31, 118, 236
The Eighteenth Brumaire of Louis Napoleon   60
The Need for a Recovery of Philosophy   24
The Poverty of Philosophy   55
The Process of Production of Capital (*see also Capital, Das Kapital* vol. I)   58
The Process of the Circulation of Capital (*see also Das Kapital* vol. II, *Capital* vol. II)   56
theory production   1, 4, 5, 8, 21, 26, 27, 32, 50, 72–84, 85, 91, 96, 113, 118, 131, 137, 141, 142
Theses on Feuerbach   24
Tocqueville, Alexis De   99, 148

INDEX

Toobin, Jeffrey   223–226, 227
torts   12, 147
Tracy, Antoine Desttut de   86, 87
Trotsky, Leon   44, 47, 100
Trump, Donald   99, 110, 166, 224, 233
Trumpian Republicans   234

underclass   10
U.S.S.R.   45, 138, 173
Unger, Roberto Mangabeira   22, 28–29, 98, 192, 194, 195, 196, 197, 198, 199, 200, 213, 215–216
United States Supreme Court   30, 120, 163, 164
University of Pennsylvania   98

wage(s)   31, 33, 57, 61, 63, 80–81, 101, 122, 150, 203, 219, 221, 222, 223, 233
West, Cornel   22, 28–29, 103, 112, 113, 229, 232
Wheen, Francis   18, 40
Wikipedia   80, 81, 149
Williams, Patricia   33
Wittgenstein, Ludwig   8, 49
worker   6, 47, 61, 62, 63, 64, 74, 76, 77, 79, 80, 82, 101, 149, 203, 218, 219, 223
working class   10, 62, 112, 219

Yale Law School   98
Young Hegelians   12, 52–53